OpenVMS Performance Management

Joginder Sethi

GW01003422

Digital Press

Boston • Oxford • Melbourne • Singapore • Toronto • Munich • New Delhi • Tokyo

Digital Press™ is an imprint of Butterworth–Heinemann, Publisher for Digital Equipment Corporation.

℞ A member of the Reed Elsevier group

Typeset by: Graham Douglas, Bath, UK

Library of Congress Cataloging-in-Publication Data

Sethi, Joginder.
   OpenVMS performance management / Joginder Sethi.
     p.   cm.
   Includes index.
   ISBN 1-5558-126-9 (pbk. : acid-free paper)
   1. Operating systems (Computers) 2. OpenVMS   I. Title
QA76.76.063S47 1995
005.4'469--dc20   95-22244
                                                CIP

The publisher offers discounts on bulk orders of this book.
For information, please write:

Manager of Special Sales, Digital Press
Butterworth–Heinemann
313 Washington Street
Newton, MA 02158–1626

Order number: EY–Q793E–DP

10 9 8 7 6 5 4 3 2 1

Printed in the United States of America

Acknowledgment

I would like to thank all those who have helped in the preparation of this second edition, particularly my two children who patiently put up with me chained to the word processor. My wife, for her patience and encouragement; to Gerald Marsh who stimulated much of my thinking and has also been a tireless reviewer of the first edition; to Peter Mann who provided me with valuable research material, without which some of the information in this book would not exist; to Jeff Ashwell who actively supported and encouraged my work; and to Maninder Uppal who reviewed the text in detail – making many suggestions which I have incorporated. Finally, my humble thanks go to DECUS committee for encouraging me to produce the second edition.

Contents

Preface   xi
Overview: Performance Management   xiii

Part A Memory Management   1

1 Introduction to VMS Memory Management   3
   Introduction   3
   Understanding VMS memory management V5.5-n   4
      an overview
   Changes to pool management V6.0   8

2 Secondary Caches (Free and Modified Page Lists)   13
   Introduction   13
   Free list   13
   Modified page list   14
   Some suggestions for determining the size of   18
      secondary caches
   Process working sets (balance set)   19

3 Automatic Working Set Adjustments   21
   Introduction   21
   Memory management terminology   21

4 What is Pagefaulting?   31
   Introduction   31
   CPU power (VUP rating) and pagefault rates   31
   Checking the pagefault rate   32
   Soft faults   33
   Hard faults   34
   System pagefaults   35
   Dead page table scans and degradation in system   36
      performance
   What is pagefault thrashing?   38

5 **Managing Pagefiles**   **41**

   Introduction   41

   Combining the pagefile with the dumpfile when   42
     disk space is limited

   Reducing the use of pagefile when memory is plentiful   43

   Processes and pagefile usage under VMS   44
     versions 4 and 5

6 **Swapper Trimming and Swapping**   **47**

   Swapper trimming and how it works   47

   Swapping and how it works   48

   Checking the swapping activity using Monitor and DCL   48

   Controlling swapping for optimal performance   52

   Steps to take when your swapfile space gets full   54

7 **Estimating Memory Needed**   **57**

   Introduction   57

   How to tune a system after adding memory (V5)   58

   How to tune a system after adding memory (V6)   58

8 **Using Memory Efficiently (Rules of Thumb)**   **61**

   Introduction   61

Part B   Disk I/O Management   65

9 **Understanding the Different Components of a Disk**   **67**
Transfer

   Introduction   67

   The components of a disk transfer   67

   Factors to consider when selecting disks   67

   Rules of thumb for selecting disks   69

10 **Raid and Storage Works**   **71**

   Development of RAID – a background   71

   Storage Works   79

11 **Rules of Thumb for Diagnosing Disk I/O Limitations**   **83**

   Introduction   83

   Commands to investigate possible I/O problems   83

   Determining direct I/O operation rate and queue length   84

   Determining average response time   87

	Determining hot disks/determining the problem device	89
	Determining the user with the top I/O rate	89
	Determining programs affecting the I/O rate	90
	Determining files opened affecting I/O rate	90
12	**Rules of Thumb for Unplugging a System Disk Bottleneck**	**95**
	Introduction	95
13	**Disk and HSC Load Balancing**	**101**
	Introduction	101
	HSC load balancing – rules of thumb	102
14	**Adjusting Disk Cluster Sizes for Performance**	**105**
	Introduction	105
	Disk cluster size and its effect on performance	105
15	**Caching, File System Activity and Performance**	**109**
	Towards a better understanding of the XQP and associated caches	109
	The file system caches	109
	Measuring file system caches performance	111
	Adjusting caching parameters	113
16	**Volume Shadowing and Performance**	**115**
	Introduction	115
	Volume shadowing features and terminology – a summarization	116
17	**MSCP Disk Server and Performance**	**119**
	MSCP Parameters	119
	Displaying and interpreting MSCP server statistics	120
18	**Disk Striping**	**123**
	Introduction	123
	Performance tuning considerations for striping disks	125
	Analyzing the performance of existing stripesets	127
19	**Additional Techniques to Reduce the I/O Workload**	**129**
	Introduction	129
	Backup and restore	138
20	**VMS File System Methodology, Fragmentation and Performance**	**141**
	Understanding the file system methodology	141

Window turns	144
Split I/Os	144
File system procedure for accessing data	145
What is disk fragmentation?	145
What is file fragmentation?	146
Problems of fragmentation	147
Curing the problems of fragmentation – rules of thumb	148

Part C   RMS Management and Application Optimization   153

21	**RMS Management**	**155**
	Introduction	155
	Types of buffering – local and global	156
	How are global buffers allocated?	157
	How RMS global buffers work in a VAX cluster	157
	SYSGEN parameters controlling global buffers	158
	Instances when global buffers are not used	162
	Points to remember about global buffers	162
	Optimizing bucket sizes for index files	163
22	**Rules of Thumb for Designing Files**	**165**
	Introduction	165

Part D   CPU Management   173

23	**CPU Management**	**175**
	Introduction	175
	Alpha AXP	176
24	**Scheduling and Scheduling States**	**181**
	What is scheduling?	181
	Scheduling states	181
24	**Locking and CPU Performance Management Within Clusters**	**191**
	Understanding the basics of lock mastering	191

Calculating the relative lock cost of a VAX cluster system 194
Rules of thumb for handling locks within a cluster 195
ENQs to VUPs ratio – some notes 195

26 **Diagnosing CPU Limitations** **197**
How to determine if the CPU forms a bottleneck 197
Developing a better understanding of CPU modes usage 201
+ some rules of thumb

27 **Rules of Thumb to Reduce CPU Limitations** **205**
Rules of thumb 205

Part E Changing SYSGEN Parameters 211

28 **Changing SYSGEN Parameters** **213**
Introduction 213
The role of AUTOGEN 214
Some useful AUTOGEN commands 215
Starting to use AUTOGEN for the first time 216
A word of warning about AUTOGEN 218
Making changes to SYSGEN – rules of thumb 219

Part F Tuning Layered Products 221

29 **Tips to Tune All-In-1 Under OpenVMS** **223**
Introduction 223
User authorization file (UAF) parameters 223
SYSGEN parameters 224
Page and swap file(s) 225
Rules of thumb – boosting All-IN-1 initialization process 226
Disk housekeeping 227
Global buffering for shared files 228
Maintenance of ALL-IN-1 files 229

30 **Tuning OpenVMS for TCP/IP** **231**
Introduction 231
Configure TCP/IP software optimally 231

Reduce the impact of overheads generated by TCP/IP software   232

31 **Tuning VMS for X-Windows**   **235**
    Introduction   235
    X-Windows tuning methodology   235

32 **Optimizing PATHWORKS Performance**   **239**
    Points to remember before installing PATHWORKS   239
    Guidelines to optimize PATHWORKS   240

Part G Optimizing RDBMS   243

33 **Understanding Relational Database Management Systems** **245**
    (RDBMS)
    Introduction   245

34 **Tips to Optimize ORACLE Applications**   **247**
    Introduction   247
    Some suggestions to improve the performance of your   249
        ORACLE applications

35 **Tips to Optimize Rdb Applications**   **265**
    Guidelines to optimize Rdb RDBMS   265

36 **Tips to Optimize INGRES Applications**   **273**
    Some suggestions to optimize INGRES applications   273

    Index *(general)*   **281**
    Index *(of parameters)*   **295**

x

Preface

If you hate computer manuals and haven't got time to waste this is the book you are looking for. The intended audience is the systems manager, database administrator, capacity planning/performance analyst, or applications analyst who wants to be able to tune his applications quickly and without wading through dozens of different books.

OpenVMS Performance Management is a concise assembly of hints and recommendations in just one easy to read book. The author of this book has a profound belief that the best advice is delivered in the fewest sentences, and it is that advice which is most likely to be put into practice. Oracle, Ingres, Rdb, X-Windows, ALL-IN-1, PATHWORKS – are all discussed, along with disk I/O, CPU, and memory management, with an attempt to help tune the applications built around them within a limited time and limited budget. On the other hand, if you do have surplus time and money...

Overview   Performance Management

This book is intended to assist those searching for guidance in OpenVMS performance management and application design. A variety of performance-related topics are discussed and guidelines are given, with examples on how to relieve specific problems. In this way, the reader can evaluate each technique and decide if it is applicable to their environment or not.

The book has been written to be a reference guide. It does not provide you with any magic solutions, because there are none. In most instances it will provide the reader with sufficient information to develop a good understanding of the issues involved and apply the techniques applicable to their environment.

The methods outlined in this book cannot be adopted uncritically, and a good system manager or a database administrator should not feel restricted to the guidelines given in this book, different approaches should be used where necessary – if the nature of the problem requires it. The techniques described in this book have proved more than adequate to solve a wide variety of performance and design problems but are by no means applicable to every type of configuration.

This book contains a large amount of information on a variety of performance-related topics including memory management (V5 and V6), disk I/O management, disk/file fragmentation, RMS local and global buffering, application design and optimization, CPU management, specific application tuning (ALL-IN-1, PATHWORKS, X-WINDOWS, and TCP/IP), RDBMS (ORACLE, INGRES, and Rdb), and making changes to SYSGEN parameters. There is a danger that some readers may feel that they are being subjected to an information overload. To obtain the maximum benefit from this guide, I recommend that the reader should concentrate on chapters of special interest to them.

Remember, system performance management is not just about meddling with SYSGEN parameters. Long before you consider getting into SYSGEN you must have a complete understanding of many items which constitute the normal behavior on your system. Below is a list of some of the main items which I think you should know.

Hardware configuration – disks (total number, capacity, transfer rate, etc.), total memory, CPU capacity, terminals population, network connectivity.

Software configuration – layered products, installed images, location of data files and application images, location of page and swap files, etc.

User environment – average number of users per day, distribution of users on nodes, applications used by various users, etc.

Operational issues – backups, batch runs normal/abnormal. Contingency procedures for hardware and software applications.

Workload environment – average number of users per day, peak and off-peak period, average response time, peak response time, peak and off-peak usage of CPU, memory and disk utilization, page fault rate, known problems, bottlenecks, etc.

VMS tools – Accounting, Monitor, Autogen, Sysgen, Authorize, etc.

Performance management tuning is a process which allows the most benefit to be obtained from the existing hardware and software, without harming user productivity, through the iterative adjustment of system/software parameters and the optimization of application design. It involves regular monitoring, trouble-shooting and the optimization of these resources to meet users' existing and future requirements. It comes from attention to detail and requires a disciplined approach from the developers, users, and people managing those systems.

Bear in mind, that a carefully administered performance management program can also help to minimize the chances of a sudden
degradation in performance and assist in isolating the precise
causes of declining performance and cure most of the performance
ills.

Part A   Memory Management

1   Introduction to VMS Memory Management

Introduction

VMS stands for Virtual Memory System and memory on a VMS system under V5.n but not under V6.n (for V6.n see *Changes to pool management V6.0*, on page 8, for details) is made up of 512-byte pages. On a VMS system, for a program to begin execution, only a portion of program needs to be in physical memory. The remaining memory which cannot fit in physical memory is stored on disks as virtual pages (512-byte blocks) in many forms, such as page, swap, and image files.

The VMS memory management system is responsible for all aspects of memory utilization on a Digital DEC VAX. These include management of both the physical and the virtual memory. Management of physical memory tasks include: the assignment of physical pages of memory to the elements needing memory, sharing memory and protecting memory for private use.

Virtual memory management tasks include: mapping of virtual memory to physical memory using tables, ensuring the availability of virtual memory, and management of virtual memory via working set lists. On a VMS system, memory is the most critical resource and should be available in abundance. But unless memory is utilized effectively it can have a disastrous affect on the performance of a computer system. Ineffective use and/or shortage of memory degrades performance by increasing the disk I/O and CPU consumption.

The two main components of the memory management sub-system are the pagefault handler and the swapper. The pagefault handler implements VMS virtual memory support and the swapper enables the system to utilize the physical memory available more effectively. A VMS system is designed to fault, but for optimal performance it is essential that memory management activities such as, paging and swapping are kept to a minimum.

While investigating performance problems, memory must be the first resource that is investigated for bottlenecks. Do not allow lack of memory to cripple the performance of a DEC VAX. Effective application of memory throughout the system can sometimes help reduce disk I/O and enhance performance. For anyone who is interested in applying memory effectively, it is important that they have a good understanding of the demands placed on memory by the existing workload.

This chapter will enable you to understand the fundamentals of VMS memory management mechanisms, develop a good knowledge of process and system parameters affecting memory management performance, understand terms used in discussing memory management, diagnose memory limitations, use memory more efficiently, and to use both DCL commands and VMS utilities to observe processes and systems for memory related statistics.

Memory is comparatively cheap and can be increased without the need to pay any additional software fees.

Understanding VMS memory management V5.5-n: an overview

Introduction

Physical memory on a VMS system is made up of 512-byte pages and can easily be divided into four major sections as shown in Figure 1.1.

Figure 1.1: VMS physical memory layout

VMS Fixed (Nonpaged dynamic memory)
VMS Variable (Paged Dynamic Memory)
Secondary Caches (Free and Modified page list)
Process Working sets (Balance set)

Nonpaged dynamic memory, more commonly known as nonpaged pool, consists of data structures such as device drivers, interrupt service routines, and process control blocks. It is the most commonly used of the storage areas. The three lookaside lists: small request packet (SRP), intermediate request packet (IRP), and large request packet (LRP) are the most frequently used nonpaged pool data structures. This part of the memory is controlled by two SYSGEN parameters NPAGEDYN and NPAGEVIR. Although referred to as 'fixed', this part of memory is potentially expandable during normal system operation. Figure 1.2 lists the SYSGEN parameters relevant to each lookaside lists.

Figure 1.2: SYSGEN parameters controlling lookaside lists (V5.n)

List Name	Controlling SYSGEN Parameters
SRP	SRPCOUNT, SRPCOUNTV, SRPSIZE
IRP	IRPCOUNT, IRPCOUNTV
LRP	LRPCOUNT, LRPCOUNTV, LRPSIZE

Figure 1.3: The uses of the lookaside lists (V5.n)

Lookaside List Name	Some Uses of Lookaside Lists
SRP	Interrupt dispatch blocks, Window control blocks, Timer queue requests, etc.
IRP	Device controller blocks, Job (Quota) control blocks, I/O device unit control blocks, I/O request packets, Lock Requests (Resource Control Blocks).
LRP	Used by DECNET for receiving messages from other nodes, allocation of device drivers.

Knowing when to adjust the lookaside list cache values for V5.5-n

Use the DCL command SHOW MEMORY/POOL/FULL to display information about paged and nonpaged pool areas. A sample display of an SRP Lookaside List is shown below. The display contains information on current and initial allocations for the three lookaside lists and the nonpaged pool along with the initial size and the largest free block for paged pool. The sample data in Table 1.1 show that the initial size and/or setting of 1529 packets for the IRP lookaside list was not enough to meet the demands placed on the system and additional request packets had to be allocated to grow to 1693 packets, the 'Current Total Size'.

If using VMS V5.n then all three lookaside lists (SRP, IRP, and LRP) should be checked for pool expansion periodically. If you find that a lookaside lists has extended, increase the initial allocation of the list using MODPARAMS.DAT to its 'Current Total Size'. In VMS V6.n these lookaside lists require no external tuning. When you find that the SRP has expanded, verify that OPCOM is running. This is because DECnet and print symbiont use SRPs to send messages to the operator mailbox. If OPCOM is not running then the messages from the mailbox are not removed and written to the operator log. In this case, start OPCOM using:

    $@SYS$SYSTEM: STARTUP OPCOM

Note: Log in as a SYSTEM user to execute the above command or ensure you have the necessary privileges if you are restarting OPCOM from another account. VMS Variable (paged dynamic memory) consists of data items which need not be memory resident and can include data structures such as, global section descriptors, known installed images header lists, the extended XQP I/O buffer cache, shareable logical name tables, access control list elements, and data structures required by the install utility to describe known images. It is controlled by the SYSGEN parameter PAGEDYN and is created as a set of demand zero pages. It expands on demand through pagefaults. For NPAGEDYN and PAGEDYN the free space size should be at least 30–40% of the current size, provided there is sufficient memory available. For PAGEDYN the largest contiguous block should be at least 20000 bytes. A value below that can result in INSUFFICIENT DYNAMIC MEMORY errors.

Table 1.1   Display from SHOW MEMORY/POOL/FULL

System Memory Resources

Small Packet (SRP) Lookaside List	Packets	Bytes	Pages
Current Total Size	2383	228768	447
Initial Size (SRPCOUNT)	2383	228768	447
Maximum Size (SRPCOUNTV)	7149	686304	1341
Free Space	652	62592	
Space in Use	1713	166176	
Packet Size/Upper Bound (SRPSIZE)		96	
Lower Bound on Allocation		32	

Table 1.1   (continued) Display from SHOW MEMORY/POOL/FULL

I/O Request Packet (IRP) Lookaside	Packets	Bytes		Pages
Current Total Size	1693	297968		582
Initial Size (IRPCOUNT)	1529	269104		526
Maximum Size (IRPCOUNTV)	4000	704000		1375
Free Space	550	96800		
Space in Use	1143	201168		
Packet Size/Upper Bound (fixed)		176		
Lower Bound on Allocation		97		
Large Packet (LRP) Lookaside List	**Packets**	**Bytes**		**Pages**
Current Total Size	68	112064		219
Initial Size (LRPCOUNT)	48	79104		155
Maximum Size (LRPCOUNTV)	192	316416		618
Free Space	24	39552		
Space in Use	44	72512		
Packet Size/Upper Bound (LRPSIZE + 80)		1648		
Lower Bound on Allocation		1088		
Nonpaged Dynamic Memory				
Current Size (bytes)	914432	Current Total Size (pages)	1786	
Initial Size (NPAGEDYN)	785408	Initial Size (pages)	1534	
Maximum Size (NPAGEVIR)	1745920	Maximum Size (pages)	3410	
Free Space (bytes)	66144	Space in Use (bytes)	848288	
Size of Largest Block	38128	Size of Smallest Block	16	
Number of Free Blocks	140	Free Blocks LEQU 32 bytes	31	
Paged Dynamic Memory				
Current Size (PAGEDYN)	594432	Current Total Size (pages)	1161	
Free Space (bytes)	262000	Space in Use (bytes)	332432	
Size of Largest Block	253408	Size of Smallest Block	16	
Number of Free Blocks	76	Free Blocks LEQU 32 Bytes	33	

Using the system dump analyzer (SDA) to check which data structures are depleting the pool resource

You can use the SDA to determine which data structures are depleting the pool resources. Investigate the data structures taking up too much space and if possible rectify the situation by taking the necessary action.

7

Sample commands:

```
$ANALYZE/SYSTEM
SDA > SET OUTPUT filename
SDA > SHOW POOL/SUMMARY
SDA > EXIT
```

If you find that the window control block data structure is the reason, then you can rectify this by making your files/disks contiguous. If you find that the PAGEDYN is mostly filled with LNM or LOG packets, then you may have excessive logical name creation problem. If you find that most of the PAGEDYN is unknown, then it is possible that you have defined large ACP caches, but there is not enough pool space to support these caches.

Changes to pool management V6.0

In this section I introduce some of the important changes which directly affect the performance of applications running under OpenVMS. These are not necessarily listed in the order of any importance.

Lookaside lists configuration and management (pool management)

Prior to OpenVMS V6.0 there were four regions of nonpaged pool consisting of three lookaside lists and a variable allocation region. See *Understanding VMS memory management V5.5-n: an overview*, on page 4, for details. In OpenVMS V6.0 Digital have introduced a new automatic nonpaged pool allocator and deallocator that automatically adapts to the workload's changing demand. Under the new mechanism allocator consists of only one region, the size of which is defined by the system parameters NPAGEDYN and NPAGEVIR.

This new mechanism for the management of nonpaged dynamic storage pool has simplified the system management process and reduced the possibility of system performance degradation and system downtime. Prior to V6.0, depletion of lookaside lists required the intervention of system managers to make modifications to system parameters and reboot the system. See the *Introduction*, on page 3, for details.

In version 6.0 the nonpaged pool area and the lookaside (SRP, IRP, and LRP) lists are put together into one region and therefore the following SYSGEN parameters are now obsolete:

IRPCOUNT, IRPCOUNTV, SRPCOUNT, SRPCOUNTV, SRPSIZE,
LRPCOUNT, LRPCOUNTV, LRPSIZE, LRPMIN

Because of these changes in nonpaged pool management the following is either no longer relevant or has changed:

1. MONITOR POOL display is no longer relevant and has been removed.

2. DCL command SHOW MEMORY now displays the total number of bytes represented by both variable pool and the lookaside lists in a single line identified as Nonpaged Dynamic Memory.

3. SDA command SHOW POOL display pool statistics differently from previous releases. The display now represent the combined total of variable pool and the 80 (see *The structure of the new lookaside lists*, on page 10, for details) lookaside lists.

How is the nonpaged pool area initially sized under OpenVMS V6.0?

During the upgrade process V5.5-n SYSGEN values are used to initially size the nonpaged pool area. The new NPAGEDYN parameter value is calculated using the formulas shown below, and the greater resultant value is chosen:

(LRPCOUNT*1792) + (SRPCOUNT*128) + (IRPCOUNT*192) + NPAGEDYN

or

(19000*No. of Nodes) + 750736
(essential for the OpenVMS VAX upgrade)

NPAGEVIR is calculated as 4 times the value of NPAGEDYN.

Note: Once the upgrade is complete and the new system has been running for at least 48 hours you must run AUTOGEN in FEEDBACK mode to resize the nonpaged pool area.

The structure of the new lookaside lists

The new structure consists of 80 lists spanning in range from 1 to 5120 bytes, in 64-byte increments (64, 128, 192, 256... 5120 bytes). These lookaside lists require no external tuning. They are implemented as self-relative, interlocked queues which are automatically prepopulated during bootstrapping based on previous demand by the SYSINIT process which reads the SYS$SYSTEM:LISTPREPOP.DAT file. Under version 6.0 this new structure exists in three forms listed below:

- allocated
- free in a lookaside list
- free in general pool.

Each list continuously adapts its number of packets based on changing demand during the life of the system.

How does the nonpaged pool memory allocation routine work?

On demand, the request packet size is rounded upwards to the next multiple of 64 bytes. The structure of the list is examined to see if there is free corresponding packet. If available, it is allocated from the corresponding list otherwise a request is made for allocation from the variable length pool. If the size of the request packet is greater than 5120 bytes it is then satisfied from the variable length pool.

The purpose of nonpaged pool memory reclamation

The purpose of memory reclamation is to conserve nonpaged memory. The deallocation routine is responsible for returning the packets to the lookaside list. Surplus packets from the lookaside lists are returned to the variable-length general pool, these are the excess packets allocated during demand spikes. The first three lists are excluded from the reclamation process. The reclamation takes place every 30 seconds. The lists are reclaimed in two phases. The first phase is referred as *gentle phase*, in this phase one packet is reclaimed on each run for lists 4 through to 80. The second phase is known as *aggressive reclamation*, this routine is invoked before pool expansion is performed in an attempt to increase the variable-length pool list. During this reclamation phase, a packet may be reclaimed even if doing so leaves the list empty.

Pool checking

The SYSGEN parameter POOLCHECK allows you to check pool management statistics if set to 1, by default it is set to 0 which means no pool management statistics are checked.

2 Secondary Caches (Free and Modified Page Lists)

Introduction

Free and modified page lists make up the secondary caches and are designed to cut I/O to disk. The idea is to have as large caches as possible, but not so large as to degrade the performance of the system by taking memory away from user processes. If the caches are large enough they will ensure that most of the faults are to memory and not to disk. VMS is very efficient in handling pagefaults to memory. Hard faults consume approximately 50% of extra system resources and therefore must be avoided.

Free list

Free list contains pages of memory which can be allocated to users and overwritten (ie it is the list of all the free physical memory pages). Free list is also used by VMS paging mechanism. When a process is in need of additional memory, VMS allocates it from free list providing there are sufficient free pages available. Parameters which control the size of free page list are described below.

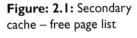 **Figure: 2.1:** Secondary cache – free page list

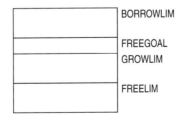

BORROWLIM

FREEGOAL
GROWLIM

FREELIM

BORROWLIM

The user's WSLIMIT is not allowed to grow beyond its WSQUOTA value until there are at least BORROWLIM pages on the free list. It is the size that the free list has to reach before a user process is allowed to grow above its WSQUOTA. If your working set quotas such as WSQUOTA, WSDEFAULT, and WSEXTENT are properly tuned, then there is less need for a process to borrow memory. The value of BORROWLIM should never be more than one-half of the user memory.

FREEGOAL

Defines the desired size of the free page list. Once the free list has fallen below the FREELIM value, the swapper attempts to make it the size of FREEGOAL. Ensure that this parameter is large enough to minimize the execution of SWAPPER.

FREELIM

Defines the lower limit specifying the minimum size of the list. The value of this parameter should be quite small. When the size of the free list falls below the FREELIM value, VMS starts looking elsewhere to support growing memory demands. To improve paging performance ensure that working set quotas are adequate for all user processes.

GROWLIM

This is the size that free list must reach before a user's WSSIZE is allowed to grow beyond its WSQUOTA value and has not reached its WSEXTENT size. The value of this parameter should never be more than one-quarter of the user memory.

Modified page list

The modified page list contains pages that may have been modified since they first appeared in memory. Pages in the modified list cannot be overwritten by other user processes. Once per second, VMS executive checks to see whether the modified page list needs flushing. If so, pages are written to the mass storage in clusters, after which those pages are allocated to the free list.

Whenever a process releases a page of memory which has been written onto, that page is placed on the modified page list. Parameters which control the size of the modified page list are described below. Since the release of version 5.0, a number of changes have been made (by Digital) to the modified page writer in order to achieve greater throughput. Multi-threading was introduced, which now enables it to initiate up to 127 I/O requests concurrently. The SYSGEN parameter MPW_IOLIMIT controls this feature. The default value of this parameter is 4.

Figure 2.2: Secondary cache – modified page list

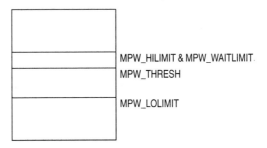

MPW_HILIMIT & MPW_WAITLIMIT.

MPW_THRESH

MPW_LOLIMIT

A new parameter MPW_LOWAITLIMIT has also been introduced which allows the processes to be released at a higher value.

MPW_HILIMIT
Defines the maximum size of the modified page list. When the modified page list reaches this size, some pages are flushed out to the page file.

MPW_WAITLIMIT
Forces a process to wait when the modified page list is full until it is emptied.

Warning: MPW_WAITLIMIT and MPW_HILIMIT should be approximately the same, but it should never be set below MPW_HILIMIT, otherwise the system will hang.

MPW_LOLIMIT
Defines the lower limit for the modified page list (ie it defines the minimum number of pages that will reside on the modified page list). When reduced to this size, pages are written to the page file. Set it to about half the value of MPW_HILIMIT.

Tip: Be careful while setting the upper limit size: a value too high may take away the much needed memory from the processes; a value that is too low may result from the excessive flushing of the pages to the page file. This parameter set to approximately 10% of the total physical memory often results in good performance.

MPW_THRESH

Suggests that modified page list is ready for trimming when it grows beyond this value (ie acts as a trigger for the modified page list writing). Set it to (approximately) less than 12% of balance set memory. To reduce and/or to disable excessive writing of the modified page list set it to its highest possible value.

MPW_LOWAITLIMIT

This parameter specifies the threshold at which the processes in the MPWBUSY state are allowed to resume. It decides when a process may start using the modified page list again once the flushing is triggered. Prior to VMS version V5, processes stayed in MPWBUSY state until the size of the modified page list was cut down to MPW_LOLIMIT. This parameter can significantly enhance the performance of fast processors with large memories by reducing the amount of time spent in the miscellaneous wait state MPWBUSY.

Use:

    MPW_LOWAITLIMIT = MPW_HILIMIT - (MPW_WRTCLUSTER * 2)

to set the value of this parameter.

MPW_IOLIMIT

Specifies the number of I/Os outstanding to the modified page writer. In previous versions of VMS (prior to VMS V5), the modified page writer was single-threaded and could only write one cluster of pages at a time (ie it could not have more than one I/O outstanding, so bottlenecks were possible under peak loads). Under VMS version 5, it can initiate a maximum of 127 concurrent I/O requests. The default value of this parameter is 4. Set the value of this parameter to 8 or above and place the page files on fast disk drives to achieve the maximum benefit of this new parameter. Each I/O operation request requires approximately 752 bytes of permanent nonpaged pool allocation. This is calculated from:

    176 + (6 * MPW_WRTCLUSTER)

MPW_WRTCLUSTER

Defines the maximum number of pages that the modified page writer can cluster before writing it to the page file (ie it determines the number of pages that can be written to the page file in a single I/O operation). The default value is 120.

Relationship among the modified page writer parameters

AUTOGEN forces the following relationship among the modified page list SYSGEN parameters:

```
MPW_WAITLIMIT >= MPW_HILIMIT
MPW_LOWAITLIMIT <= MPW_HILIMIT
MPW_LOWAITLIMIT >= MPW_LOLIMIT
```

Some events which trigger modified page writing

1. When the modified page list exceeds the limit defined by the SYSGEN parameter MPW_HILIMIT.

2. When the free page list fall below its limit defined by the SYSGEN parameter FREELIM.

3. During system shutdown.

4. When a process needs to reuse its working set list entry (WSLE) containing a page that is dormant but still maps transition pages on the modified page list.

5. When a writeable global section with pages on the modified list is deleted.

Some suggestions for reducing the frequent flushing of modified page lists

Frequent flushing of the modified page list can degrade system performance. Modified page list is flushed out to the page file until the number of pages on the list reaches:

```
MPW_LOLIMIT (before VMS 5.2)
MPW_LOWAITLIMIT (since VMS V5.2)
```

The entire list can be flushed for any one of the reasons described in *Some events which trigger modified page writing*. The most common reason for the flushing of the modified page list is the release of a working set list entry to make room for another page. How then can we reduce the frequent flushing of Modified Page List? The answer is not to allow programs to reduce the working set sizes. Check the working set sizes by using:

SHOW PROCESS/CONTINUOUS/ID = n

If the working set size equals the WSEXTENT value, increase the size of WSEXTENT and SYSGEN parameter WSMAX accordingly. Ensure that the page files are at least 50% free. Use multiple page files of equal size.

Check the swapping activity on your system; if high, then check the free space. Swap files should be at least 25% free. Set it to twice the value of the SYSGEN parameter WSMAX.

Check for a high system fault rate, using MONITOR PAGE command. If greater than 1, check the 'Paged Dynamic Memory' with the DCL command SHOW MEMORY. It should be at least 40% free. Make changes if necessary using MODPARAMS.DAT and reboot. If the problem persists, adjust the value for the system working set using the formula:

SYSMWCNT = GBLPAGES/128 + PAGEDYN/512 + 370

This provides an initial estimate of SYSMWCNT. If necessary, add more memory and increase the working set sizes.

Some suggestions for determining the size of secondary caches

I have followed the guidelines shown below for various DEC VAX sites and found them to be useful – some adjustments were made to achieve the optimal balance of hard and soft faults. To get the correct balance of the hard and soft faults on your system, some adjustments to the values suggested below may be necessary.

FREELIM
Set to 1000 + (100*(n–5)), where n is the number of megabytes of memory. But it should never be less one page per process.

FREEGOAL
Set to three times the value of FREELIM.

BORROWLIM
For small machines, set to approximately 20% of the total physical memory. For large machines, set to approximately 8% of the total physical memory.

GROWLIM
Set to about 45% of the BORROWLIM value.

Process working sets (balance set)

Balance set consists of pages mapped onto physical memory for each user process in memory. It is a set of resident working sets controlled by the SYSGEN parameter BALSETCNT. It defines the number of processes that can reside in memory concurrently. It should be set to lower than MAXPROCESSCNT. Use the command SHOW MEMORY to see if you are using all your BALANCE SET SLOTS. If all the 'balance set slots' are used, the swapper swaps out a process to free a slot for a new process.

To reduce BALANCE SET SWAPPING, set the SYSGEN parameter BALSETCNT to MAXPROCESSCNT-2.

If you wish to accommodate more processes on your system you might need to increase the values of MAXPROCESSCNT and BALSETCNT. These two values are fairly close and BALSETCNT should never be greater than MAXPROCESSCNT. If the BALSETCNT value is set too low, then very few processes will be able to reside in memory simultaneously, resulting in the rest of the processes being outswapped. Other parameters associated with balance slot memory consumption are listed below.

MAXPROCESSCNT
This parameter defines the maximum number of processes that can run on a system. If there are more than BALSETCNT processes, then some processes working set slots are written to swap slots. Do not allow AUTOGEN to tune BALSETCNT for you as VMS version 5.4 drastically reduces the value of this parameter which results in a large number of processes being outswapped and increasing the likelihood of performance degradation.

Specify your own value in MODPARAMS.DAT. For instance, on a system where MAXROCESSCNT is 100, specify a value of 98 for BALSETCNT in MODPARAMS.DAT as follows:

```
MIN_BALSETCNT = 98
```

This will force the AUTOGEN to use the value of BALSETCNT specified in MODPARAMS.DAT.

VIRTUALPAGECNT

Determines the maximum number of virtual pages that can be allocated to a process. Four bytes of permanently resident memory are reserved for every 128 virtual pages. Set it to the value of dump file plus 3000 pages.

PROSECTCNT

Determines the number of section descriptors that each process can hold. An additional 32 bytes are added to the fixed portion of the process header per section descriptor.

WSMAX

Defines the upper limit that any process working set list may grow to. It should be set equal to the highest WSEXTENT value on your system. Do not set it too high, as this parameter is used in reserving memory for process headers for active processes on your system. If the value set is too high, it will unnecessarily reserve large amounts of space which could be made available for user processes. Balance slot bytes for active process headers is calculated as follows:

Number of Active Processes * ((WSMAX * 4)+PROSECTCNT*32) + (VIRTUALPAGECNT/32))

The operating system allows a number of processes to run concurrently including the supervisor (executive) system. Each process is given its own virtual address space. A portion of this virtual space is mapped onto the physical memory.

3   Automatic Working Set Adjustments

Introduction

VMS operates a sophisticated memory management mechanism known as automatic working set adjustment (AWSA) which enables processes to acquire additional memory to optimize program performance (when there is abundant memory available). This section refers to memory management terminology, the SYSGEN parameters controlling processes memory environment, and defines the AWSA algorithm as employed by VMS.

Memory management terminology

Working set size and working set list size

Working set can be defined as the set of pages that a process can access without a pagefault. In other words, the working set size corresponds to the number of pages that a process owns in physical memory. You can calculate the working set size of active processes by adding the values returned by the DCL lexical function:

F$GETJPI(pid,"PPGCNT") *and*
F$GETJPI(pid,"GPGCNT").

The working set list size defines the maximum number of pages a process may have in its working set before it must release a page to add a new page. VMS uses first-in-first-out technique for page replacement. Working set list size is always greater than or equal to working-set size: it bounds the working set size – this ensures that a process does not tie up memory required by another processes on the system.

Parameters controlling the working set list sizes

WSDEFAULT, WSQUOTA and WSEXTENT values define the working set limits (upper limits) for a process. Initial values are assigned at the account creation stage (using AUTHORIZE) and are derived from the user authorization file (UAF).

WSDEFAULT (working set default)
Defines the initial working set limit for a process at image activation. At most sites this limit is set below the WSQUOTA value. There is no reason to do this with the latest versions of VMS, as it simply slows down the image activation process.

WSQUOTA (working set quota)
Defines the next (general limit). Process requiring additional memory are authorized to grow to its WSQUOTA value under all circumstances.

WSEXTENT (working set extent)
Defines the final limit. Memory-hungry processes may be able to extend the working set space to this limit providing there is sufficient free memory available on the system.

Warning: Be careful while assigning WSQUOTA values; if the quota values are too big, it is possible that you system could run out of memory.

WSEXTENT is limited by the SYSGEN parameter WSMAX. A process's extent region cannot be greater than WSMAX. You should set WSMAX to the maximum number of pages required by any process on your system.

Figure 3.1: Working set limit parameters

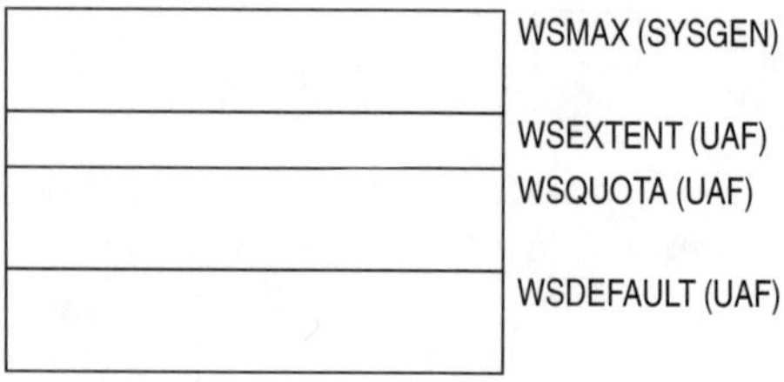

WSMAX (SYSGEN)

WSEXTENT (UAF)
WSQUOTA (UAF)

WSDEFAULT (UAF)

Understanding automatic working set adjustment algorithm

Working set list grow mechanism

For each process, VMS collects pagefault statistics over the period defined by two SYSGEN parameters: QUANTUM and AWSTIME. By default, these two parameter values are equal (ie exactly the same). At the end of a QUANTUM period VMS checks to see if a process has also reached the end of its automatic working set adjustment interval; only then does it proceed to perform AWSA.

The first part of the adjustment is performed by checking whether the pagefault rate is greater than the SYSGEN parameter PFRATH (this parameter defines the upper limit of acceptable pagefaulting for all processes). If the pagefault rate is greater than PFRATH, then the working set list is increased by WSINC entries (a SYSGEN parameter that specifies the number of pages by which the limit of the working set is automatically increased at each adjustment interval). This way, VMS allocates additional working set list entries to a process and to use these entries a process must pagefault to make them valid.

Working set growth limits

There is a second level of limit which is defined by the UAF parameter WSQUOTA (working set quota). The working set quota is allowed to grow up to the value of this parameter under all circumstances. Always check the number of processes running on your system including the amount of free memory available, before assigning quota values.

Can a process grow beyond its WSQUOTA value?

The third and final level of limit is defined by the UAF parameter WSEXTENT (sets the maximum number of pages to which a process can grow). The area between quota and extent is known as the *loan region*. When a process is faulting heavily it can grow above its WSQUOTA limit, providing there are at least BORROWLIM pages on the free list. If there are not enough free pages the process working set list is not incremented, and the process can then only replace old pages for new. In other words, it must give up some pages in order to acquire new pages. Before allowing a process to grow above its WSQUOTA value, VMS also ensures that the process has not already reached its WSEXTENT.

What happens when too many processes are attempting to add pages?
When a number of processes are attempting to add pages at once, VMS stops the growth of the processes that have already grown above their quota value. Such processes must give up some of their page allocation to read in new pages. Other processes are allowed to grow providing there are a sufficient number of free pages on the free page list as indicated by the SYSGEN parameter GROWLIM.

Can memory be taken away from the processes?
For the processes which are generating less than PFRATL faults VMS decreases the working set list size by WSDEC pages providing PFRATL is a non-zero value. This reduction, as with growth, takes place at QUANTUM end, normalized over AWSTIME. No process is reduced below the SYSGEN parameter AWSMIN (which defines the lowest number of pages to which a process's working set can be decreased by VMS).

Why is the default value for PFRATL and WSDEC zero?
When an image is first activated, the process in control of that image faults heavily to bring in the sections of image executable code. Heavy pagefaulting results in a rapid increase in the working set list size. Once an image is loaded, most processes reach their ideal working set list size and generate a reduced level of faulting or no faulting at all. This means that if WSDEC was set to a non-zero value, the VMS AWSA mechanism will reduce the size of the working set list and you will notice that processes are continuously faulting as the working set size grows and shrinks. This is because VMS attempts to keep its pagefault rate within the limits defined by PFRATH and PFRATL.

Automatic working set decrementing, if enabled, removes working set pages from processes which are pagefaulting less than PFRATL. This often introduces more pagefaulting and can affect system performance and results in high kernel mode activity.

Is working set decrementing degrading system performance?
If you suspect that working set decrementing is affecting your system performance, use the DCL command SHOW SYSTEM to check if the working sets for processes are oscillating – ie 'Ph.Mem' keeps increasing and shrinking for many processes. If the above is happening, check the amount of memory available on the system using SHOW MEMORY/FULL and MONITOR PAGE. If there is

plenty of free memory available on the system, then AWSD could be affecting the performance of your system. You must then turn off AWSD by setting the SYSGEN parameter PFRATL to zero using MODPARAMS.DAT. You may also use SYSGEN to set PFRATL to zero immediately as it is a dynamic parameter.

Working set adjustments for interactive processes

User processes working set limits are derived from the User Authorization File (UAF). For interactive processes these values may be increased or lowered using the DCL command (providing you have the appropriate privileges):

```
$SET WORKING_SET/QUOTA=n
```

You may also change the value of the extent region:

```
$SET WORKING SET/EXTENT = n
```

If you wish to make a permanent change, then you must make those using AUTHORIZE. The procedure assumes that you have the necessary privileges to make these changes to the UAF entries, and AUTHORIZE has previously been invoked. Once in AUTHORIZE, use the MODIFY command to make the necessary changes:

```
UAF > MODIFY username/WSQUOTA = n/WSEXTENT = n
UAF > EXIT
```

Working set adjustments for batch jobs

For batch jobs, if no quota limits are specified when the job is submitted, the process obtains those by default from the user UAF entries. It is best to determine the quota values for each job and submit the jobs with the required limits as shown below:

```
$SUBMIT/QUEUE=queue_name/WSDEFAULT = n-
/WSQUOTA =n/WSEXTENT=n program_name
```

If you intend to run memory-intensive jobs through a batch queue, then you may prefer to set high working set values for that batch. This is done when a queue is first initialized as follows:

```
$INITIALIZE/QUEUE=queue_name/-
BATCH /WSDEFAULT=n /WSQUOTA=n /WSEXTENT=n
```

If a queue is already running, then you must stop the queue using the DCL command:

```
$STOP/QUEUE queue_name
```

Use the DCL INITIALIZE command as shown above and then start the queue using:

```
$START/QUEUE queue_name
```

You can also set high quota values for a batch queue, then these quota values apply to all jobs submitted to that queue for execution. To display the characteristics of a batch queue, type:

```
$SHOW QUEUE=queue_name /FULL
```

You may also change the characteristics of a batch job before the job starts to execute by using:

```
$SET QUEUE/ENTRY=n /WSQUOTA=n /WSEXTENT=n batch_queue_name
```

where n with /ENTRY qualifier is the entry number of your job within the queue.

Adjusting working set limits for detached processes

All detached jobs take their working set limit values from the PQL_D SYSGEN parameters unless they have been explicitly specified using the RUN command. For each quota field in the UAF there is an equivalent PQL_D parameter – see Figure 3.2.

Figure 3.2: Showing detached processes working set limit parameters

UAF Quota Field	Equivalent PQL Parameter
WSDEFAULT	PQL_DWSDEFAULT
WSQUOTA	PQL_DWSQUOTA
WSEXTENT	PQL_DWSEXTENT

There is also a second set of PQL parameters:

```
PQL_Mquota_name parameters
```

which specify the absolute minimum working set limits for a process. When you log in as a VMS user, initially your process is created using the PQL_D limits, only later to be replaced with your

UAF working set limits, that is only if the UAF values are greater than the absolute minimum values specified by PQL_M parameters.

All PQL parameters are dynamic (except PQL_DWSDEFAULT and PQL_MWSDEFAULT) and providing you have the appropriate privileges you can change them using the SYSGEN utility as described in Part E. Only change the PQL parameters if you are absolutely sure that it is the detached processes which are affecting performance due to insufficient working set limits.

Displaying working set limits

You may display the working set limits specified by your system manager using the command:

$SHOW WORKING_SET

Table 3.1   Output from SHOW WORKING_SET

Working set / limit=512	/Quota=1024	/Extent=2048
Adjustment enabled	Authorized Quota=1024	Authorized Extent=2048

Calculating the 'ideal' working set size for a particular image

There are several techniques available to measure the 'ideal' working set size, but the most common technique is to run the image on a system with ample free memory, from an account with WSEXTENT set high (approximately equal to the value of WSMAX, but not greater than WSMAX). You should then monitor the process from another terminal using the DCL command:

$SHOW PROCESS/CONTINUOUS/ID = < pid-number >

Watch the display closely for the VIRTUAL PAGE size and the WORKING SET size when the program is running. The virtual page size indicates the amount of memory the executable would use if it were all in memory. The working set size indicates the number of pages currently available to the program. You may notice that the 'working set' grows rapidly soon after the image is executed and then starts to level off. If the working set does not level off and equals the WSEXTENT value and stays there, it proves that the process needs a larger working set to reduce pagefaults.

You can re-execute the program with larger WSEXTENT and WSMAX values and determine the working set size, but the program may require more memory than available on your system. You may have to accommodate high page faulting when this image is run unless you can add more memory and tune the processes working set sizes accordingly.

Changes to memory management V5.5-n

Prior to VMS V5.4–3 inactive processes retained unused memory until the process finished automatically or the memory was reclaimed by trimming and/or swapping. On memory-deficient systems this frequently restricts the growth of active processes and results in excessive page faulting. Since the introduction of VMS V5.4–3 memory management has changed dramatically, a new mechanism called 'proactive memory reclamation' has been introduced which can detect memory deficiency before the resource is completely depleted. The SYSGEN parameter MMT_CTLFLAGS controls proactive memory. This new feature recovers memory from idle and periodically executing processes as follows.

Proactive memory reclamation – idle processes

This allows VMS to remove pages from the process working set without reducing their working set sizes. The procedure is triggered when the free list reaches FREEGOAL, and enables the system to free up memory for other processes. Memory is reclaimed from idle processes in LEF or HIB state, with no activity at all for LONGWAIT seconds. Working set pages are reduced to SWPOUT-PGCNT, but the working set size remains unchanged. This enables the processes to add pages to their working sets quickly when additional pages are needed.

Proactive memory reclamation – periodically executing processes

This mechanism is triggered when the size of the free list drops below twice the value of the SYSGEN parameter FREEGOAL. The procedure reclaims memory from processes which wake up occasionally and then return to sleep. Working set size is not reduced as with the memory reclamation from idle processes.

The mechanism watches for processes that are only active for a very small percentage of the time ($< 1\%$ over a given period). Once such processes are detected, 25% of the pages in the working set are released to the free list. This process is iterative and after the next period of time (provided free list is still below 2*FREEGOAL) the pseudo-idle process could see another 25% of its pages in use removed. Obviously by removing 25% each time the process never ends up with no pages at all and by not reducing the work set size the process can quickly recover memory if it needs to.

Changes to memory management V6.0

Proactive memory reclamation

In OpenVMS V6.0 the value of the SYSGEN parameter MMG_CTLFLAGS is set to 3 by default. In the previous versions of VMS this value was set to 253. As explained in *Changes to memory management V5.5-n*, on page 28, this parameter controls the proactive memory management and memory reclamation mechanism under OpenVMS. A value of 3 ensures that proactive memory management system is enabled. For details on proactive memory management, see *Changes to memory management V5.5-n*, on page 28.

Users working set quota values under V6.0

OpenVMS V6.0 now supports working sets up to 512 Mb. The maximum value of the system parameter WSMAX has been raised to 1048576.

Extended addressing (XA)

Under OpenVMS V6.0 XA is supported on VAX 6000-600, VAX 7000-600 and VAX 10000 systems. This characteristic enlarges both the physical and virtual addressing architecture of these processors. Physical memory capacity has increased from 512 Mb to 3.5 Gb. Extended physical addressing (XVA) increases the system virtual address space from 1 Gb to 2 Gb. S1 space is appended to S0 space to create a single region of system space.

Virtual balance slots (VBS)

Prior to OpenVMS V6.0 the number of concurrent memory resident processes was limited by the size of system virtual address space. Whenever this limit was exceeded, user processes were swapped out according to the criteria defined in Chapter 6. Excessive swapping can have a serious impact on system performance (see Chapter 6 for details). With the introduction of OpenVMS V6.0, VBS allows you to have unlimited number of user processes residing concurrently through timesharing of the available virtual address space.

The system parameter MMG$GB_VBSS_ENABLE allows you to enable and disable VBS.

4   What is Pagefaulting?

Introduction

A virtual page begins life as a block of an image file. A process activates the image and VMS maps the pages loaded to a process's address space. When a process references a page of virtual memory that is not contained in its address space, it generates a pagefault. Depending upon the circumstances this page reference request may be satisfied from the physical memory or the disk. A VMS system is designed to fault but excessive amounts of pagefaulting can have a disastrous affect on the overall system performance and must be minimized for optimal performance.

The most common reason for high pagefaulting is the inappropriate allocation of working set sizes controlled by the three SYSUAF parameters: WSDEFAULT, WSQUOTA and WSEXTENT – see *Understanding automatic working set adjustment algorithm*, on page 23, for details.

CPU power (VUP rating) and pagefault rates

The number of pagefaults per second your VMS machine can handle is directly related to the VUP rating (speed) of the CPU. In general, a DEC VAX CPU can handle approximately 100 faults per second per VAX unit of processing (VUP), before incurring additional CPU overhead. Table 4.1 contains suggested threshold values for various DEC VAX CPUs. Use these suggested values as a yardstick to measure the overall pagefault rate performance. Maximum overall page rates often vary with the type of processor (uniprocessor or multiprocessor), workload and types (mix) of application running on a machine. These figures are to be used as a guideline, your workload and your knowledge of the applications environment are the best determinants of an acceptable pagefault rate for your configuration. If your configuration exceeds the threshold values suggested in Table 4.1, then you should take appropriate steps to minimize the overall page fault rate and improve memory responsiveness, especially if these are sustained over a long period of time.

Table 4.1   Suggested page rate values (threshold)

Maximum Suggested Page Fault Rate Per Second (Approximate Values)	DEC VAX Processors	Maximum Suggested Page Fault Rate Per Second (Approximate Values)	DEC VAX Processors
30	M VAX 1, VAX 11/725, VAX 11/730	800	VAX 8820, 6330
60	VAX 11/750	900	VAX 6330, 6340, 6350, 6420, 6510
75	MVAX II, VAX 2000	1500	VAX 6430
80	VAX 11/780, VAX 8200	2000	VAX 6440, 6520
100	VAX 8250	2500	VAX 6460, 6530
150	VAX 11/785, VAX 8300	3000	VAX 9210, 9410
200	MVAX 3110	3500	VAX 6540
250	MVAX 3120, 3500, VAX 6210, VAX 4200	5000	VAX 9220, 9420
300	VAX 8530, 8600, 6310	7000	VAX 9430
350	VAX 6320, 6410, VAX 4300	9400	VAX 9440
490	VAX 8650, VAX 8700, VAX 8810	1750	VAX 4500
		1800-8000	VAX 6610, 6620, 6630, 6640

Checking the pagefault rate

Check the pagefault rates (hard, soft, global, demand, system, etc.) using the MONITOR utility command: $MONITOR PAGE/ALL.

Table 4.2   Summary output from MONITOR PAGE command

VAX/VMS Monitor Utility PAGE MANAGEMENT STATISTICS				
	CUR	AVE	MIN	MAX
Page Fault Rate	47.37	61.83	9.90	134.50
Page Read Rate	31.46	37.70	5.65	81.41
Page Read I/O Rate	7.87	5.85	0.95	11.81
Page Write Rate	4.19	8.63	0.00	25.74
Page Write I/O Rate	0.02	0.12	0.00	0.39
Free List Fault Rate	4.22	4.23	0.89	9.46
Modified List Fault Rate	6.00	12.95	1.32	29.64

Table 4.2 (continued) Summary output from MONITOR PAGE command

Demand Zero Fault Rate	8.64	10.20	0.65	26.65
Global Valid Fault Rate	20.32	28.09	4.96	66.94
Wrt In Progress Fault Rate	0.00	0.03	0.00	0.12
System Fault Rate	1.18	0.81	0.13	2.63
Free List Size	5602.00	1240.66	132.00	5602.00
Modified List Size	669.00	638.70	32.00	1209.00

Total pagefault rate is the sum of all hard faults and soft faults. Different varieties of hard and soft faults are discussed below.

Soft faults

A soft pagefault occurs when a process makes a reference to a virtual page that is not in its working set and the request is satisfied from the physical memory. There are several varieties of soft faults and these can be measured using the MONITOR PAGE command. Each soft fault involves some CPU overhead but compared to hard faults, the CPU overhead associated with soft faults is very small. Soft pagefaults is the sum of:

> Free List Fault Rate, Modified List Fault Rate, Demand Zero Fault Rate, Global Valid Faults and Wrt In Progress Fault Rate.

Global valid faults
A soft fault which occurs when a page reference request is satisfied by mapping a shared page that is already valid (already in another process's working set). It is useful to increase the global valid fault rate and thereby reduce the hard fault rate by installing images as shared images. Use the VMS INSTALL utility to install the image as a /SHARED image.

Demand zero faults
Demand zero fault rates are basically the result of image activations. Image activation is part of VMS and is unavoidable. Excessive use of DCL procedures are sometimes the cause of high image activation. If more than about 35% of the aggregate paging activity is attributed to demand zero fault rate, it is possible that the system is suffering from excessive image activations. By issuing a MONITOR PAGE command demand zero pagefaults can be observed. Total fault rate for this type of fault should not exceed

50% of the overall fault rate. As suggested above install the most frequently and concurrently used images as shared images to reduce the amount of image level activity.

Free list faults
Pagefaults which can be satisfied from the secondary cache (free page list) and are mainly the result of inappropriate working set sizes allocations.

Modified list faults
Pagefaults which can be satisfied by referencing the modified page list (secondary cache). Also the result of insufficient working set quota sizes.

Hard faults

A hard page fault occurs when a process makes a reference to a virtual page that is not in its working set and the request is satisfied from the page or image file on the disk. In other words, hard faults involve a disk I/O operation and are undesirable. There are certain types of hard faults which cannot be avoided on a VMS system. For example, to execute an image (a program instruction), VMS must load the executable image file (a portion of an image file) into its physical memory.

Calculating hard pagefault rate

To determine the hard pagefault rate, subtract the sum of soft faults (Free List Fault Rate, Modified List Fault Rate, Demand Zero Fault Rate, Global Valid Faults, and Wrt In Progress Fault Rates) from the overall Page Fault Rate.

Hard Page Fault Rate = Page Fault Rate – Soft Faults

On average, the total number of hard faults should not exceed 10% of the overall faults. Each hard fault involves some CPU and disk overhead; it is approximately 50 times more expensive than a single soft fault. It is likely that your secondary page caches are too small to support a desirable hard and soft fault ratio. You may also use MONITOR STATES command to check which processes are waiting for hard pagefaults to be satisfied.

System pagefaults

The system executive (like any other process) needs a working set (physical space in memory) in which to execute. A non-zero value in the System Fault Rate column of the MONITOR PAGE display (see Table 4.2) means that the VMS operating system is pagefaulting and needs additional memory. It is possible for all user processes to halt until this type of fault is satisfied.

The SYSGEN parameter SYSMWCNT controls the system working set space. Increase the value of this parameter if the average system fault rate is greater than 1%, but only if additional memory is available. Any additional memory allocated to the system working set is permanently allocated to the system and therefore is no longer available for user processes. A system reboot is necessary to make this parameter active.

Follow the guidelines detailed in Part E while making changes to SYSGEN parameters. Keep the system fault rate to an absolute minimum (below 1 fault per second) regardless of the VUP rating of your DEC VAX.

Do not take the risk of introducing and/or increasing the system fault rate by decreasing the working set size of the system account.

It is recommended that you use AUTOGEN feedback mechanism to increase the SYSGEN parameter SYSMWCNT until the average system fault rate is under 1 per second.

The system working set is made up of the pageable portions of the system, RMS, and the paged dynamic pool. Using the command $SHOW MEMORY/FULL system memory cache allocation can be displayed as shown in Table 4.3, page 36.

To calculate a SYSMWCNT value for machines with High Fault Rate, use the following formula to calculate an approximate initial value for SYSMWCNT.

SYSMWCNT= GBLPAGES/128 + SPTREQ/5 + PAGEDYN/1024

Table 4.3   SHOW MEMORY/FULL command display

	Total	Free	In Use	Modified
Physical Memory Usage (pages):	Total	Free	In Use	Modified
Main Memory (32.00Mb)	65536	2560	62627	349
Slot Usage (slots):			Resident	Swapped
Process Entry Slots	100	28	72	0
Balance Set Slots	97	27	70	0
Fixed Size Pool Areas (packets):	Total	Free	In Use	Size
Small Packet (SRP) List	2383	652	1731	96
I/O Request Packet (IRP) List	1693	551	1142	176
Large Packet (LRP) List	68	24	44	1648
Dynamic Memory Usage (bytes):			In Use	Largest
Nonpaged Dynamic Memory	914432	67584	846848	38128
Paged Dynamic Memory	594432	262000	332432	253408
Paging File Usage (pages):		Free	Reservable	Total
Disc$VAXVMSRL053:[SYS1.SYSEXE]SWAPFIL.SYS		10600	10600	10600
Disc$VAXVMSRL053:[SYS1.SYSEXE]PAGEFILE.SYS		84436	31024	100000
FISTDISK:[SYS1.SYSEXE] PAGEFILE.SYS:1		83695	31397	99992

Of the physical pages in use, 7229 pages are permanently allocated to VMS

Dead page table scans and degradation in system performance

What is a dead page table scan and how does it affect system performance?

When a process needs to pagefault another page into its working set but the working set is full (ie it is equal to its WSEXTENT value), VMS has to remove a page from the working set for the new page. The procedure used to remove a page from a process working set is described in steps below.

1.   VMS scans the process working set list searching for a candidate page to remove.

2.   If the candidate page is a process page table, VMS checks to see if it is an inactive page table page. If no entries point to any pages in the working set, the page is marked as a 'dead page table page'. An inactive page table page does not contain entries pointing to pages currently in the working set.

3. VMS then selectively removes these pages from the modified page list to the backing storage. Prior to VMS V5.2 if any of the dead page table pages were found in the modified page list, the entire modified page list was flushed from memory to the backing storage.

Determining the number of dead page table scans occurring on your system

Use the system dump analyzer (SDA) utility to determine the dead page table scan count as follows:

```
$ANALYZE/SYSTEM
SDA> READ SYS$SYSTEM:SYSDEF
SDA> EXAMINE PMS$GL_DPTSCN
SDA> CONVERT <the hexadecimal value displayed above to decimal>
```

Rules of thumb to tune your system to reduce the dead table scans

Dead page table scans occur when a process working set is full; therefore, there are several possible options to let you reduce the number of dead page table scans.

1. You can increase your working set sizes, especially the value of WSEXTENT using AUTHORIZE. It may be necessary for you to increase the value of the SYSGEN parameter WSMAX in conjunction with WSEXTENT.

2. You can allow the working set sizes to grow more quickly. For this, decrease the value of PFRATH and increase WSINC.

3. Switch off Automatic Working Set Decrementing by setting PFRATL=0 in MODPARAMS.DAT.

4. Do not allow programs to adjust their own working set list sizes using system services.

5. Add more memory and adjust working sets accordingly.

What is pagefault thrashing?

When you observe that a VMS system is performing excessive amounts of I/O to the pagefile (paging) and consuming a great chunk of CPU time in the process, it is in fact pagefault thrashing.

Causes of pagefault thrashing and remedies

There are many causes of thrashing. Some of these are discussed below. Thrashing can occur when working set limits defined by WSQUOTA and WSEXTENT defined using AUTHORIZE are not adequate for user processes. Digital's layered products are getting more and more sophisticated with every new release, and as such require more memory to run.

Users (system managers) often forget to alter the working set quota for the accounts running such tools and layered products. Application programs are often enhanced and sometimes these changes require additional memory, but the working set limits are not increased to meet the additional memory requirements.

When a system process is not meeting its memory requirements, it could experience excessive soft pagefault rates. You can reduce the overall impact of pagefaulting on the system by increasing the working set limits of the user accounts running such layered products and/or applications. If your system is memory deficient, then you must acquire additional memory to meet the demand or restrict the simultaneous use of memory-intensive applications or run applications in a batch queue with elevated working set limits.

Thrashing can also occur if the RMS buffers specified for files and/ or bucket sizes are extremely large and the working set limits are not large enough to adequately support that type of operations. Be careful while specifying buffer values: large buffers can cause more I/Os in the form of hard faults. RMS buffering helps you reduce the amount of physical I/O to the disk, but try finding an optimal value for each application during the testing stage. Setting values too high does not necessarily enhance performance.

The most common cause of pagefault thrashing are applications with poor locality of reference in memory: especially programs written in FORTRAN using large multidimensional arrays which are stored with the rightmost index changing more rapidly, where working set limits are not adequate to support the large arrays.

So, as each data element is referenced VMS fetches the page with the data element, reads or updates the array element, and then fetches another page. When the working set limits are reached (when it is full), recently retrieved pages are flushed out to make room for new array elements (new pages). Flushed out pages go on the free page list or the modified page list. If they go on the modified page list then it is possible that they may be written out to a disk, resulting in additional disk I/Os.

When the flushed out pages are needed again, they are faulted back into the working set. To retrieve the pages from the disk a hard fault is necessary unless it is on the free page list.

Scientific applications usually have large arrays, for which this process may be repeated several thousand times and must be avoided.

The solution lies in writing such an application in other high level languages – such as BASIC – where multidimensional arrays are handled differently. Failing this it becomes desirable to change the order in which the arrays are handled in FORTRAN, that is, reverse the order of the array indices.

5

Managing Pagefiles

Introduction

For optimal performance it is essential that your pagefile is contiguous and at least 50% free on a busy system. Check your operator console for error messages relating to pagefile fragmentation and pagefile space. The errors shown below indicate that your pagefile is not large enough to support the current paging activity on your system. It may be necessary for you to either increase the size of your existing file or create secondary pagefiles. The best solution is to create secondary pagefiles if possible on separate disks.

```
SYSTEM-W-PAGEFRAG, Pagefile badly fragmented, system continuing
SYSTEM-W-PAGECRIT, Pagefile space critical, system trying to continue
```

If the pagefile gets full, the system performance will degrade and there is a danger that the system may hang. Also, processes may enter into a RWMPB or RWMPE state. However, processes can enter into a RWMPB or RWMPE state even if the pagefile is not full. For details see Chapter 24: *Scheduling states*. Use the DCL command SHOW MEMORY/FILES to display information on each of the pagefiles on your system. For optimal performance ensure that there is at least 50% of the pagefile space free on each of the pagefiles on a busy system. Use the methods described below to increase the size or the number of pagefiles on your system.

Increasing the size of the primary pagefile on the system disk

Firstly, ensure that there is sufficient free disk space available on your system disk. Try not to exceed the performance threshold utilization of any of the disks on your system. Performance thresholds for RA-series disks is 85% utilization. Performance thresholds details on other types of disks can be found in Chapter 11: *Rules of Thumb for Diagnosing Disk* I/O *Limitations*. After checking the amount of free disk space available, run the command procedure:

```
$@SYS$UPDATE:SWAPFILES
```

to increase the size of the primary pagefile on your system disk. Note that this procedure does not affect the size of secondary pagefiles on your system and it is necessary to reboot the system for the increase in size to become effective. Also, the procedure may not grant you all the requested space.

Creating and installing secondary pagefile(s)

The number of secondary pagefiles you can create on a system is controlled by the SYSGEN parameter PAGFILCNT. Check the value of this parameter before creating/installing another pagefile. If the value of this parameter equals the number of pagefiles on your system, then you must increase the value of this parameter using MODPARAMS.DAT. It is necessary to reboot your system after this change. To avoid rebooting of the system always set the value of PAGFILCNT one higher than the total number of files on your system. This will leave a free slot for you to install a secondary pagefile on the system while it is running, without rebooting. Use SYSGEN to create/install new pagefiles:

```
$RUN SYS$SYSTEM:SYSGEN
SYSGEN>CREATE disc:[000000]PAGEFILEn.SYS/SIZE=newsize
SYSGEN>INSTALL disc:[000000]PAGEFILEn.SYS/PAGEFILE
SYSGEN>EXIT
```

The above procedure creates the pagefile on the specified disk and makes it known to VMS by installing it. After running the above utility, add the INSTALL command to the SYPAGSWP_FILES.COM procedure in SYS$MANAGER so that pagefiles are automatically installed on each reboot.

Combining the pagefile with the dumpfile when disk space is limited

This method is useful when the disk space is limited. To combine the two files together the pagefile must reside on the system disk. VMS cannot write system dumps to a non-system disk. The procedure to combine the two files together is:

1.   SET DEFAULT SYS$SYSTEM.

2. RENAME SYSDUMP.DMP *.OLD.

3. Modify MODPARAMS.DAT and set the value of SAVEDUMP
    and DUMPSTYLE to 1.

4. Reboot the system and delete SYSDUMP.OLD to free disk
    space.

5. Use the SYSGEN utility to increase the size of your pagefile as
    follows:

```
$ RUN SYS$SYSTEM:SYSGEN
SYSGEN > CREATE SYS$SYSTEM:PAGEFILE.SYS/SIZE=new size
SYSGEN> EXIT
```

Note: new size should be at least your memory size plus 1030 blocks.

6. To save a crash dump for analysis, include the following
    commands in SYS$MANAGER:SYSTARTUP V5.COM

```
$MOUNT disc: label
$ANALYZE/CRASH SYS$SYSTEM:PAGEFILE.SYS
SDA > COPY disc:[CRASH]SYSDUMP.DMP
```

7. Reboot the system.

Reducing the use of pagefile when memory is plentiful

When there is plenty of free memory, and the pagefile is less than
50% free, and there are processes with high fault rates, increase the
WSQUOTA and/or WSEXTENT sizes to decrease the pagefault rate
and keep more in physical memory.

Note: You must not increase the WSEXTENT size beyond the
WSMAX value. It may be necessary for you to increase the size of
WSMAX accordingly.

Use the DCL command MONITOR/PROCESS TOPFAULT to find
out top pagefaulting processes.

Figure 5.1: Sample output from MONITOR PROCESS/TOPFAULT

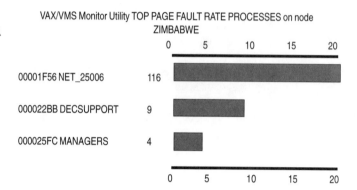

VAX/VMS Monitor Utility TOP PAGE FAULT RATE PROCESSES on node ZIMBABWE

Processes and pagefile usage under VMS versions 4 and 5

Under VMS version 4, a process could use only one pagefile during its life cycle, a pagefile containing the most space available was allocated to the process. Since VMS version 5, a process may use different pagefiles during its lifetime. However, this depends on how much space VMS perceives each pagefile to have.

Pagefile allocation mechanism under VMS version 5

Under version 5, all processes are allocated a 'current' pagefile, and the number of pages are reserved for these processes in their 'current' pagefile. Use the command shown below to check the number of pages reserved in any pagefile.

Table 5.4   Output From SHOW MEMORY/FILE

```
$ SH MEM/FILES/FULL
DISK$VAXVMSRL5:[SYS0.SYSEXE]SWAPFILE.SYS
```

Free Blocks	19760	Reservable Blocks	19760
Total Size (blocks)	20000	Paging File Number	1
Swap Usage (processes)	1	Paging Usage (processes)	0

This file is used exclusively for swapping

```
DISK$VAXVMSRL5:[SYS0.SYSEXE]PAGEFILE.SYS
```

Free Blocks	16932	Reservable Blocks	-59666
Total Size (blocks)	50000	Paging File Number	5
Swap Usage (processes)	0	Paging Usage (processes)	47

This file can be used for either paging or swapping

The above table shows the reservable figure as negative. This indicates that the pagefile is over-committed and more pages have been reserved than are available. It does not necessarily indicate a problem. Once a process has used up the reserved pages in its 'current' pagefile, VMS assigns a new pagefile as a 'current' pagefile to the process and reserves space in there for the process. The new pagefile could well be the same as the old pagefile. For each pagefile on your system it performs the following calculation and then picks the file which gives the smallest result:

(pagefile size – reserved pages) / pagefile size

Note: The system does not use the free space figure as in version 5. For version 5, it is recommended that all pagefiles are of similar sizes for optimal performance.

6 Swapper Trimming and Swapping

Swapper trimming and how it works

On VMS V5.n systems, Swapper manages physical memory on a system-wide basis using swapper trimming and swapping. VMS reclaims memory from processes using a sophisticated procedure known as *swapper trimming*, detailed below.

First-level trimming

Swapper trimming is invoked when there are fewer than FREELIM (number of free pages on the free list fall below the value of the SYSGEN parameter FREELIM) pages in the free page list. First-level trimming ensures that the processes which are above their WSQUOTA limit are trimmed back to their WSQUOTA value, giving the remaining processes a chance to acquire free pages for their needs.

Swapper trimming triggering mechanisms and validations

Firstly, a check is made on the modified page list to ensure that there are at least the number of pages as indicated by the SYSGEN parameter MPW_THRESH to make it worthwhile to flush it to the disk and free its pages for the free page list. However, if writing of the modified list would not bring it to the level of pages as specified by the value in FREEGOAL, the system decides not to flush the modified page list to the disk, and triggers first-level trimming. This ensures that the processes which are above their WSQUOTA value are trimmed back to their WSQUOTA value.

Second level of trimming

If still more memory is required, second-level trimming is initiated. This is where idle processes are trimmed back to the value of the SYSGEN parameter SWPOUTPGCNT.

Is swapper trimming affecting your system performance?
To find out if swapper trimming is affecting your system performance, first find out which processes are faulting heavily on your
system using:

MONITOR PROCESS/TOPFAULT

Make a note of the process identification numbers (PIDs) and then
examine the behavior of those processes using the DCL command:

SHOW PROCESS/CONTINUOUS/ID = n

If you find that the working set size of these processes is close to
their SWPOUTPGCNT or WSQUOTA values then swapper
trimming is definitely affecting your system performance and you
must take steps to remedy the situation.

Swapping and how it works

As a last resort, if the second level of trimming fails to free enough
memory as demanded by the processes, the system resorts to
swapping: where complete process are swapped to disk. Swapping
involves removing a complete process from memory and placing it
on a disk (with swapfiles), to free memory for other processes. Each
swapping operation generates a large amount of disk I/O; frequent
swapping often cause disk or channel contention. Swapping
imposes substantial system overhead: it has to stop the process,
write its entire contents to a disk (a slow device), and later start that
process again by bringing its contents into memory. If your
swapfile happens to be on the same disk as the system disk, then all
other activities to that disk grind to a halt while swapping is taking
place.

Checking the swapping activity using Monitor and DCL

Swapping imposes a high system overhead. Those processes
swapped out must be swapped back into memory in order to run.
For this reason avoid swapping altogether, if possible, or at least
keep it to a minimum. Use the commands described below to
check swapping. Use the command SHOW SYSTEM to see if any
processes show up with the <swapped out> comment. Use MONITOR

STATES and MONITOR SYSTEM to see if there are any processes in
an outswapped state as shown below:

- **LEFO (local event flag wait outswapped)** usually waiting for a
  terminal I/O.
- **HIBO** – hibernating outswapped
- **SUSPO** – suspended outswapped
- **COMO** – computable outswapped

Table 6.1   Output from SHOW SYSTEM

Pid	Process Name	State	Pri	I/O	CPU	flts	Ph.Mem
				sh system VAX/VMS V5.4 on node node name			
00000101	SWAPPER	HIB	16	0	0 00:06:51.29	0	0
00000105	ERRFMT	HIB	8	39202	0 00:01:40.37	85	138
00000106	OPCOM	HIB	7	29768	0 00:01:12.61	1791	176
00000107	AUDIT_SERVER	HIB	10	5665	0 00:00:21.72	1365	507
00000108	JOB_CONTROL	HIB	9	559178	0 00:19:52.47	407	548
00000109	IPCACP	HIB	10	7	0 00:00:00.26	79	152
0000010A	TP_SERVER	HIB	9	197791	0 00:08:08.52	170	266
0000010B	VIDEO_SERVER	HIB	13	56033	0 00:01:38.54	227	343
0000010C	NETACP	HIB	10	36436	0 00:04:51.70	401	564
0000010D	EVL	HIB	6	627	0 00:00:02.26	747965	66 N
0000010E	REMACP	HIB	8	488	0 00:00:00.41	75	67
0000010F	VAXsim V1.5-127	HIB	8	6522	0 00:00:26.37	828	407
0000D510	INQ	LEF	8	994	0 00:00:03.22	1324	329
0000CE11	CONF_GR	LEF	6	819	0 00:00:03.51	1753	1024
00000113	NCP	HIB	6	153	0 00:01:50.20	1139	312
0000BC17	GAMISC	LEF	8	1160	0 00:00:04.93	1770	222
0000D418	PTINP	LEF	9	794	0 00:00:03.03	1455	261
000011A	RMSRV_ABSDD_1A	HIB	3	555861	0 00:11:17.21	2186	744
000011B	SYMBIONT_0001	HIB	6	1561172	0 00:37:42.36	66712	553
000011E	SYMBIONT_0002	HIB	6	36301	0 00:02:21.19	80615	201
00010320	TUFFSB1	LEF	5	267	0 00:00:01.19	1128	725
0000DE21	L2R	LEF	5	726	0 00:00:03.81	1793	225
0000dF22	GET	LEF	8	805	0 00:00:03.57	1515	238
00000123	SERVER_0001	HIB	10	3145	0 00:00:02.89	107	170
0000BB27	05E2 CRTOFF	HIB	7	226	0 00:00:01.49	1677	489
00000128	RTMON	HIB	10	610	0 00:00:00.49	97	148
0000C62B	ROUGH	LEF	5	1453	0 00:00:05.35	2738	252
0000C633	ST400_LTA7555	HIB	4	307	0 00:00:02.36	1885	372
0000DO34	NOSTRO	LEF	7	679	0 00:00:02.97	1381	1032

Table 6.1   (continued) Output from SHOW SYSTEM

Pid	Process Name	State	Pri	I/O	CPU	flts	Ph.Mem
0000D938	SERVER_00C7	LEF	6	188	0 00:00:00.97	863	323 N
0000E239	TRMMON_T7555	LEF	8	214	0 00:00:00.79	927	971 S
0000CF3A	SFSTAT_T7555	LEF	6	74	0 00:00:00.50	783	1037 S
0000E93B	NET_24687	CUR	4	296	0 00:00:01.33	836	330 N
0001063D	RANDOM_T7555	LEF	8	64	0 00:00:00.53	836	868 S
0000D940	0761_PRTIO	HIB	6	84	0 00:00:00.41	305	543 S
0000C64C	DIS	LEF	8	17184	0 00:00:43.48	6846	285
0000FF61	TUFFSD2	LEF	5	816	0 00:00:03.36	2060	1001
0000CE73	MASTER1	LEF	4	6007	0 00:00:06.42	975	734
0000D474	1NS_SERVER01	HIB	5	48434	0 00:04:55.06	1225	1226
0000EF76	1NS_SERVER02	HIB	6	48134	0 00:04:53.45	1274	1286
0000EC77	1NS_SERVER03	HIB	5	54902	0 00:05:25.92	1295	1340
0000E378	1NS_SERVER04	HIB	6	50046	0 00:05:00.12	1279	1286
0000F07A	1N0STROINPUT	HIB	6	815	0 00:00:00.83	572	445

Figure 6.1: Graphical output from Monitor States

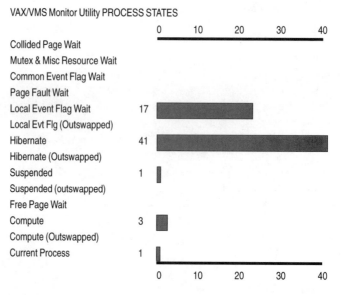

Processes in a COMO state must be swapped back into memory at some stage in order to execute. Sometimes, to bring a process back into memory, VMS may swap out a process. Firstly, record the monitor statistics for all classes for a given period (peak time) and then perform a summary display for MONITOR STATES as follows:

```
$MONITOR/INPUT = directory:filename/SUMMARY-
/NODISPLAY/BEGIN=time-
/END=time STATES/ALL
$PRINT MONITOR.SUM
```

Note: Submit the above commands as a batch job.

Table 6.2   Tabulated output from MONITOR STATES display

VAX/VMS Monitor Utility PROCESS STATES (%)				
	CUR	**AVE**	**MIN**	**MAX**
	(%)	(%)	(%)	(%)
Collided Page Wait	0.00	0.00	0.00	0.00
Mutex & Misc Resource Wait	0.00	0.12	0.00	1.00
Common Event Flag Wait	0.00	0.00	0.00	0.00
Page Fault Wait	0.00	0.08	0.00	1.00
Local Event Flag Wait	32.00	40.54	29.00	51.00
Local Evt Flg (Outswapped)	0.00	0.00	0.00	0.00
Hibernate	22.0	27.06	22.00	30.00
Hibernate (Outswapped)	0.00	0.00	0.00	0.00
Suspended	1.00	1.00	1.00	1.00
Suspended (Outswapped)	0.00	0.00	0.00	0.00
Free Page Wait	0.00	0.00	0.00	0.00
Compute	0.00	0.22	0.00	2.00
Compute (Outswapped)	0.00	0.00	0.00	0.00
Current Process	1.00	1.00	1.00	1.00
PLAYBACK		**SUMMARIZING**		

If you find that there are many processes in the outswapped state, you then use MONITOR IO and check the inswap rate (this gives the rate at which the working sets were read into memory from the swap file). It should be kept as low as possible and should be less than one process per second.

If you find that the inswap rate is greater than 1 then you must take steps to remedy the situation as outlined in the following sections.

Table 6.3   Summary output from MONITOR SYSTEM

VAX/VMS Monitor Utility I/O SYSTEM STATISTICS			
	CUR	**AVE**	**MIN**	**MAX**
Direct I/O Rate	22.89	27.96	9.91	47.67
Buffered I/O Rate	9.73	12.37	7.79	20.56
Mailbox Write Rate	0.88	0.92	0.68	1.24
Split Transfer Rate	1.34	1.68	0.46	4.00
Log Name Translation Rate	11.64	13.47	9.29	29.26
File Open Rate	1.37	1.64	1.02	2.87
Page Fault Rate	50.16	46.90	34.37	101.59
Page Read Rate	5.13	5.85	4.05	11.71
Page Read I/O Rate	0.96	1.09	0.72	2.29
Page Write Rate	0.00	0.00	0.00	0.00
Page Write I/O Rate	0.00	0.00	0.00	0.00
Inswap Rate	0.00	0.00	0.00	0.00
Free List Size	53797.00	55239.89	50406.00	60980.00
Modified List Size	6621.00	6108.55	4534.00	7074.00
PLAYBACK	**SUMMARIZING**			

Controlling swapping for optimal performance

Constant swapping is much more expensive than paging. If at all possible avoid it altogether, or at least try to keep swapping to a minimum. The guidelines below, if followed, may enhance the performance of your DEC VAX. The best solution is to have plenty of memory, as it is cheaper than both the disk drives and the CPU.

Checking to see if swapping is really necessary on your system

Using the commands described above check to see if your system is really swapping, and if swapping is degrading the performance of your system. You may then proceed to check if swapping is really necessary on your system as follows.

Plenty of free memory but no free balance set slots

Use the SHOW MEMORY command to check the amount of free memory on your system. If you consistently find that there is ample free memory, yet processes are being swapped out, check the SHOW MEMORY output to see if all the BALANCE SET SLOTS are in use. If all the balance set slots are in use, then VMS must swap out a process to free a slot for a new process. This is called BALANCE SET SWAPPING.

▸ **Minimizing the effect of balance set swapping** – to reduce balance set swapping, increase the SYSGEN parameter BALSETCNT to:

    MAXPROCESSCNT – 2

However, it may be necessary to increase the size of both the parameters to accommodate additional processes on the system. Make these changes using MODPARAMS.DAT and AUTOGEN as described in Part E.

▸ **Memory is scarce** – lack of memory can induce swapping on your system. Use the commands SHOW MEMORY and MONITOR PAGE to check the number of free pages on your system. If the number of free pages is low and swapping is affecting performance, the best solution is to add more memory. As mentioned above, swapping becomes necessary on a DEC VAX that is deficient in memory for the workload it is required to handle. If you find that processes on your system are spending enormous amounts of their time lying idle, then swapping may enhance performance but the best solution is to add more memory.

If you wish to induce swapping to compensate for memory then you may increase the size of system parameter SWPOUTPGCNT to encourage swapping of idle processes. Set it to approximately 20% less than the typical WSQUOTA value on your system. This will ensure that processes are swapped out and not trimmed back to the minimum working set quota value (SWPOUTPGCNT), which is too small for efficient execution. Be careful, if the inswap rate becomes excessive then readjust values for optimal performance using MODPARAMS.DAT and AUTOGEN.

▸ **Reduce swapping by controlling batch/interactive jobs run concurrently** – if memory is really tight, you may also reduce the number of processes allowed to operate concurrently both interactively and as detached batch jobs. You can reduce the concurrent running of batch jobs by stopping the queue using the DCL command STOP/QUEUE/RESET <queue> and then starting it again, this time imposing the limit using:

    START/QUEUE/JOB_LIMIT= 1 <queue>

The value of the SYSGEN parameter MAXPROCESSCNT may also be lowered, but change it in conjunction with AUTOGEN as it may require readjustment of the associated system parameter BALSETCNT described above.

▶ **Reducing working set quotas to minimize swapping** – you   may decide to reduce the working set quotas for interactive jobs (as well as detached) but bear in mind this will increase pagefaulting on your system. To lower the working set quotas (WSQUOTA and WSEXTENT) values use AUTHORIZE and to lower the values of detached jobs alter the value of PQL_DWSQUOTA, and PQL_DWSEXTENT using SYSGEN but only in conjunction with the rules specified in Chapter 28 – *Changing SYSGEN Parameters.*

▶ **Controlling programs making calls to system service $GETJPI** – application programs which keep track of other processes on the system using system services $GETJPI can induce more swapping. This is because $GETJPI service can cause a process to become computable. VMS then must bring that process into memory to service the $GETJPI call. To reduce swapping, check if the process is already swapped before issuing $GETJPI service.

▶ **Ensure the file system code is being shared by all processes** – the default value of the SYSGEN parameter ACP_XQP_RES is 1, which enables processes to share the file system code. Ensure that it has not been altered.

▶ **Install frequently used images** – images   used   frequently   and concurrently by multiple users should be installed as /SHARED, this saves memory by allowing several users to reference a single copy of the program in memory.

Steps to take when your swapfile space gets full

Swapfile should never be more than 70% full and should also be contiguous. Use the SHOW MEMORY/FULL command to display information on these files. If the swapfile starts to fill up, the system performance begins to degrade with processes going into RWSWP state. In VMS version V5.n, less swapfile space is required because of the change in allocation algorithm and the space is allocated just before it is required.

Prior to VMS V5.n, swapfile space was allocated when the process was created; even if the process never swaps out. If you find that the disk space is more than 70% full then you must consider adding and/or increasing the swapfile space. You may use any of the methods described below to add more swapfile space.

Increasing the size of primary swapfile

Use the command shown below to increase the size of the primary swapfile:

```
@SYS$UPDATE:SWAPFILES
```

This procedure will enable you to alter the size of the swapfile on the system disk only. It does not affect other files on other disks.

Add secondary swapfile(s)

The SYSGEN parameter SWPFILCNT controls the number of swapfiles that can be created on your system. The default value of SWPFILCNT is 4. If you wish to have more swapfiles than specified by SWPFILCNT then increase the value of this parameter in MODPARAMS.DAT. It is necessary to reboot the system after this change.

Reduce demand for swapfile space

Space in swapfile is allocated up to the value of WSQUOTA. Use AUTHORIZE to reduce the WSQUOTA value for users processes so that processes use less space in the swapfile. Remember, processes are still allowed to grow to their WSEXTENT value despite the lowering of WSQUOTA value.

Install a secondary pagefile

Pagefiles can also be used for swapping. Using a pagefile for swapping can degrade the overall performance of your system. It is recommended to keep swapping separate from paging. Only use a pagefile for swapping as a last resort. Check the PAGFILCNT parameter to create a secondary pagefile. Install the file once it is created. The procedure to create and install a secondary pagefile is:

```
$RUN SYS$SYSTEM:SYSGEN
SYSGEN> CREATE disc_name:[0000003]PAGEFILE2.SYS/SIZE = new_size
SYSGEN > INSTALL disc_name:[000000]PAGEFILE2.SYS/PAGEFILE
SYSGEN> EXIT
```

Use MONITOR DISK/ITEM=QUEUE to establish if an I/O queue exists for the disks on which these files are residing.

7   Estimating Memory Needed

Introduction

Use the equation below to determine the amount of memory you may need to sustain and/or improve existing performance levels.

```
Amount of memory needed estimate =
    Pages permanently allocated to VMS + MPW_HILIMIT
        + 1600
        + MAXIMUM OF (FREEGOAL, 1000)
        + (Max. no. of processes on the system * average WSQUOTA)
```

The steps below explain the above equation in detail:

1. Get the amount of space allocated to VMS from the display of DCL command SHOW MEMORY.

2. To the memory allocated to VMS, add the SYSGEN parameter MPW_HILIMIT.

3. Add either 1000 or the SYSGEN parameter FREEGOAL, whichever is greater.

4. Add 1600 pages for system process working set.

5. Multiply the average WSQUOTA value for all the processes by MAXPROCESSCNT, then add this value to the above total.

Note: This value does not take into account the global pages shared between processes and you may find that the value estimated is greater than the actual memory in use.

How to tune a system after adding memory (V5)

After the installation of new memory boards, VMS will automatically configure the new memory when it reboots. You need not do anything for this to occur. Use the DCL command SHOW MEMORY to check the current memory size.

If you do not see all the memory, get your Digital representative to check the memory boards. On some systems it is either necessary to delete and/or recreate the console file MEMCONFIG.DAT. See your console manual specific to your DEC VAX for instructions. Once it is established that the memory has been correctly installed, you must do the following:

1. Run AUTOGEN to let VMS make adjustments to performance related SYSGEN parameters.

2. Make adjustments to working set sizes if necessary.

3. Adjust the size of system dump file SYSDUMP.DMP or the page file PAGEFILE.SYS, whichever you are using for crash dumps.

How to tune a system after adding memory (V6)

Prior to the introduction of OpenVMS V6.0 memory was configured automatically at boot-time. In V6.0 it is necessary to adjust some SYSGEN parameters, working set sizes and the size of the dump file. With the introduction of V6.0 the maximum value for SYSGEN parameter PHYSICALPAGES that can be set has been increased from 1048756 pages (512 Mb) to 7340032 pages (3.5 Gb). The procedure described below, if followed, will enable you to configure and tune memory after the upgrade under V6.0.

1. Modify MODPARAMS.DAT to add the line show below:

    MEMSIZE = 2048 * amount of memory in megabytes

2. Invoke AUTOGEN as shown below.

    @SYS$UPDATE:AUTOGEN SAVPARAMS SETPARAMS

3. Install additional memory and reboot the system.

4. Comment out the line added in step 1.

5. Add the following statement to MODPARAMS.DAT

   PHYSICALPAGES = Ttl no. of pages of memory

6. Run AUTOGEN as follows:

   @SYS$UPDATE:AUTOGEN SAVPARAMS REBOOT

7. Amend dumpfile size to cater for new memory size.

8   Using Memory Efficiently (Rules of Thumb)

Introduction

This section contains some suggestions which may enable you to use memory more efficiently.

Set WSDEFAULT to be the same as WSQUOTA

For memory-rich systems, WSDEFAULT should be set to the value of WSQUOTA. It reduces the amount of paging required at image activation and speeds up the image activation. Be careful if you are still running VMS version 2.0: it may then disable AWSA (automatic working set adjustment) on your system. It is a *myth* that setting WSDEFAULT lower than WSQUOTA conserves memory.

Working set limits for development accounts

Development and testing should, if possible, be performed on a separate machine away from the live environment. Compiling and linking are resource-hungry activities; if they are to be performed on the same machine, the development accounts should at least be kept on a disk separate from the live data. The following guidelines for their working set limits should be taken into account.

Compiling and linking small programs
The WSQUOTA value for programs which handle small amounts of data manipulation and are accessing that data on a per record basis should be in the region of 512 pages.

Compiling and linking large programs
Programs which handle large amounts of data in memory (storing arrays, performing internal sorts, etc) should have a large WSQUOTA value of at least 1024 pages.

For interactive live users

Set WSQUOTA to the largest value required by a program and WSEXTENT to the highest number of pages you anticipate a process will ever need.

Set up separate batch queues for running large (CPU and memory intensive) programs with large working set limits. You can assign WSQUOTA and WSEXTENT values at the initialization stage using:

INITIALIZE/QUEUE or START/QUEUE

You can also specify working set limits when you submit jobs to the batch queue using SUBMIT.

Installing images as shared images

In order to save memory, images used concurrently by multiple users should be installed as /SHARED. This allows several users to reference a single copy of the program in memory. Use the INSTALL utility to install it as an shared image. Before installing the image as a shared image ensure that there are a sufficient number of GBLSECTIONS and GBLPAGES free. You can check this while in INSTALL with:

INSTALL > LIST/SUMMARY/GLOBAL

If you have to increase the value of the GBLSECTIONS and GBLPAGES make sure you use AUTOGEN so that other associated parameters are also automatically adjusted. Images installed using /OPEN/HEADER/SHARED take up approximately two pages of nonpaged dynamic memory.

Suspend processes exceeding WSQUOTA value when memory is tight

When memory is tight and the system is page faulting heavily and there are processes which are above their working set quota, you may suspend some of those large processes temporarily using the DCL command: SET PROCESS/SUSPEND. As soon as the process is suspended, SWAPPER leaps into action to trim the working set size of the process to the value of SWPOUTPGCNT (minimum number of pages under which a process can reasonably operate).

Ensure that trimming has taken place by using the DCL command:

SHOW PROC/CONTINUOUS/ID=pid

resume the process as soon as possible using the DCL command:

SET PROCESS/RESUME

This procedure will enable you to release memory for other processes, and as long as memory is very tight this process will not be able to grow above its WSQUOTA limit. Before suspending a process, check that it is not sharing files with other processes on the system.

Limit working set sizes when memory is tight

Discourage borrowing when memory is scarce by restricting the growth of the WSEXTENT limit. Keep it equal to or only a little bit greater than WSQUOTA. Also, reduce the size of the working set quota for processes, if necessary. But remember, it will increase page faulting for those processes.

Add more memory

As a last resort you should acquire some additional memory and configure it using AUTOGEN.

Part B

Disk I/O Management

9 Understanding the Different Components of a Disk Transfer

Introduction

Disk performance is primarily concerned with the speed with which I/O operations can be completed (ie the time it takes to retrieve the required disk blocks). This is dependent on a number of factors such as seek time, rotational delay and the data transfer capacity of the disks – including their controllers. The following section describes the components of a disk transfer.

The components of a disk transfer

The components of a typical I/O request for a VAX-11/780 processor running under VMS are shown in Table 9.1. This shows that the majority of the time is spent performing a seek (58%) and wait (20%) for the desired sector to appear under the heads. On a fragmented disk this is made worse by the fact that the information is not contiguous and therefore seek times are longer. Because of fragmented disk space it takes disk heads additional time to seek the location of the data. Transfer time is dependent on the amount of data to be transferred.

Factors to consider when selecting disks

The key issue when selecting disks is the amount of time it takes to complete an I/O operation. This is dependent on a number of factors such as transfer rates, seek rates, rotational delay and the nature of the application (eg database design including access methods).

The service time required to complete an I/O operation is made up of four elements:

Service Time = Seek + Rotational latency + Data Transfer + Bucket Search

Table 9.1   Components of a disk transfer detailing breakdown
(transfer on VAX-11/780 – four to eight block size)

Components and Breakdown	%	Influencing Device

I/O request pre-processing
    Call to QIO system service
    QIO validates/queues request
    Driver sets control registers to start the transfer
	4	Host CPU Speed

Controller delay Controller sets/initiates the request to the hardware	2	DISK Controller type (HSC,UDA50, MASSBUS,etc)
Seek time Driver position heads to the correct cylinder	58	Controller type as above

Rotational latency
    disk rotates until the requested sector is under read /
        write heads.
	20	Rotational speed of disk
		Firmware in controller

Transfer time
    Amount of data transferred
    Controller Buffer Space
    Contention for the bus
	12	Controller throughput
		Controller seek
		Controller buffering
		Rotational speed
		Data density
		Disk format
		Bus contention

I/O post processing
    Returning status to the requesting process
    Setting the requested event flag
    Calling the scheduler to make the process
        computable
    Queuing the requested AST, if any
	4	Host CPU speed

The major part of servicing an I/O request (as shown in Table 9.1) is consumed by the physical hardware movement (ie seek + rotational delay). The single most expensive component of a disk input/output operation is the seek rate.

Rules of thumb for selecting disks

1. *When data transfer speed is critical* – (ie for applications where a large amount of data transfer is involved) give greater consideration to disk transfer rates.

2. *When accessing of data is mostly random* – (ie for applications with mostly random access) give greater consideration to seek rates.

3. *Large files and random access* – if the disk is to contain large files and the access to these files is random, then greater consideration should be given to the cylinder capacity within the disks. Disks with large cylinders give better performance when measured in terms of seek times per megabyte.

10   Raid and Storage Works

Since the early 1990s there have been some very dramatic improvements in CPU performance; most recently, but not exclusively, characterised by Alpha. It was clear that in many respects the I/O sub-system was being left behind, and certainly in terms of percentage increases of performance over the same time period the I/O sub-system is now much more of a bottleneck than the CPU.

This chapter attempts to discuss the most common approach taken by the industry generally to attempt to deal with this disparity, whilst still using rotational platter designs, namely RAID (redundant array of independent disks), and briefly consider the DEC offering: *Storage Works.*

Development of RAID – a background

Two trains of thought were going on in the industry through this time. One was the need for openness – principally created from the hype concerning UNIX. The second was the need to improve I/O sub-system reliability – which, if you were still using old RA-type devices you were probably only too well aware of.

Technology too had advanced dramatically in the I/O sphere. There was no longer a need to have huge platters housed in very large cabinets: the 5.25-inch disk was becoming accepted as a standard and improvements in disk-coating technology and head design facilitated the development of significantly higher information-storage densities. Together with these developments, SCSI (small computer systems interconnect) appeared as an industry standard. Once this was accepted there was greater market competition and hence prices fell.

In early 1990, a proprietary 1.2 Gb 9-inch disk – then the latest technology – would have cost about $30,000. By early 1995, 1.4 Gb

5.25-inch SCSI disks cost in the region of $1200. The change in price over this period was so dramatic that some suppliers of RAID products redefined RAID as *redundant array of inexpensive disks*.

Technology continued to move forward and the 5.25-inch disks were superseded by 3.5-inch disks with even higher information densities: 4 Gb being the highest commercially available at the time of writing, with expectations of 20 Gb within a few years.

So it was now possible to buy physically small – hence lower power consumption – disks at very low prices. Although somewhat faster than the previous offerings they were still mechanical devices and hence prone to failure. RAID was first christened by the University of California at Berkeley in 1987. The primary aim of RAID was to use these new disks in such a way so as to protect the data against loss by failure of a disk. Of the many different methods devised so far, some have become commercially accepted while others are limited to specific uses. In all cases a few things are consistent:

- several physical disks appear to the system as a single logical disk

- additional processor power (usually built into the RAID device) handles all the I/Os and determines how the data will be stored and recovered

- if a disk fails, I/O will continue to be processed, by rebuilding the data in some way

- most systems offer the facility to remove the damaged disk, replace it with a new disk and the data on it will be automatically rebuilt.

Types of RAID

RAID variants go under the inventive names of RAID 0, RAID 1, RAID 2 and so on. We will discuss each in turn.

RAID 0

This is not strictly RAID at all in that it has no redundancy: if a disk fails the data is lost. It is included because it is marketed under that name but is really a totally different product. Many years ago DEC acknowledged the speed of I/O as being a problem and looked at ways using the then limited technology of accessing data more quickly (there were no ESE50s). DEC produced a software solution called *striping*. The idea was simply that if a file could be broken down into several small pieces and the pieces could be read (or written) simultaneously to different disks then the whole I/O operation would complete much quicker. To be effective the I/Os had to be relatively large, but generally it worked. RAID 0 is an implementation of striping.

Data efficiency	100%
Read efficiency	Improved for large I/Os but same for small I/Os
Write efficiency	Improved for large I/Os but same for small I/Os
Data recovery	None

RAID 1

Is also a design that has existed for many years. DEC introduced *volume shadowing* to primarily overcome the problem of data loss by disk failure. The solution, again initially implemented in software only, was to duplicate every write I/O to two or more disks – this meant each disk had a duplicate: should the primary disk fail the duplicate copy could be used immediately. There were also some performance gains on read operations since any of the disks in the volume set could be read to obtain the required information: so the first disk to deliver the information cancelled the I/O request to each of the others. Write operations are slower since each I/O has to be duplicated to each disk.

Theoretically, there is no limit to the number of duplicate disks for each primary disk; however, in practice, no more than two duplicates are ever required – and rarely more than one. This tends to be the most expensive option in terms of cost per gigabyte due to the very low data efficiency.

Data efficiency	50% for 2 volume sets, 33% for 3 volume sets
Read efficiency	133% for 2 volumes, 150% for 3 volumes
Write efficiency	Depends upon the implementation, where data is cached and if concurrent writes can be achieved. However, writes are almost always slower under RAID 1
Data recovery	Duplicate data available with processing overhead. Rebuild of replacement disk is simple read then write operation

High cost and absence of significant gains in performance means that very few suppliers offer a RAID 1 option. However, if fast data-recovery is very important and it is a transaction-processing system (high volumes of small write operations) this may be considered.

RAID 0+1

This is, as the name suggests, a combination of RAID 0 (striping) and RAID 1 (shadowing). Effectively, there is a stripe set to achieve performance improvements and this is shadowed (all disks are duplicated) to achieve redundancy. It is a straightforward concept which is easy to market but the data efficiency is poor; consequently, the cost per megabyte is high. It is unlikely that the performance gains will be significantly higher than using either RAID 3 or 5 which are also commercially available.

Data efficiency	50% for 2 volume sets
Read efficiency	Improved due to both the striping and shadowing
Write efficiency	For large I/Os write performance is improved due to the striping but worsened due to the shadowing. For small I/Os write efficiency is always poor
Data recovery	Immediate with no overhead until all the disks in a single shadow set fail. Then there is no recovery. Rebuild is simple

RAID 2

This is not commercially available so will not be fully discussed; however, the concept has two features worthy of note. Firstly, all the disks are synchronized so they all rotate at exactly the same speed and maintain a constant latency. Secondly, the I/O data is divided into bits or bytes (depending upon the implementation) and each bit (or byte) is written to a different drive – hence even very small I/Os are written to all available disks. The combination of very fine granularity of file and the synchronized files ensure very fast I/Os for large files but no improvement for small files because the latency is the same on every disk. Redundancy is achieved by having a separate disk, or disks, for error correction data. The error correction method is called Hamming code.

RAID 3

In RAID 3 the disks are again synchronized and the data is finely divided, typically at byte level, though several implementations use 2 byte divisions. A separate disk is provided for error correction using simple XOR methods. Assuming four data disks and one parity disk, then for each I/O the data will be finely divided across all four data disks with an XOR function being used to create the parity disk information. Because the error correction is achieved using XOR, a simple binary operation, it is performed with very simple CPU instructions – hence it is very fast. There is little or no detectable overhead in reconstructing the data even if a disk does fail.

Data efficiency	$n/(n+1)$ where n is the number of data disks
Read efficiency	Good for large I/Os but adequate for small I/Os
Write efficiency	For small I/O requests it is not efficient but for large I/O requests it is efficient
Data recovery	If the parity disk fails, no action is required. If a data disk fails then data is recovered by reading all disks and performing simple binary operation

RAID 4

This is not commercially available for the reasons outlined below; however, as it is closely related to RAID 3 it warrants some discussion. In RAID 4 the disks are again synchronized but the data is far less finely divided: typically 512-byte blocks written to each disk. A separate disk is provided for error correction using simple XOR methods. This is best suited to large I/Os because there is no gain for small I/Os.

Assuming there are four data disks and one parity disk then each I/O for 8192 bytes will be divided into 16 blocks of 512 bytes with 4 blocks being written to each data disk at the same time. Blocks 1, 5, 9 and 13 to the first disk; blocks 2, 6, 10 and 14 to the second disk; and so on. Also, at the same time, 4 ECC blocks will be written to the parity disk using an XOR of the 16 data blocks. Blocks 1, 2, 3 and 4 forming the first parity block; blocks 5, 6, 7 and 8 forming the second; and so on. Because the error correction is achieved using XOR, which is a very simple binary operation, this is performed with very simple CPU instructions and is hence very fast. There is little or no detectable overhead in reconstructing the data even if a disk does fail.

However, there is one significant disadvantage to RAID 4 and it concerns the parity disk. If any data block (a single 512-byte block in the example above) is changed, then several I/Os are required: a write I/O to the particular data field itself (which could be on any one of the data disks) and a write I/O to the parity disk. However, calculating the parity value itself is a little complicated because it depends upon the data in all the other blocks which make up this parity block. It is not necessary to read all the other data blocks, which would then have an overhead on every single disk, but it is necessary to know that both the data and the old parity block value is about to be replaced. The actual chain of events is shown below:

1.   Read the old data and the old parity block (this happens concurrently due to the disk synchronization).

2.   Calculate the new parity block using an XOR of the old parity block and the old data blocks (effectively removes the effect of the old data block on the parity block) then XOR the new data block with this value. This calculates the new parity value.

3.   Write the new data and the parity block (again this happens concurrently due to disk synchronization).

So there are four I/Os, and two of these are always to the parity disk, hence it is easy to see how the parity disk could fairly quickly be saturated if there are frequent writes to single blocks. To make matters worse, because both I/Os are to the same physical address on the disk, it takes on average one and a half full rotations of the disk to complete the operation.

Data efficiency	$n/(n + 1)$ where n is the number of data disks
Read efficiency	Improved for large I/Os, same for small I/Os
Write efficiency	Much worse for small I/Os, improved for I/Os large enough to write to all disks. There is the possibility of saturating the parity disk
Data recovery	If the parity disk fails no action is required. Otherwise data is rebuilt by reading all the disks and performing XOR operations. No recovery if more than one disk fails. Rebuild requires reading of all disk and simple binary operations

RAID 5

This is similar to RAID 4; however, the parity chunks are spread across all the disks instead of to a single parity-disk. This has significant advantages in write performance over RAID 4 because the distribution of the parity information prevent one disk becoming saturated.

The need to perform two read operations and two write operations to complete a single write I/O request remains – as does the extra rotation of the disk. The following table shows how RAID 5 would distribute data and parity information across a five-volume set.

	DISK 1	DISK 2	DISK 3	DISK 4	DISK 5
Segment 1	LBN0	LBN1	LBN 2	LBN 3	XOR 0
Segment 2	LBN 4	LBN	LBN 6	XOR 1	LBN 7
Segment 3	LBN 8	LBN	XOR 2	LBN 10	LBN 11
Segment 4	LBN 12	XOR	LBN 13	LBN 14	LBN 15
Segment 5	XOR 4	LBN	LBN 17	LBN 18	LBN 19
Segment 6	LBN 20	LBN	LBN 22	LBN 23	XOR 5

The write operation under RAID 5 is not atomic and hence it is possible for a power failure to occur during a write operation and an inconsistency to exist between the data and the XOR value which is undetected. This is called a *write hole.*

Data efficiency	n/(n+1) where n is the number of data disks
Read efficiency	Improved for large I/Os, same for small I/Os
Write efficiency	Improved for large I/Os, same for small I/Os
Data recovery	If any disk fails then recovery of that data can be achieved from the remaining disks. If two or more disks fail data cannot be recovered. Rebuild requires all disks to be read

RAID 6

This is similar to RAID 5 except that two redundant disks are used and a different error correction algorithm, Reed–Solomon ECC, is used. This has an adverse impact on write performance but the redundancy is far more effective in that any two disks can fail and the data can still be recovered. Hence, very high MTBF (mean time between failures) can be achieved. This is not commercially available, although it is used in some specific applications.

Data efficiency	n/(n+2) where n is the number of data disks.
Read efficiency	Improved for large I/Os, same for small I/Os
Write efficiency	Improved for large I/Os, same for small I/Os
Data recovery	Up to two disks can fail and the data can still be recovered. Rebuild again require significant disk I/O and more complex binary operations

Other types of RAID

Several other types of RAID have been defined (generally variations on the above) which are vendor specific:

RAID 7	is RAID 4 with a cache and parallel operations
RAID 10	is what has now become commonly known as RAID 0+1
RAID 35/RAID 53	are variants of RAID 3 and RAID 5 attempting to take the good bits of each and find ways of overcoming some of the downsides

Most implementations of RAID will also offer some form of caching which is either an optional extra or is incorporated into the unit. Caching is necessary if you have small I/Os and want to see some significant performance increase.

RAID devices – the current position

Most commercially available RAID sub-systems have a number of SCSI connections and their own processor internal to the RAID cabinet so the RAID device appears to the host system as a disk – or a number of disks. All the distribution of data across physical disks, data recovery and checking is performed internally to the RAID device. Hence there is no additional load placed on the host system. Invariably, such systems offer a variety of diagnostic tools, warning and performance indicators plus other bells and whistles which you may, or may not, want.

There are, however, two other possibilities that are commercially available. It is also possible to buy RAID controller boards that fit into the host CPU cabinet and onto the host CPU back plane. These have one (or a number of) SCSI connection(s) to which the disks are physically attached. The processing is done on the controller board and hence does not affect the CPU power of the system, but it does use the host's PSU (power supply unit) and will fail if the host system fails. Thus, if the host system fails it may not be possible to use a separate host system and continue processing. The other downside of this is that another single point of failure is introduced; consequently, because of additional hardware, the MTBF is reduced.

The final option is where the RAID software actually runs on the host system. Two obvious examples being disk-striping software (RAID 0) and *host-based shadowing* (volume shadowing phase II).

Both of these options have an impact on the host processor.

Most commercially available systems allow the removal of a failed disk by physically pulling it from its housing and replacing it with another; rebuilding the data can then commence on the new disk. However, there are still a few commercially available systems that will not function correctly if a disk is removed whilst the system is working. A controlled closedown of all, or part of, the RAID sub-system is required to replace such a disk. Most currently available RAID sub-systems are truly 'hot swapable', but it is well worth checking.

Some RAID sub-systems are actually configured with a spare disk which is automatically brought into use if one of the RAID set disks fails or shows signs of potential failure.

The next question to arise is 'What happens to the I/O performance of the system when a rebuild is in progress?' Fortunately, most manufacturers have considered this and provide a user-variable switch that controls how great (or small) an impact there is. If you need the disk rebuilt quickly then this can be achieved – at the price of reduced I/O performance to the host. If I/O performance to the host is paramount then the rebuild will take longer with a different switch setting. But again, not all manufacturers have this feature so you should check.

Finally, there is one last word of warning. The SCSI bus, or busses, that are used to connect the RAID device, or devices, have a limited bandwidth. There is little point in putting an I/O sub-system that is capable of handling 10 Mb per second on the end of a bus that can only handle 4 Mb per second!

Storage Works

DEC did not enter the RAID arena particularly promptly. There seemed to be a philosophy that RAID was just one part of the general I/O sub-system problem. DEC seemed to want to achieve several things from their new I/O sub-system, not just what was offered by RAID.

These were:

1. To escape from their very protective proprietary system culture and show a positive and strong commitment to openness.

2. To incorporate all the other I/O sub-system components: CDs, solid state disks etc., into a single unified approach to input/output sub-systems.

3. To introduce a new packaging system that could be used by all vendors of I/O sub-systems using either DEC's or their own products.

The solution took some time in arriving but was heralded by considerable marketing talk about a product then called *Storme*. When it did arrive, however, it was clear that DEC was not just marketing another RAID system: they were actually trying to bring the whole concept of the I/O sub-system up to date.

Storage works – some details

The first thing worthy of note are the cabinets themselves. There are five basic cabinets all designed to hold the same basic building blocks: starting with a small 'pizza box' for desktop use which will hold three 3.5-inch devices or two 3.5-inch devices and one half-height 5.25-inch device. This has one SCSI connection.

Next is the shelf unit which will hold seven 3.5-inch devices or various combinations of 3.5-inch and 5.25-inch devices. This may have two SCSI connections.

The next unit can hold 24, 3.5-inch devices or eight 5.25-inch devices and various combinations in between. This unit also has space for controllers and up to eight power supply units.

The last unit which still works on single-phase power supply will potentially hold 70, 3.5-inch devices.

The data centre unit requires three-phase power supply and holds up to 168, 3.5-inch devices (ie approximately 600Gb of magnetic disk storage) – all this in under nine square feet of floor space.

The advantage of these systems becomes clear when one sees the variety of different devices that can all be incorporated into these units:

- Various magnetic disks from 0.5 Gb to 4 Gb

- Solid state disks, from 107 Mb to 856 Mb

- DLT tape units, potentially able to hold 140 Gb

- DAT, QIC and 8mm tape units

- 5.25-inch compact disks

- A variety of controllers – including some for RAID

- Dual power supply and cooling options

and many more!

11   Rules of Thumb for Diagnosing
Disk I/O Limitations

Introduction

I/O sub-systems could become a limiting factor for any number of reasons: insufficient number of storage devices; insufficient speed of the storage and associated devices; poorly designed application placing excessive demands on specific devices; improper system configuration; inefficient use (or lack of) of RMS buffering; file fragmentation; inappropriate working set quotas; lack of memory/ inefficient use of memory. To isolate potential I/O bottlenecks, examine the I/O statistics at system, device and process levels.

Commands to investigate possible I/O problems

MONITOR IO
Shows I/O rates per second including number of files being opened every second (FILE OPEN RATE) and file fragmentation (SPLIT TRANSFER RATE). It also displays the number of logical name translations being performed.

MONITOR DISK/ITEM=ALL
This command shows the I/O rate and the queue length for all the disks on your system for a particular node. In general, a long queue length indicates that the device is inundated with I/O requests and is unable to keep up with the demand, so I/O requests must wait before being serviced.

MONITOR MSCP
Shows server statistics such as Fragmented Request Rate, Extra Fragment Rate and Buffer Wait Rate.

MONITOR CLUSTER
Displays cluster-wide disk statistics including the current, average, minimum and maximum.

MONITOR FCP
This shows the WINDOW TURN RATE, indicating the number of times VMS had to map another portion of file headers. The WINDOW TURN RATE and the SPLIT TRANSFER RATE are good indicators of file fragmentation.

MONITOR PROCESS/TOPDIO
Shows processes responsible for most of the 'Direct I/O Operations' on the system.

MONITOR FILE_SYSTEM_CACHE
Shows the effectiveness of caches (Hit Rates and Attempt Rates).

SHOW DEVICE/FULL device name
Displays device name, device type, blocks available, blocks free, cluster size, extent size, cache size, etc.

SHOW DEVICES/SERVED
Shows devices status, size, I/O requests waiting to be serviced, etc.

SHOW DEVICE/WINDOWS
Shows window count, window size, and segmented windows for files open.

MONITOR RMS
Shows I/O statistics relating to files. Useful for producing a list of hotfiles.

Determining direct I/O operation rate and queue length

I/O operation rate is the rate of I/O operations completed for disks that are mounted. The direct I/O operation rate and the queue length statistics for each disk can be obtained using the command:

MONITOR DISK/ITEM=ALL

Observe these disk statistics at peak usage time for about 10 to 20 minutes. The above command provides disk statistics for mounted disks only. It displays all system and user I/O statistics as illustrated in Table 11.1.

Table 11.1   Example MONITOR DISK output

VAX/VMS Monitor Utility Disk I/O Statistics on node ZURICH

I/O Operation Rate	CUR	AVE	MIN	MAX
255DUA0: (HSC004) VMSRL5	4.17	5.13	2.43	7.48
255DUA1: (HSC004) LAYERED	8.01	4.63	0.83	9.50
255DUA2: (HSC004) SUPPORT	12.85	5.86	0.25	18.07
$255SDUA3: (HSC004) PAGESWAP1	2.56	1.91	0.43	3.51
255DUA4: (HSC004) USERDISK4	0.60	0.88	0.19	2.69
255DUA5: (HSC004) PMS1_SHARE1	1.10	0.56	0.05	1.66
255DUA6: (HSC000) SPAR_SCRATCH	0.00	0.00	0.00	0.00
255DUA8: (HSC000) SPAR_BACKUP	0.00	8.37	0.00	21.17

VAX/VMS Monitor Utility Disk I/O Statistics on node ZURICH

I/O Request Queue Length	CUR	AVE	MIN	MAX
255DUA0: (HSC004) VMSRL5	0.14	0.18	0.08	0.27
$255SDUA1: (HSC004) LAYERED	0.41	0.32	0.03	0.66
255DUA2: (HSC004) SUPPORT	0.21	0.28	0.00	0.82
255DUA3: (HSC004) PAGESWAP1	0.12	0.11	0.01	0.29
255DUA4: (HSC004) USERDISK4	0.03	0.02	0.00	0.13
255DUA5: (HSC004) PMS1_SHARE1	0.00	0.02	0.00	0.11
255DUA6: (HSC000) SPAR_SCRATCH	0.00	0.00	0.00	0.00
255DUA8: (HSC000) SPAR_BACKUP	0.00	0.67	0.00	5.18

Table 11.2 provides suggested I/O loading rates and Table 11.3 provides queue length characteristics for DEC RA-series disks.

An RA-series disk can normally handle a maximum of 25–40 I/O operations per second using a HSC controller. The figures shown are independent of host CPU configuration. Always begin by checking the system-wide I/O operation rate and queue length statistics.

System-wide I/O threshold can be obtained by multiplying the total number of RA-series disks by 25.

Table 11.2   Suggested approximate I/O load rates for RA & RF series disks
(an HSC controller may enable you to achieve higher performance)

Device	I/O requests per second	Device	I/O requests per second
ESE20	1500	RF30	25.0
RA60	12.0	RF35	30.0
RA70	28 0	RF71	29.0
RA71	30.0	RF72	30.0
RA72	30.0	RF73	30.0
RA81	22.0	RK07	15.0
RA82	22.0	RM03	20.0
RA90	30.0	RM05	20.0
RA92	32.0	RM80	22.0
RP04	20.0	RP07	25.0
RP05	22.0	RP06	22.0

Table 11.3   Queue length characteristics

Queue Length	Load
less than.20	Light
.20 to.50	Moderate
Over.50	Heavy

Direct I/O operation rate provides an indication of system-wide disk I/O activity. When deciding on standards for the disk operation rate, and the I/O request queue length, it is necessary to consider what is most important – high throughput of a disk, or improved response time for the users. Use the standard average rates shown below for improved response times.

- disk operation rate: 15 I/Os per second
- I/O request queue length: 0.5.

For high throughput of a disk the I/O request queue length should be kept high so that there is always work waiting for the disk, but this has a detrimental affect on the response times. If improved response times are required, then the queue length needs to be very short, which in turn means that a lower operation rate should be expected. Check the average I/O rates and queue lengths.

A low I/O rate together with a big queue length means that the I/O to the disk comes in bursts.

Determining average response time

Introduction

Average response time gives you a means of checking the relative performance of your disks. It indicates the perceived delay from the norm. Normally, disks with greater than average response time of 25 to 40 milliseconds (for RA-series disks) are good candidates for improvements. Ideally, average response time for an RA-series disk should be approximately 35 milliseconds. The average response time for any type of disk is calculated as follows:

$$\text{average response time (milliseconds)} = \frac{\text{average queue length}}{\text{average I/O rate}} \times 1000$$

▸ **Example** – to calculate the average response time for the system disk from the MONITOR output shown in Table 11.1. Average response time in milliseconds for VMSRL5:

$$= (0.18/5.13) \times 1000$$
$$= 35 \text{ ms}$$

Disks showing greater than average response times are either seek intensive or data transfer intensive. Disks exhibiting high operation rates are most likely to be seek intensive, whereas disks with low operation rates and large queue lengths of greater than 0.50 are usually data-transfer intensive.

▸ **Always watch out for exceptions** – a disk may have a low operation rate and a large queue length, and itself is not data transfer intensive, but is being blocked by data transfer from another disk on the same channel. It is possible that the I/O to the disk comes in bursts.

Causes of artificially high disk response time

A disk can show a higher than expected response time due to any of the following:

1. *The disk is fragmented.* Badly-fragmented disks can cause high disk-response times. Use the DCL commands MONITOR IO and MONITOR FCP to detect disk fragmentation. MONITOR IO will identify the 'Split Transfer Rate' whereas MONITOR FCP will identify the 'Window Turn Rate'.

   As explained above, SPLIT TRANSFER RATE identifies how many I/Os had to be broken up into several I/O requests to complete the requested data transfer. WINDOW TURN RATE also indicates file fragmentation. SPLIT TRANSFER RATE and WINDOW TURN RATE of under two per second is adequate for most installations.

2. *I/Os from other cluster nodes are omitted.* When several different nodes are accessing a common disk, running MONITOR DISK from one node often show high disk response time, because not all the I/Os from the other nodes are being accounted. To resolve the problem, collect data on all nodes or use the DCL command MONITOR CLUSTER.

3. *Incorrect queue lengths.* The disk queue length can get corrupted and set to an artificially high value, resulting in high disk response times. Use the following DCL command to check for corruption:

   ```
   MONITOR DISK/ITEM=ALL/INTERVAL = 1
   ```

   A non-zero queue length with zero I/O rate will confirm this corruption.To reset the value, first dismount and then remount the disk. If this does not resolve the problem, then a system reboot is necessary. If it is not possible to apply any of the methods described above, then use the following formula to calculate a more accurate disk response time:

   $$\text{average disk response time} = \frac{A - B}{C} \times 1000$$

   where:

   A = average queue length
   B = minimum queue length with zero I/Os
   C = average I/O operation rate

4. *Backup was running while the disk I/O was being measured.* Do not run backup during normal working hours if possible or do not measure response time while backup is being run.

5. *Pagefile(s) were on the same disk.* Disks holding pagefiles often show high disk response times. Flushing of the modified list can generate several concurrent I/Os to the pagefile, resulting in a high queue length for that disk for short periods, even if the overall I/O rate is low. This in turn can result in higher than normal disk response time.

6. *The I/O operation rate was too low.* A low I/O rate of under five per second can also produce high response times because of the way the response time is calculated. Even a small queue length can generate an artificially high response time. Recalculate the response time when the system is busier.

7. *The disk was too busy, inundated with requests.* It can be perfectly valid. To alleviate the problem, redistribute the load and/or redesign the application.

Determining hot disks/determining the problem device

Use the command MONITOR DISK/ITEM=ALL and watch out for disks with a queue of pending requests, especially those with a queue length of greater than 0.50. A queue indicates contention for that disk or controller and is normally the result of one of the following two conditions:

- the disk is not fast enough
- the disk is being saturated with requests.

Once the problem disk is isolated, the cause of the problem needs to be found and remedial action taken to improve performance as suggested in the sections that follow.

Determining the user with the top I/O rate

Use the command $MONITOR PROCESS/TOPDIO to display the processes responsible for high I/O activity. The user-id of all such processes is displayed, including the I/O rating as shown below.

Use this user-id to display the process details as shown in the next section.

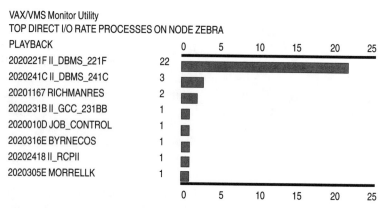

VAX/VMS Monitor Utility
TOP DIRECT I/O RATE PROCESSES ON NODE ZEBRA
PLAYBACK

2020221F II_DBMS_221F	22	
2020241C II_DBMS_241C	3	
20201167 RICHMANRES	2	
2020231B II_GCC_231BB	1	
2020010D JOB_CONTROL	1	
2020316E BYRNECOS	1	
20202418 II_RCPII	1	
2020305E MORRELLK	1	

Figure 11.1: Output from
MONITOR PROCESS/TOPDIO

Determining programs affecting the I/O rate

Once a process that consistently issues a significant number of direct I/Os is identified, use the command:

SHOW PROCESS/Continuous/ID=user-id

to obtain more information about the process and the image being run. Afterwards, using your knowledge of the system and the application in question, follow the steps in the next section to show files open by that process.

Determining files opened affecting I/O rate

It is possible to find hotfiles without the use of special tools. Use a series of steps/commands described below to determine 'hotfiles' on your system:

$SHOW DEVICE/FILE volume name

to show all open files on a disk of your choice.

Table 11.4   Output from SHOW DEVICE/FILES

$SH DEV/FILES DUA1

Files accessed on device DUA1: date time

Process Name	PID	File Name
	00000000	[00000031NDEXF.SYS;1
	00000000	[ST500.DAT]ENVPAR.GSD;1
	00000000	[STS(X).DAT]FNCTBL.GSD;1
	00000000	[ST500.DAT]CURTBL.GSD;1
	00000000	[ST500.DAT]KONSTS.GSD;1
	00000000	[ST500.DAT]MONCOM.GSD;1
	00000000	[ST500.DAT]TCPROC.GSD;1
	00000000	1ST500.DAT]SWSERV.GSD;l
BUNNELLBSRO1	00002AIB	[BUNNELLBSR]LOGIN.COM;1
BUNNELLBSROl	00002AIB	[BUNNELLSBSR.OA]BUNNELLBS.PST;1
BUNNELLBSRO1	00002A1B	[BBUNNELLBSR.OA]ACTITEM.DAT;2
SHACKELLJASS	00002D38	[SHACKELLJA]LOGIN.COM;2
SHACKELLJASS	00002D38	[SHACKELLJA]SHACKkLLJ.PST;l
SHACKELLJASS	00002D38	[SHACKELLJA]DOCDB.DAT;65
SYNGEAPOS	00002D14	[SYNGEAP]LOGIN.COM;l
SYNGEAPOS	00002D14	[SYNGEAP.OA]SYNGEAP.PST;l
SYNGEAPOS	00002D14	[SYNGEAP.OA]ACTITEM.DAT;2

Table 11.5   Retrieval pointers (extents)

Dump of file 1D1A3:[ALLIN1.DATA_SHARE]OA$DAF_E DAT
File ID (2880,7,0) End of file block: 78552 Allocated: 78552

File Header

Header area

Identification area offset:	40
Map area offset:	100
Access control area offset:	255
Reserved area offset:	255
Extension segment number:	0
Structure level and version:	2, 1
File identification:	(2880,7,0)
Extension file identification	(O,0,0)
VAX-11 RMS attributes	
Record type:	Variable
File organization:	Indexed
Record attributes:	Implied carriage control

Table 11.5   (continued) Retrieval pointers (extents)

Record size:	0
Highest block:	78552
End of file block:	78553
End of file byte:	0
Bucket size:	4
Fixed control area size:	0
Maximum record size:	2000
Default extension size:	100
Global buffer count:	16
Directory version limit:	0
File characteristics:	Contiguous best try
Map area words in use:	127
Access mode:	0
File owner UIC:	[SYSTEM]
File protection:	S:RWED, O:RWED, W:E
Back link file identification:	(13664,1,0)
Journal control flags:	<none specified>
Active recovery units:	None
Highest block written:	78552

Identification area:

File name:	OA$DAF_E.DAT;40
Revision number:	4035
Creation date:	
Revision date:	
Expiration date:	<none specifed>
Backup date:	

Map area:

Retrieval pointers

Count:	12	LBN:	284829
Count:	306	LBN:	465354
Count:	102	LBN:	475725
Count:	1530	LBN:	489588
Count:	714	LBN:	501897
Count:	204	LBN:	502713
Count:	204	LBN:	503127
Count:	102	LBN:	516129
Count:	102	LBN:	520707
Count:	204	LBN:	538344
Count:	1020	LBN:	544572
Count:	34578	LBN:	549957

Checksum: 329187

You may then use MONITOR RMS to measure the I/O rates for these files. At this stage check these files for fragmentation, if any, by issuing the following command:

DUMP/HEADER/BLOCK:COUNT=0 device:filename

A fragmented file will have a number of extents (retrieval pointers), shown in the MAP AREA at the end of the dump, containing a count field and a LBN field. The count field is the number of contiguous blocks within the extent, whereas the LBN field shows the logical block number to the start of the extent. See Table 11.5 for a dump of a file.

If the free disk space is not contiguous and the file is fairly large, it is highly probable that the file will contain many extents. Response time for fragmented disks is greater due to the added disk movements required to position the head to the different segments of a file. If file fragmentation is a problem follow the remedial procedures relevant to file fragmentation.

12 Rules of Thumb for Unplugging a System Disk Bottleneck

Introduction

System disk I/O performance can often be improved dramatically by simple means as described below. If your system disk is a bottleneck then the following might help to reduce the I/O load.

Ensure page and swap files are contiguous

Both of the above files should be contiguous and should never be more than 70% used. You can establish the current usage by executing the command $SHOW MEMORY/FILE/FULL.

Table 12.1 Example SHOW MEMORY/FILE output

UD4:[PAGESWAP]PAGEFILE.SYS;1			
Free Blocks	2329	Reservable Blocks	-45663
Total Size (blocks)	54929	Paging File Number	3
Swap Usage (processes)	99992	Paging Usage (processes)	55
	0		
This file can be used for either paging or swapping.			

If you find that more than 70% of the file is in use then extend the size of these files by executing the SWAPFILES command shown below.

When extending these files or creating secondary page and swap files ensure there is sufficient free space (at least 20%) left on the disk (ie after the creation or extension of these files). If there is not enough free space then you will have to move these files onto a less heavily used disk as shown in the next section. Since the release of version 5, a significant change in VMS now allows a process to use up to four page files simultaneously.

It is always best to create secondary files on a less heavily utilized disk than to extend the existing page and swap files on the system disk. It is more efficient to have four small page files spread over four different spindles than one large page file on a single spindle.

To expand a page and/or swap file execute:

    $ @SYS$UPDATE:SWAPFILES.COM

When creating new page/swap files ensure that there is sufficient free space on the disk and that the files are contiguous.

Move page or swap file or both to another disk

Relocation of these files ensures that I/O is equally distributed across the system's physical disks. If you have multiple page and swap files, always relocate the largest of these to achieve the best results. The main objective behind the relocation of files is to minimize the amount of contention for use of the following:

- availability of disk head for seeks
- availability of channels for data transfers.

Reduced contention results in better overall response and minimizes CPU blocking. Pagefiles tend to be more active with high hard fault rates. Poor distribution of pagefiles may frequently lead to processes in a PFW (pagefault wait) state waiting for pagefile I/O completions. It is advisable to move the secondary page and swap files to a less active disk. But if you wish to move the main file to a different spindle then this is achieved by executing:

    @SYS$MANAGER:SYPAGSWPFILES.COM

automatically at boot time. This procedure mounts the page and swap files disks and installs the files so that they are no longer needed on the system disk.

Move frequently-accessed files to another disk

After the successful relocation of page and swap files if the system disk is still I/O bound, relocate key files such as: SYSUAF.DAT, VMSMAIL.DAT, NETUAF.DAT, JBCSYQUE.DAT, RIGHTSLIST.DAT to a less active disk. *Do not forget* to alter or to assign new logical names for these files.

On a cluster, commands involving queue manager interaction such as SUBMIT, SHOW QUEUE and PRINT can impose heavy I/O on the queue file JBCSYQUE.DAT; it is vital that you move this file off the system disk. Before moving JBSCYQUE.DAT from the system disk ensure all queues are stopped and produce a list of all outstanding entries. Issue the following commands to stop all queues: $STOP/QUEUE/MANAGER.

To restart the queues type:

    $START/QUEUE/MANAGER device:directory JBCSYQUE.DAT

Do not forget to alter your system startup file with the new location. Note that QUEMANAGER has been re-written since the introduction of VMS V5.4-3 and VMS V6.0.

Use global buffers

Global buffering is the most effective way of minimizing disk I/O operations. Consider the use of global buffers for greater memory savings on shared files, do not use local buffers for files shared by multiple users. Use global buffers on shared system files such as SYSUAF, file primarily used for reading.

Use global buffers for index, and relative files (shared files only) on your system. You can request global buffers on a *per file* basis. The system parameter RMS_GBLBUFQUO represents total number of global buffers available on a system. Global buffers consume GBLPAGES as well as GBLPAGFIL and GBLSECTIONS. Make sure you have enough GBLSECTIONS and GBLPAGES free before introducing global buffering. You can check this when in INSTALL as follows: INSTALL >LIST/SUMMARY/GLOBAL. Global buffers allow the index portion of a file to be cached in memory thus reducing physical I/Os during an index traversal. Providing there is no shortage of memory and the file in question is small, you may cache the entire file in memory, but if the memory is somewhat restricted, try at least caching the index in memory. The procedure to set global buffers is explained below.

Figure 12.1: Using
Global Buffers

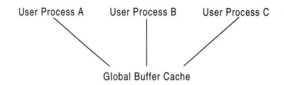

Setting global buffers

1. Produce file statistics by using:

   $ANALYZE/RMS/STATISTIC filename

2. Check the count of index blocks

3. Check bucket size

4. Check memory availability

5. Global buffer count should be the sum of all index blocks (providing there is enough free memory)

6. Declare the global buffers using the DCL command:

   $SET FILE/GLOBAL_BUFFER=n filename

   where n ranges from 0 to 32767 and a value of 0 (zero) disables global buffering. The total number of global pages required by the global buffers is the product of the total number of buffers declared and the bucket size, including some additional overhead. Use the command: MONITOR RMS/ITEM = CACHING/FILE = filename to obtain local and global cache statistics.

7. Decompress system libraries and optimize performance. Decompress the system library files to reduce disk I/O and CPU time required for library operations. Decompressing system libraries consumes additional disk space but enhances performance when linking modules and executing HELP. Decompress library files by using:

   $@SYS$UPDATE:LIBDECOMP.COM

Table 12.2   Example output from ANALYZE/RMS/STATISTIC command

RMS File Statistics
1DIA3:[ALLIN1.DATA SHARE]CALACCESS.DAT;1
FILE HEADER
    File Spec: 1DIA3:[ALLIN1.DATA SHARE]CALACCESS.DAT;1
    File ID: (13683,1,0)
    Owner UIC: [ALLIN1]
    Protection: System: RWED, Owner: RWED, Group: RWE, World: RWE
    Creation Date: 17-APR-1986 18:39:54.46
    Revision Date: 14-JAN-1992 12:57:58.94, Number: 126
    Expiration Date: 1-JAN-2000 00:00:00.00
    Backup Date: 15-JAN-1992 22:44:59.83
    Contiguity Options: none
    Performance Options: none
    Reliability Options: none
    Journaling Enabled: none
RMS FILE ATTRIBUTES
    File Organization: indexed
    Record Format: fixed
    Record Attributes:
    Maximum Record Size: 63
    Longest Record: 63
    Blocks Allocated: 18, Default Extend Size: 0
    Bucket Size: 2
    File Monitoring: disabled
    Global Buffer Count: 0
FIXED PROLOG
    Number of Areas: 1, VBN of First Descriptor: 2
    Prolog Version: 3
AREA DESCRIPTOR #0 (VBN 2, offset %OX'0000')
    Bucket Size: 2
    Reclaimed Bucket VBN: 0
    Current Extent Start: 16, Blocks: 3, Used: 2, Next: 18
    Default Extent Quantity: 0
    Total Allocation: (not accumulated for this file)
STATISTICS FOR AREA #0
    Count of Reclaimed Blocks: 0
KEY DESCRIPTOR #0 (VBN 1, offset %X'0000')
    Index Area: 0, Level 1 Index Area: 0, Data Area: 0
    Root Level: 1

Table 12.2 (continued) Example output from ANALYZE/RMS/STATISTIC command

Index Bucket Size: 2, Data Bucket Size: 2

Root VBN: 7

Key Flags:

    (0) KEY$V_DUPKEYS 1

    (3) KEY$V IDX COMPR 1

    (4) KEY$V INITIDX 0

    (6) KEY$V KEY COMPR 1

    (7) KEY$V REC COMPR 1

Key Segments:

Key Size: 30

Minimum Record Size: 30

Index Fill Quantity: 1024, Data Fill Quantity: 1024

Segment Positions: 0

Segment Sizes: 30

Data Type: string

Name: ""

First Data Bucket VBN: 4

STATISTICS FOR KEY #0

Number of Index Levels:	1
Count of Level 1 Records:	4
Mean Length of Index Entry:	32
Count of Index Blocks:	2
Mean Index Bucket Fill:	6%
Mean Index Entry Compression:	59%
Count of Data Records:	63
Mean Length of Data Records:	63
Count of Data Blocks:	8
Mean Data Bucket Fill:	74%
Mean Data Key Compression:	86%
Mean Data Record Compression:	36%
Overall Space Efficiency:	43%

The analysis uncovered NO errors.

13   Disk and HSC Load Balancing

Introduction

Disk load balancing is the even distribution of the disk I/O load across the less active disks thus increasing overall responsiveness of the system by reducing the amount of competition for:

- seek operations through available heads
- data transfer operations through available channels.

This is the most effective way to reduce I/O queues and to improve I/O performance. You can also reconfigure disks to specific channels and hence reduce overall response time for the device and also reduce the amount of CPU blocking. Use the command shown below to identify hot files during peak hours.

First, use the command SHOW DEVICE/FILE drive name: to check which files are open, then pick the files you feel are most active and issue the command SET FILE/STATISTICS filename.ext for those files. Lastly, use the command:

```
$MONITOR RMS/ITEM = ALL/FILE = filename.ext
```

to see which files are hit most. Now you can spread them over multiple disks and/or controllers. Products, such as VPA, DECPS and SPM have the ability to pick hotfiles information.

Do not move any files before developing a complete understanding of the applications and data files in use.

Note: When planning load balancing, do not forget to consider the natural growth of files. Remember the capacity performance thresholds for the disks in questions when redistributing files.

HSC load balancing – rules of thumb

HSC load balancing is also critical to I/O performance. This section will provide you with some basic guidelines to enable you to configure your HSC for maximum efficiency. Some of the vital points you should be aware of while configuring your HSCs are discussed in the following sections.

Do not put shadow sets on the same interface cards

If busy drives are connected to separate requester cards then multiple reads and writes can be performed simultaneously; this is because only one device can transfer data at any one time when all of the drives are on the same requester.

Distribute heavily used drives evenly among (interface) requester cards

Distribute busy drives evenly among the interface (requester) cards. A requester card can support up to four devices, but only one device can transfer data at any one time. Greater performance can be achieved if there are fewer heavily used drives on any one requester card, especially if the size of transfers is large.

Do not configure drives of varying transfer rates on the same requester card

Install faster drives on higher requester cards to reduce the possibility of data bus contention and ensure maximum performance. For example, you should not connect an RA81 and a RA90 to the same requester card, this will limit the performance of the RA90 to the equivalent of RA81

Connect your 'active' disks to higher priority requester

Heavily used drives should be connected to higher priority requester card. This is because if there are two requestors contending for the data bus simultaneously, the higher priority requester wins.

Check and adjust I/O credit rating between the HSC and VAX nodes

I/O credits are the total number of outstanding I/O requests a VAX node can have with an HSC. Any I/O requests beyond this credit value, established when the HSC is connected, are queued within the VAX until an outstanding I/O is complete. These I/Os are excluded from the HSC seek optimizations and unnecessarily delay I/O operations. In total, an HSC can support approximately 400 of such credits. The default value per node is approximately 24 credits. Use the DCL command:

```
MONITOR SCS/ITEM=SEND_CREDIT
```

to detect credit waits. Increase this value using the SET CREDIT command if necessary.

Use the utilities shipped with the HSC operating system to obtain information for optimal load balancing, shadowing and HSC caching
The latest version of CRONIC operating system for the HSC includes the utility LGUTIL which can be used to obtain HSC-related performance statistics. Data collected through this utility can be used to determine the possible performance benefits of volume shadowing, load balancing and HSC caching. To use the utility, see the appropriate manual for details.

Do not overload your HSC K.DSI channels
Each HSC requester card can support up to four disks but only one disk at a time can transfer data back. If data transfer is taking place and another disk is also ready to transfer the data, then it must wait until the first transfer is complete. The probability of this happening is very small but increases, and can affect performance when all four disks on a requester channel are busy transferring large chunks of data. It is always a good practice to keep at least 1 channel free for contingencies such as a channel failure.

Do not have both A and B buttons pressed in if your disk is not dual ported
If your disk is not dual ported (ie there is only one connection to the disk) then you must release the port button for the port which is not connected. This will prevent your system performing unnecessary checks and speed-up operations.

14 Adjusting Disk Cluster Sizes for Performance

Introduction

When the file system within VMS creates and/or extends a disk file, the amount of disk space allocated is measured in units called clusters. A cluster is the basic unit of space allocation on disk. Clusters are blocks grouped together at disk initialization. A disk cluster size can range from 1 to 65,535 blocks. A disk cluster size is set at the time the disk is first initialized. Use the DCL command:

    INITIALIZE/CLUSTER = cluster_size device_name:

to specify the cluster size for a disk. You cannot specify the cluster size for disks already mounted. A default value of 3 is used by VMS if no /CLUSTER qualifier is specified.

Warning: 'INITIALIZE' erases all data from the disk.

Use the DCL command SHOW DEVICE/FULL device_name: to check the cluster size of mounted disks. A disk file called BITMAP.SYS holds information on used and available clusters on a cluster. It contains a bit for each cluster on the disk. These bits are modified on the allocation of disk space.

Disk cluster size and its effect on performance

The larger the cluster size, the smaller the BITMAP.SYS and the more effective the bitmap cache

As explained, the file BITMAP.SYS holds the storage allocation map for each cluster on a disk volume. There is a 'bit' for every cluster on the disk and each 'bit' indicates whether the cluster is allocated to a file or not. The size of the file BITMAP.SYS is directly proportional to the number of clusters on the disk. A large cluster size reduces the size of BITMAP.SYS; this is because it has to store less information on a reduced amount of clusters.

As this file becomes smaller in size, the VMS file system is able to hold more of it in its cache memory, thus improving the bitmap cache effectiveness and reducing volume rebuild time. The VMS file system sometimes scans this file several times before creating and/or extending a file. A small file held in memory can speed up such operations.

There are also some disadvantages associated with large cluster sizes. The main disadvantage is that too much disk space is wasted, since a file with only a few bytes of information will still occupy the number of blocks in 'one' cluster – because disk space is allocated by cluster. Use the DCL command:

```
$DIRECTORY/SIZE=ALL/GRAND
```

to report on the differences between used and allocated space. A large cluster size also creates problems with finding extents which match the file sizes. A large cluster size is not recommended for disks holding a vast quantity of small files. It is not ideal for ALL-IN-1 type of applications where a large number of small word processing documents are created.

Do not use the default cluster size of 3 for large drives. Always consider the free space availability and file sizes before adjusting the cluster size. Care must be taken while setting the cluster sizes for disks. Ideally the cluster size should be a factor of cylinder size in blocks. Use the DCL command SHOW DEVICE/FULL device_name: to obtain information sectors (blocks) per track, tracks per cylinder, and cylinders per drive for the disk of your choice.

A large cluster size can reduce the number of 'window turns'
A large cluster size can reduce the number of 'window turns' on a fragmented file. Window turns are detrimental to good system performance. By default the file system stores up to 7 'retrieval pointers' per file and if the file contains more than 7 fragments, additional I/Os are required to make all the data accessible.

When a file is opened by the system this part of the extent map is held in window control block (WCB). If the user issues a read to the block not in memory, the file system refreshes the WCB with new pointers. It can also constitute of a file header read thus resulting in an additional seek unless the information is stored in the file header cache. A retrieval pointer points to at least one cluster. A large cluster size can hold more blocks for a file within the WCB. A large cluster size increases the likelihood of that block being part of the WCB. Further details on 'window turns' and how to reduce them can be found in *Curing the problems of fragmentation - rules of thumb*, on page 148.

A large cluster size can reduce the number of split I/Os

A large cluster size ensures that a greater number of disk blocks are contiguous, thus decreasing the likelihood of split I/Os.

15   Caching, File System Activity and Performance

Towards a better understanding of the **XQP** and associated caches

In order to make improvements in the performance of disks it is essential that the reader has a little insight into the workings of VMS file system and its caches. To develop a complete understanding you are advised to read *Understanding the file system methodology*, on page 141.

VMS directory and file structures are supported both by RMS (record management services) and XQP (extended QIO processor). RMS is responsible for implementing a record structure within a file and the different methods of accessing that data, whereas XQP is responsible for implementing the file structure on disks. The file system (here referred to as XQP) treats disks as direct access devices and manages them by keeping track of disk blocks. These blocks are identified using logical block numbers (LBN) in the range of 0 to n-1, where n relates to the total number of blocks on the disk. The file system is responsible for translating all virtual I/O requests issued by either RMS or the user directly into logical requests. It translates the virtual block number into LBN and thus acts as a mapper between the file structure and the disks. The file system uses VMS caching (described below) to reduce the I/O load and provide quicker file access.

The file system caches

The VMS file system allocates a number of buffers (caches) to support its I/O operations. This multiple buffer nature of the caching system helps the file system to load several blocks of different information simultaneously into its memory. By doing so, the file system can avoid certain I/O operations and hence provide faster file access.

The seven file system caches which are used to improve the disk I/O performance

BITMAP CACHE

Assists in the allocation and deallocation of disk space. It contains blocks from the storage bitmap file, BITMAP.SYS. This file contains one bit for each block on the disk including a complete record of blocks in use. The file system accesses this cache when the new allocation requests cannot be specified using the extent cache.

EXTENT CACHE

Also associated with allocation and deallocation of disk space for file creation, deletion, extension, and truncation. It describes a number of free disk block areas. The file system attempts to allocate space from this cache first on file creation and/or extension. Only when it fails to satisfy the request from the extent cache, is bitmap cache searched.

FILE HEADER CACHE

Associated with the opening, closing, creation and deletion of files. It is simply a set of file headers (which reside in INDEXF.SYS) maintained in memory to prevent excessive I/O. The index file contains information on control blocks, home block, boot blocks and file headers.

FILE ID CACHE

A list of file identifiers (header slots) which helps to eliminate unnecessary I/O to the index file INDEXF.SYS.

DIRECTORY DATA CACHE

Is associated with file lookups. It helps to reduce the need for sequential searches.

DIRECTORY FCB CACHE

Is also associated with file lookups. A cache lookup may be performed on file creation, deletion, or extension.

QUOTA CACHE

Is associated with disk quotas. It helps to reduce the excessive I/O to QUOTA.SYS which records all disk usage for user processes when disk quotas are enabled.

Table 15.1   File system caches and associated SYSGEN parameters

Cache Description	Name Used in MONITOR display	Associated SYSGEN Parameters
Directory File Control Block	Dir FCB	ACP_DINDXCACHE
Directory Data	Dir Data	ACP_DIRCACHE
File Header	File Hdr	ACP_HDRCACHE
File Identification	File ID	ACP_FIDCACHE
Extent	Extent	ACP_EXTCACHE
		ACP_EXTLIMIT
Quota	Quota	ACP_QUOCACHE
Bitmap	Bitmap	ACP_MAPCACHE

Measuring file system caches performance

There are two possible ways of checking the performance of these caches. You can use the MONITOR FILE_SYSTEM_CACHE utility to examine performance effectiveness. This is done through hit rates where 'Hit%' is the percentage of times that a required block was found in the cache. A high hit rate (nearing 100%) is an indication of optimal performance. If a cache misses then a disk I/O is required. We need to keep disk I/Os down to a low level - say 1 per second per cache. So we need to ensure:

$$\frac{\text{attempt rate} \times (100 - \text{Hit \%})}{100} < 1$$

A hit rate below 80% indicates that an adjustment (ie a slight increase) is required in the value of the associated SYSGEN parameters (ie those which affect caching). Remember, the higher the hit percentage, the greater the effectiveness. This is only achievable if the caches are large enough to keep the hit percentage high. On average, a hit rate of 80% is normally acceptable but keep an eye on the attempt rates. If the attempt rate is also high, then the hit rate should ideally be nearing 100%. Window turns are also an indication of poor caching. Use the MONITOR FCP utility to examine the window turn rate (see Table 15.3 for sample output). Window turns are associated with file header operations and mapping.

Table 15.2   Sample Output from MONITOR FILE_SYSTEM_CACHE

VAX/VMS Monitor Utility
FILE SYSTEM CACHING STATISTICS
on node ZLW01
SUMMARY

		CUR	AVE	MIN	MAX
Dir FCB	(Hit %)	99.00	98.06	95.0	99.00
	(Attempt Rate)	3.26	2.28	0.45	6.15
Dir Data	(Hit %)	96.00	92.93	85.00	97.00
	(Attempt Rate)	3.99	3.16	0.56	7.78
File Hdr	(Hit %)	79.00	86.34	79.00	92.00
	(Attempt Rate)	3.53	2.60	0.64	5.73
File ID	(Hit %)	100.00	99.91	97.00	100.00
	(Attempt Rate)	0.03	0.15	0.03	0.42
Extent	(Hit %)	99.00	99.66	98.00	100.00
	(Attempt Rate)	0.68	1.80	0.51	5.63
Quota	(Hit %)	0.00	0.00	0.00	0.00
	(Attempt Rate)	0.00	0.00	0.00	0.00
Bitmap	(Hit %)	100.00	95.45	0.00	100.00
	(Attempt Rate)	0.00	0.00	0.00	0.02

Table 15.3   Sample output From MONITOR FCP

VAX/VMS Monitor Utility
FILE PRIMITIVE STATISTICS
ON NODE ZL01
SUMMARY

	CUR	AVE	MIN	MAX
FCP Call Rate	4.89	3.81	0.94	9.17
Allocation Rate	0.08	0.19	0.06	0.40
Create Rate	0.03	0.15	0.03	0.41
Disk Read Rate	0.82	0.49	0.06	131
Disk Write Rate	0.61	0.84	031	1.85
Volume Lock Wait Rate	0.00	0.00	0.00	0.01
CPU Tick Rate	2.60	1.96	0.46	4.67
File Sys Page Fault Rate	0.10	0.18	0.02	0.48
Window Turn Rate	0.12	0.11	0.02	0.42
FIle Lookup Rate	3.24	2.20	0.41	5.94
File Open Rate	0.48	0.87	0.24	1.95
Erase Rate	0.00	0.00	0.00	000

It is usually fragmentation which is responsible for the poor performance of these caches.

Adjusting caching parameters

The effectiveness of the disk caches can be improved by making them larger. In the case of the directory data cache, its performance is likely to suffer if directory files contain more than 500 entries or if files are frequently added and deleted from directories. The performance of a directory file can be compared with an RMS indexed file, which has been subject to continuous addition and deletion of records without a file reorganization. It is important that you are familiar with AUTOGEN, and that you always use MODPARAMS.DAT file for changes – this file is used for input by AUTOGEN.

If the hit rate is low and you need to increase the size of the associated parameter, change it in co-ordination with AUTOGEN. AUTOGEN can make corresponding adjustments to both nonpaged dynamic memory (NPAGEDYN) and paged dynamic memory (PAGEDYN) if necessary under version 5. Only increase the value by 10% of its original value at a time, then observe the performance for a little while. If necessary increase it again by another 10%. Do not hesitate to revert to the original settings if it does not result in a quantifiable gain. Remember to reboot the system to make these changes effective.

In a cluster environment the XQP on each node acts independently and builds its own cache. Each node should therefore be examined independently for its performance of caches. It is important that VMS file structures are operating without undue overhead as caching holds the key to disk performance and ultimately to system performance. However, do not waste memory by allocating too large a value to these caches and always make the changes in co-ordination with AUTOGEN (unless you want your system to hang).

16

Volume Shadowing and Performance

Introduction

Volume shadowing allows you to declare two disks on the same HSC controller to be copies of each other. To VMS they appear as one disk. The HSC controller ensures that the shadow disk is an exact copy of the master disk by replicating all I/O operations to the shadow set.

Volume shadowing is very good for maintaining effectiveness and resilience. Most sites use shadowing to protect themselves from disk failures. In addition, there are performance gains to be achieved if shadowing is introduced for disks with a high read to write ratio. Shadowing is faster for reading (giving approximately 50% improvement over reads) because the HSC will accept the data from whichever disk can access the data first. However, it is slower for writing since shadowing has to write any data on to two disks. Experience has shown that the disks handling more than 25% of writes are not worth shadowing as there will be no gain in overall efficiency.

Volume shadow the system disk, but only after moving some of the files onto a different disk. If files such as PAGEFILE.SYS, SWAPFILE.SYS, JBCSYSQUE.DAT, RIGHTSLIST.SYS are moved, there will be a major improvement in the performance of that disk and hence of the system as a whole.

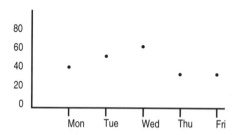

Figure 16.1: To show the benefits of volume shadowing the system disk (under uniform load throughout the week)

The graph in Figure 16.1 shows the response time for the common system disk in a cluster which was not shadowed on MONDAY, TUESDAY, and WEDNESDAY, but was shadowed on THURSDAY and FRIDAY. The disk was 80% read. During the last two days, the response went down from around 57 ms to around 28 ms. Before the introduction of volume shadowing the system disk could not cope with the load, the system performance was dreadful and the users were screaming. SPM analysis revealed a large build up of queues.

Use your HSC software to obtain read/write statistics before applying volume shadowing for performance

Run the utility LGUTIL shipped with the latest releases of the HSC operating system CRONIC to obtain read/write statistics for all disks being served by the HSC. A disk with high read to write ratio would benefit from volume shadowing.

Volume shadowing features and terminology – a summarization

1. A shadow set may contain up to three disks, data is duplicated on all disks. All disks in a shadow set must be of the same type, such as an RA90. Disk(s) containing duplicate data are members of the shadow set.

2. Shadow sets do not provide data integrity, they mainly provide resilience. You can achieve enhanced performance where the application is mostly reading the data (ie for disks with high read to write ratio).

3. One single HSC must manage the entire shadow set. If your shadow set is dual ported, then all shadow set members must

be managed by one of the two HSCs. This provides further resilience in case of an HSC failure.

4. Users cannot write to individual disks while they are members of a shadow set.

17

MSCP Disk Server and Performance

MSCP Parameters

In a VAX cluster, a mass storage control protocol (MSCP) disk server enables remotely connected disks to appear as local disks for the nodes which have the disks mounted. This enables applications on cluster nodes to have simultaneous read/write access to the disks. Parameters which control the loading, serving, and tuning of the MSCP server are discussed below.

MSCP_LOAD

This parameter specifies the loading of a server during the system boot. The default SYSGEN value is set to 0 (zero) which instructs VMS not to MSCP serve any disks from this node. This value should be set to 1 (one) if any disks are to be MSCP served from this node.

MSCP_SERVE_ALL

This instructs VMS to control the serving of remotely connected disks as follows. If set to 0 (zero) then do not serve any disks. If MSCP_LOAD is set to 0 (zero), then MSCP_SERVE_ALL is ignored completely; no disks are served. If set to 1 (one) it serves all disks; if set to 2, it only serves locally attached disks – that is non-HSC or non-RFXX.

MSCP_BUFFER

Is used to specify the number of pages of physical (nonpaged pool) memory for data transfers between client systems and the MSCP-served disks. SYSGEN default value is 128 pages. Substantial enhancement in performance can be achieved by increasing the value of this parameter, especially if there is a significant amount of fragmented I/O requests and buffer waits. Use the DCL command MONITOR MSCP_SERVER to observe the I/O traffic and buffering.

MSCP_CREDITS

This controls the number of concurrently outstanding I/O requests that may be pending for MSCP served disks from each client system. The default SYSGEN value is 4. You may benefit by increasing the value of this parameter on nodes serving many disks, but be careful, a haphazard increase can worsen performance. The value of this parameter is normally increased in conjunction with MSCP_BUFFER. If MSCP_BUFFER is set at too small a value, increasing the value of MSCP_CREDITS may degrade performance.

Displaying and interpreting MSCP server statistics

Use the DCL command MONITOR MSCP_SERVER to display MSCP_SERVER statistics. A summary of previously collected data is shown below.

Table 17.1   Sample output From MONITOR MSCP_SERVER

		VAX/VMS Monitor Utility MSCP SERVER STATISTICS ON NODE FRANKFURT			
		CUR	AVE	MIN	MAX
Server I/O Request Rate		0.00	0.72	0.00	6.23
Read Request Rate		0.00	0.53	0.00	6.21
Write Request Rate		0.00	0.15	0.00	7.17
Extra Fragment Rate		0.00	0.65	0.23	0.99
Fragmented Request Rate		0.00	0.82	0.15	0.88
Buffer Wait Rate		0.00	0.21	0.00	0.51
Request Size Rates	1	0.00	0.08	0.00	0.99
(Blocks)	2-3	0.00	0.02	0.00	0.67
	4-7	0.00	0.02	0.00	0.67
	8-15	0.00	0.00	0.00	1.63
	16-31	0.00	0.10	0.00	5.55
	32-63	0.00	0.47	0.00	0.00
	64+	0.00	0.00	0.00	0.00

To interpret the results correctly, some information on the workings of MSC server is given below.

Use of buffers within MSCP

When an I/O request is sent to a device which is MSCP-served by some other node in the cluster, the requesting node places it request with the MSCP-server software running on the node which serves that disk. After receiving the I/O request, the MSCP-server reserves some space in its MSCP_BUFFER area for the temporary storage of the data. It uses its own built-in algorithm in determining the amount of space it should reserve. It calculates the maximum and the minimum buffer space essential for the requested transfer using the following equation:

MAX_BUF_SIZE = Available buffer space/2
MIN_BUF_SIZE = Available buffer space/8

Note that the result is rounded down to the nearest block. These equations are only an approximation. The server never gives up all the available space to any one request, it reserves some space for other nodes and processes making I/O requests. After processing the I/O request, MSCP-server places that data in its special buffer area, this is because it is not intelligent enough to send the data back to the requesting node directly. The requesting node fetches its own data and passes it to the relevant application.

Interpreting the statistics

Fragmented request rate

This shows the number of I/O requests fragmented because of insufficient transfer buffer size availability. To illustrate how the buffer sizes are calculated, let us assume that a node within the cluster requested approximately 20 blocks of data and the MSCP software currently has only 31 free pages in its buffer space. Using the equations shown above it will calculate the maximum and the minimum fragment size to satisfy the I/O request.

15 = 31/2   (maximum fragment size rounded down to the nearest value)

3 = 31/8   (minimum fragment size rounded down to the nearest value)

From the above calculations you can see that there is not sufficient space available to transfer the 20 blocks of data in one go. The MSCP-server therefore breaks the request into two requests of 10 block each. It is this type of fragmentation which is shown in 'fragmented request rate'.

Extra fragment rate

Shows how frequently an incoming I/O request had to be fragmented because of insufficient transfer buffer size. Continuing with the example listed under 'fragmented request rate', and assuming that the MSCP buffer space was really lacking in memory and there were only 17 blocks of free memory available, then using the equation above, the maximum fragment size would be 8 (ie it is not big enough to fulfill 10 block I/O request).

The MSCP software halves the I/O request again. Now the system can cope with five pages of contiguous data transfer and the request is serviced in four separate I/O requests to the disk. This type of fragmented I/O is shown under 'extra fragment rate' and is considered more serious than the 'fragmented request rate'.

Buffer wait rate

As explained above, the MSCP software also calculates the minimum fragment size. Figures shown under this column indicate that there was not even a minimum amount of buffer space available to serve the I/O request. It cannot serve that I/O request until buffer space is made available by other processes. Ideally, 'buffer wait rate' should be nearer zero, a buffer wait rate of greater than zero indicates MSCP buffer area is badly fragmented and its size should be increased.

MSCP_BUFFER fragmentation results in additional I/Os to the disk and therefore detrimental to the performance of a system. A larger buffer area reduces I/O requests fragmentation and enhances performance. The sample data shown above suggests that the system would benefit from a larger MSCP_BUFFER area.

18   Disk Striping

Introduction

Disk striping is a technique to facilitate greater I/O performance and reduce disk I/O contention by joining two or more disks into a single virtual unit. In a striped set, data is stored in consecutive chunks on the combined volumes. A number of consecutive blocks exists on one physical disk before they continue on the next unit. Data can be accessed from the combined disks in parallel, on two disks joined together this almost halves the retrieval time to access the same amount of data from a single disk. This distribution of blocks across several disks is completely hidden from the application and the file system. The striping software handles the organization of data and the translation of LBNs on a particular disk. Striping is also discussed in Chapter 10: *Raid and Storage Works*.

Striping is also ideal for load balancing, especially in a shared environment where there are large number of users sharing files. A single disk can only serve one request at a time. If a large number of users are accessing the same file or a number of files on a disk, some user requests cannot be satisfied until the completion of the existing request, thereby increasing the response time of the disk. The response time increases with the increase in the number of users, effectively degrading performance of the whole system. By combining several disks into a stripe set the I/O load can be distributed evenly providing the access to the files on those disks is somewhat random. In simple words, striping takes single I/O requests and disperses it over multiple disks to increase the overall transfer rate and reduce the overall response time of a disk.

In fact, the data transfer rate increases in a linear fashion with additional stripesets. The example below gives a clear demonstration of how striping can dramatically increase the transfer rate and improve load balancing. Consider a chunk size of four blocks on a two-disk striped set, the logical blocks will span across the two disks as shown below.

Table 18.1   Allocations of chunks in a two-disk stripeset

	chunk 0	chunk 2	chunk 4
Disk Volume 1	0 1 2 3	8 9 10 11	16 17 18 19
Disk Volume 2	4 5 6 7	12 13 14 15	20 21 22 23
	chunk 1	chunk 3	chunk 5

From Table 18.1 you can see how data will be distributed on the two volumes combined together: first four blocks (0–3) will reside on disk volume 1 and LBNs (4–7) will reside on disk on disk volume 2. Likewise, the next four blocks will reside on disk volume 1. Now, if we were to retrieve the first eight blocks (0–7) from a striped set, this data transfer can take place in parallel from the two volumes: (0–3) blocks from disk volume 1 and (4–7) blocks from data volume 2. The time taken to retrieve the data will be equivalent to retrieving four block of data. Whereas, on a disk with no striping, time taken to transfer (0–7) blocks will double (8 sector times). To cut the retrieval time even further, you may create a three-member striped set where LBN (0–3) will reside on disk 1, (4–7) on disk 2 and (8–11) on disk 3. Now, if you were to access the first 12 blocks (0–11), the time taken will still be equal to four sector times because all the three disk units will be able to transfer the data in parallel.

Still using the above figure of a two-disk striped set, let us consider two requests for data: one to LBN 5 and the other to LBN 19. It is possible that these two requests are for the data from the same file or two different files or even two different users. On a non-striped disk the second request can only be serviced after the completion of the first; whereas on a striped disk this can take place in parallel. This is because the second request does not have to wait for the first request to complete. In a shared environment, when a high number of users are accessing the data, striping can dramatically reduce the average response time of a disk.

Three types of striping can be implemented: *hardware-based, file-based* and VMS *driver-based.* In the hardware-based striping multiple disks are combined together to form one disk unit.

In *file-based striping*, specific files are striped instead of physical disk units, striped files are spread across several disks. Applications accessing that data files call striping software routines to organize and retrieve data. The main advantage of file striping over disk striping is that the loss of one disk does not effect other files. A number of disks can be used to stripe a file across several disks to obtain better transfer rates. But there are also two main disadvantages of this approach: first, it requires modifications to existing applications; second, backup of individual files as one unit.

In the VMS *driver-based striping*, the VMS driver binds the multiple disks into one virtual unit. The application and the user treat the virtual device as a real disk. The striping driver is responsible for the organization and retrieval of data: it intercepts the I/O requests and passes them to individual physical device drivers. It is completely transparent to the user and the applications. Just like normal data files, striped files can be backed up and restored as normal, and they can be opened normally, etc., as usual.

Please note that striping can only be installed on systems running OpenVMS VMS V5.4 or greater, and the system must have the striping driver (STDRIVER.EXE) installed. To install a striping driver, execute the following command:

```
$ @SYS$STARTUP:STRIPE$STARTUP.COM
```

Stripesets can also be shadowed, but not directly: each member of the stripeset is shadowed individually. In the following sections, I recommend initial optimal settings to use when creating a stripeset to achieve peak performance and discuss techniques to enhance the performance of existing stripesets.

Performance tuning considerations for striping disks

Controller and disk capabilities
Before striping disks ensure that your disk controller can actually handle the increase in the data transfer rates you hope to achieve and it will not be limited by the speed of the controller. For example, the data transfer rate of a RA92 is 1.72 Mbps and KDA50 data transfer rate is 1.3 Mbps. In this case, the data transfer rate of

the RA92 will be restricted by the controller. Also note that these controllers can only process one disk request at a time and here we will be limited by the speed of the controller, despite the greater transfer rates of the disks combined together.

Consider faster controllers such as KDM70 which is also connected to I/O bus with much higher transfer rates. You will obtain maximum performance of a disk stripeset by making optimal use of the bus bandwidth of the controller in transferring data to and retrieving data from the disk stripeset. Also consider multiple controllers to obtain the maximum data transfer rate, because the higher transfer rates achieved by striping can easily surpass the ability of the controller.

Distribute stripeset members between separate controllers

Disk units members of a stripeset must be distributed between separate controllers to utilize multiple data paths for maximum efficiency.

Create files contiguously

For maximum data transfer rates ensure that your data files are created contiguously. It reduces the seek time to locate the data.

Starting location of the file

To obtain supreme data rates ensure that your file begins on the first LBN of a chunk.

Parallel transfers

Specify the transfer size of the I/O equal to the chunk (track) size in bytes, multiplied by the number of striped sets for maximum efficiency. It will ensure that the data is transferred from all units in parallel.

Specify a default chunk size of one track for applications that execute large I/Os

For applications performing very large I/Os (ie greater than 48 blocks in size) choose the default chunk size of one track to attain maximum performance.

Specify a large chunk size for applications issuing small I/Os

A large chunk size for small I/Os ensures that each I/O issued to the stripeset involves only one member. The bigger the chunk size, the greater the possibility that each I/O will involve only one disk.

This permits one I/O to be handled by one disk unit while another is queued to a second disk unit. Use the guidelines shown in Table 18.2 determine the chunk size for efficient load balancing.

Table 18.2   Chunk size for efficient load balancing

Disk type	Approximate chunk size	Disk type	Approximate chunk size
RA70	99	RA81	104
RA80	93	RF30	112
RA82	116	RF31	100
RA90	138	RF35	112
RA92	146	RF71	112
RA60	84	RF72	102

Note: By default, the STRIPE INITIALIZE command uses the number of BLOCKS per TRACK as the default CHUNK_SIZE value. For most applications this default value is optimal. Do not change this value unless absolutely necessary.

Analyzing the performance of existing stripesets

To analyze the performance of an existing stripesets, issue the following DCL command:

$ STRIPE LIST logical or physical name of the stripeset

From the display check for the following:

To analyze the transfers and how many disks are affected, note the following fields from the above STRIPE LIST display:

<= 1 chunk transfers
<= 1 trip transfers
> 1 trip transfers

Please note that the values displayed alongside the above transfer, if added together, represent the total number of transfers handled by the striping software.

'<= 1 chunk transfers' represents a single I/O request to the striping software involving only one member of the stripeset and that can be executed instantly. The striping software can issue this I/O request and instantly proceed to the next I/O without having to divide single I/O request from the OpenVMS file system into smaller I/Os to various members of the stripeset. For optimal performance this is where the bulk of transfers should take place. Remember, the increased number of single transfers means better performance and a small waiting queue.

As a rule of thumb, at least 95% of I/O transfers should involve only one member. If you find that one member transfers is less than the quoted value, then the stripeset is a prime candidate for further optimization.

Also examine the values displayed alongside the fields 'Average queue depth' and 'maximum queue length'. If you find an *average queue depth* of > 0.5 and a *maximum queue length* of > 10 then you can be sure that the stripeset is a candidate for further tuning. Now you may apply necessary changes to the chunk size to improve performance.

19   Additional Techniques to Reduce the I/O Workload

Introduction

Some of the additional techniques which may help you to enhance the performance of the I/O sub-system are described below.

Introduce volume sets (combined spindles)

You may combine two or more drives together to improve their performance. Define volume sets by binding disks together to distribute access to files requiring read and write access. This technique enables the VMS file system to create new files on the disk with the greatest amount of free space within the volume set. Volume sets enables you separate index buckets from other file areas. Using FDLs you can place index buckets on a drive different from the data area. See Chapter 10: *Raid and Storage Works*, for additional information on volume sets.

Install frequently used image executables as shared images

Performance of the concurrently and frequently used images can be enhanced by installing them as shown below. Installation of an image as a known image saves on disk I/O and hence speeds up the initial execution process. For images installed as shared, it helps to save memory by allowing several users to reference a single copy of the program in memory. Before installing the image as a shared image perform the following checks.

Check concurrent accesses
While in install use the LIST/FULL command to check the maximum number of concurrent shared accesses to an installed image.

Only if the number of concurrent accesses is greater than two, is it worth installing as a shared image.

Table 19.1   Example output from INSTALL >LIST/FULL

OA$MAIN; 19 Open Hdr Shar Prv		
Entry access count	=	1787
Current / Maximum shared	=	18 / 34
Global section count	=	5
Privileges	=	SYSNAM GRPNAM TMPMBX WORLD OPER NETMBX SYSGBL SYSPRV BYPASS SYSLCK
OA$SUBMIT;20 Open Hdr Shar Prv		
Entry access count	=	16
Current / Maximum shared	=	0 / 3
Global section count	=	2
Privileges	=	CMKRNL
UNIT_PRICING;10 Open Hdr Shar Prv		
Entry access count	=	0
Current / Maximum shared	=	0 / 0
Global section count	=	2
Privileges	=	CMEXEC
DELETE;1 Open Hdr Shar		
Entry access count	=	6051
Current / Maximum shared	=	0 / 3
Global section count	=	1
DIRECTORY;1 Open Hdr Shar		
Entry access count	=	215
Current / Maximum shared	=	0 / 3
Global section count	=	2
EDT;1 Open Hdr Shar		
Entry access count	=	2
Current / Maximum shared	=	0 / 2
Global section count	=	1

Check free space

Ensure that you have sufficient free space by using the command LIST/SUMMARY/GLOBAL when in INSTALL. The following shows some sample output from INSTALL > LIST/SUMM/GLOBAL:

```
Summary of Local Memory Global Sections
235 Global Sections Used, 22850/5850 Global Pages Used/Unused
```

If you do need to change these system parameter values, then edit the MODPARAMS.DAT file residing in SYS$SYSTEM and run AUTOGEN (for details on modifying system parameters see Part E).

Turn on image level accounting

Do this by issuing the command: $SET ACCOUNTING/ENABLE=IMAGE/NEW. IMAGE accounting consumes large amount of disk space and should only be switched on for a short period(s) of time. Use this accounting information to produce a list of frequently used executables by highest amount of processor time as follows:

```
$ACCOUNTING/TYPE=IMAGE/OUTPUT=EXECUTABLES.LIS/-
SUMMARY=IMAGE/REPORT = -
(PROCESSOR,ELAPSED,DIRECT_IO,FAULTS)
$SORT EXECUTABLES.LIS EXECUTABLES.SORT/KEY = (POS = 16,SIZE= 13,DESCEND)
$PRINT EXECUTABLES.SORT
```

Remember that if you reorganize the data disk which contains installed images, you must install them again. It is better to include all INSTALL commands in the site-specific startup command procedure: SYS$MANAGER:SYSTARTUP.COM. The other reason for this is that if your system fails or is shutdown it is essential that you reinstall all known images after the reboot. Install an image as a shared image using the command:

```
INSTALL>ADD/OPEN/SHARED/HEADER device:image name
```

Installation of an image as a shared image takes up approximately two pages of physical memory. The breakdown of the physical memory consumption is shown below.

Table 19.2 Breakdown of the physical memory consumption

Known file entry	approximately 52 bytes per image.
/OPEN	approximately 512 bytes. Eliminates directory search to locate a file because installed images are accessed by FILE ID instead of file name.
/HEADER_RESIDENT	approximately 512 bytes. Saves one disk I/O operation per file access by making the image header, memory resident.

Disable highwater marking

Highwater marking is a security feature which prevents unauthorized users from gaining access to other people's data. It is associated with the creation and extension of files and is set by default whenever a volume is initialized. It is an erase-on-allocation technique which erases previous disk blocks every time a file is created or extended. It overwrites newly allocated disk space with erase patterns to ensure users cannot read what was previously there. Unfortunately, such security checks add to the I/O load for the device.

Disable highwater marking using any of the commands shown below, unless the mechanism is required to meet elevated security needs.

$SET VOLUME/NOHIGHWATER_MARKING device_name:

Remember that you need to dismount and then remount the volume for it to be effective. Highwater marking can also be disabled when a disk is first initialised:

$INITIALIZE/NOHIGHWATER device_name:

Note that sites running VMS V5.0 or earlier may suffer a system crash with the following commands if the highwater marking is enabled on the system disk. It is advised that they disable highwater marking temporarily before invoking the commands shown:

1. Extending the size of PAGEFILE or SWAPFILE from within SYSGEN using the command CREATE

2. Using the DCL command:

    ANALYZE/DISK/REPAIR device_name:

on the system volume for a running system. Remember that disabling highwater marking improves performance.

Use the DCL command SHOW DEVICE/FULL drive_name to see if the high- water marking is enabled. Table 19.3 shows output from SHOW DEVICE/FULL.

Table 19.3   Output from SHOW DEVICE/FULL

$SHOW DEVICE/FULL device name:

Disk S1$DIAO: (DISKO), device type RF31, is online, mounted, file-oriented device, shareable, available to cluster,error logging is enabled.

Error count	0	Operations completed	8
Owner process	""	Owner UIC	[1,10]
Owner process ID	00000000	Dev Prot S. RWED, O:RWED, G:RWED, W:RWED	
Reference count	1	Default buffer size	512
Total blocks	744400	Sectors per track	50
Total cylinders	1861	Tracks per cylinder	8
Host name	"DISKO"	Host type, avail	RF31, yes
Allocation class	1		
Volume label	"DATA2_1"	Relative volume number	0
Cluster size	3	Transaction count	1
Free blocks	416460	Maximum files allowed	93050
Extend quantity	5	Mount count	2
Mount status	System	Cache name "_ 1DIA4:XQPCACHE"	
Extent cache size	64	Maximum blocks in extent cache	41646
File ID cache size	64	Blocks currently in extent cache	0
Quota cache size	0	Maximum buffers in FCP cache	1042

Volume status: subject to mount verification, file high-water marking, write-through caching enabled. Volume is also mounted on ZPLE49.

Disable SYSGEN parameter ACP_DATACHECK

The ACP_DATACHECK parameter, if set to 2 (the default is 2), performs additional security checks for every write executed by your system – introducing additional I/O overheads. Modern disks do not require these security checks. Use SYSGEN to change the value of this parameter to 0 using guidelines described in Part E.

Specify index placement for small disks with large files

By default, on the initialization of a disk, the index is placed in the middle to reduce head movements (meaning, if you do not specify /INDEX qualifier with the command INITIALIZE). The /INDEX qualifier enables you to place the index in the beginning, middle or end. For small drives holding large files, do not use the default setting as it can result in a file being fragmented if it must be placed around the index information

133

Reduce fragmentation on INDEXF.SYS for volatile disks

When initializing a disk, make use of the /DIRECTORIES=n and the /HEADERS=n qualifiers to preallocate directory and header space in INDEXF.SYS, especially for large and volatile disks. The default value is 16 for headers and 16 for directories, this can result in poor I/O performance when reading directories and file headers. For details, see *Understanding the file system methodology* on page 141.

Set SYSGEN parameter RMS_EXTEND_SIZE to 80

Setting the above parameter to 80 will reduce the overhead associated with the creation and extension of files. It is more efficient for VMS to extend a file in large blocks than it is to create several small extensions frequently. Use SYSGEN to alter the value of this parameter following the guidelines detailed in Part E. For systems holding a large number of small word processing documents, a value of 80 may not be appropriate. Check the average file sizes and the growth rate before allocating a new value to the SYSGEN parameter RMS_EXTEND_SIZE. The best solution is to specify extension sizes using FDLs (see *Understanding the file system methodology* on page 141).

Ensure your image files are contiguous

Executable image files behave as swap files; as more of the image executable code is needed, the file is accessed and loaded into memory. Less I/Os are required to load the file in memory if it is contiguous and it speeds up the execution process.

Reorganize RMS index files

RMS index files must be reorganized frequently in order to maintain efficient performance. If the file has a high growth rate (ie new records are being added to the file in thousands every day) then the file must be reorganized daily in order to restore its throughput. RMS files are reorganized using the RMS FDL utility CONVERT. The reorganization process copies the data records to a new rationalized structure, and the old version is discarded. The new structure can be defined to allow free space for new records. All the indexes associated with the file are built from scratch during the convert operation. Some of the main factors affecting the convert run times are:

- total number of data records in the file
- total number of secondary keys
- number of sort keys/files used during convert
- users working set quotas
- RMS buffering
- other technical factors.

For an example of file reorganization using CONVERT see *Option 1*, page 149.

Relink images previous to version 4.0

Some performance gains are achievable by relinking pre-version 4.0 images that reference run-time library routines. Previous versions of VMS images on execution activated all five libraries, even if only one was needed. Relinking these modules will ensure that only the required libraries are activated at execution time.

Rewrite DCL procedures as executables

Users of VMS systems, especially system managers, produce vast amounts of controlling procedures in DCL which are heavy on system resources such as CPU. This is because DCL is interpretative and therefore comparatively slow. Most commands activate an executable image imposing additional overheads. In addition to this, DCL procedures are security risks as they cannot be properly protected against hackers. It is easy for other people to examine the contents of DCL procedures. Another disadvantage is that they cannot be installed with necessary privileges for any special functions. If at all possible, try to accomplish the same task by using a compiled language. VMS provides run-time library routines which allow access to almost all DCL features from most high level languages. These images can then be installed, enabling fast execution of these images and reducing the I/O overhead involved in image activation, it also saves on memory.

Optimize the performance of VMS Libraries

Library file performance deteriorates with the fragmentation of index within the file. To make the file contiguous use one of techniques described below.

1. First extract the modules form the library, then delete the library and re-create it using the DCL command:

    LIBRARY/CREATE/MODULES:n

where n is the maximum number of modules expected. Lastly, insert the modules in the library.

2. Compress the library using the DCL command:

    LIBRARY/COMPRESS/MODULES:n

where n is the maximum number of modules expected.

Avoid direct migration of programs from PDP-II processors

PDP-11 system architecture is very different from a VAX processor which has a large virtual address space. When migrating programs from a PDP processor, try redesigning the programs to make efficient use of this large virtual address space by combining them together into one large program. It will help to reduce the image activation rate.

Reduce demand on the controller

If your investigations have proved that the bottleneck device is a controller or MASSBUS then separate the slow devices such as tapes from the fast devices such as disks. Tape drives often overload the MASSBUS.

Introduce multiple CI adapters and busses

Powerful high-end VAXs with multiple processors and interleaved memory boards might find even the XMI bus limiting. Such high-end machines can benefit from multiple CI adapters and busses.

Adjusting disk buffers for performance

Buffering reduces physical I/O at the expense of memory. The number of buffers required depends on the application. Insufficient number of buffers increases the physical read rate and an excessive number may waste memory which could be better used in other areas. Excessive buffering may also increase the pagefault rate. To determine the approximate number of buffers required for your disk, check the global statistics under nominal load. Look at the LOGICAL READ to PHYSICAL READ ratio: it should be high, never less than (approximately) 10:1. If it is low, add buffers until the ratio improves.

Examine the BUFFER WRITE WAITS, this should never be greater than zero. If it is, increase the cache size until it improves. A value greater than zero indicates that the cache is full of blocks that must be written first before any new blocks are read in. An inappropriate cache size can drastically reduce the performance of a system. Remember to experiment with buffering to find the optimal level: more buffers do not necessarily give you better performance.

Improve/maintain the performance of directories

With the introduction of VMS 5.2, restriction on directory sizes was lifted. You can now have a directory greater than 1024 blocks. Large directories performance can over time deteriorate to an unacceptable level. To prevent poor directory performance, adhere to the following:

1. *Keep the directory file small* – even though the size restriction has been lifted. Guidelines on directory sizes are shown in Table 19.4.

2. *Keep filenames unique within the directory.* This is because the way in which the file system performs directory searches.

The maximum number of filename entries a directory cache can hold per page is 33. Only the first 15 characters of the filename are stored in the cache. It usually picks up the last entry in every block for the first 33 blocks, after which the sample interval is every other block.

When a search for a file is made, it looks at its cache entries and decides on the block to begin the search. If your directory file is more than 33 blocks long, it will have to sequentially go through two blocks to find the required file. The cache begins to loose it effectiveness if all the filenames within the directory start with the same 15 characters.

Table 19.4   Guidelines on directory sizes

Maximum Directory Size	Reason
33 Blocks	If files are randomly accessed
128 Blocks	For wildcard searches

Reschedule work that heavily accesses the device at peak times

As a last resort, reschedule the application with the agreement of the users so that less demand is placed simultaneously on the heavily used direct I/O devices at peak times. Run it as an overnight batch job, if at all possible.

Backup and restore

Periodically perform full image backup and restore operations to restructure fragmented disks, especially those disks which contain dynamic files. The backup should not be an HSC backup as this will simply replicate the original fragmented structure. Do not forget to use the /IMAGE qualifier when restoring data to preserve file IDs and synonym directories. This type of backup enables you to reduce the number of window turns and split I/Os. A new, faster, backup utility was released with VMS V5.2.

Tips on tuning backup procedures

Here are some tips which can help you to tune your backup procedures and achieve maximum throughput. Factors affecting and/or limiting the performance of your backup procedures concern some UAF parameters (as well as SYSGEN parameters), and the number and the size of the files being backed up. These UAF and SYSGEN parameters are interrelated as follows:

WSDEFAULT, WSQUOTA, WSEXTENT (UAF parameters)

These parameters limit the amount of memory a process is able to consume. WSQUOTA (UAF parameter) interrelates with the SYSGEN parameter WSMAX and should never be greater than WSMAX.

FILLM (UAF parameter)

This parameter restricts the number of files that can be opened by a process at any one time. Default UAF value is 18. The maximum value is restricted by the system parameter CHANNELCNT and is limited to 2047. Each open file requires approximately 96 bytes of BYTLM. If your disk contains a vast number of average size files then you must increase the size of FILLM for optimum performance.

DIOLM (UAF parameter)

This restricts the number of direct I/O requests that can be outstanding at any one time. The default UAF value is 18.

BYTLM (UAF parameter): I/O byte count limit

The default UAF value is 8192. This limits the amount of buffer space that a process can consume for mapping files. If your disk is badly fragmented then you must increase the size of this parameter to avoid and/or reduce window turns. For a backup account tune these SYSGEN and UAF parameters together to achieve optimal performance but be careful in making adjustments to these parameters. Only alter one parameter at a time, and observe the results before making changes to other parameters.

Acquire additional hardware capacity

If none of the solutions suggested in this section help you to improve performance, you probably need to acquire additional high performance disk drives. *Do not* just go and buy additional disks: the solution may lie in replacing the existing disks with disks that has faster transfer rates – also check the controller capacity.

Warning: Do not overload your controller or bus, the result can be disastrous.

It is vital that you understand your workload distribution and your I/O subsystem to acquire the right hardware for your site (whether this being a new bus, or a controller or disks). Before placing the order for a new drive or a set of new drives to meet your demand for the disk space, consider the following:

Evaluate the I/O throughput requirement

Do this for the applications you are currently supporting and those you wish to support for all groups of users. Obtain/calculate the I/O statistics per second and pass this information to the relevant supplier. They can help you find the best fit to suit your application.

Check what is important

Is it the number of requests per second or the transfer rate? It may help your supplier to suggest you a relevant controller to go with your disks.

20   VMS File System Methodology, Fragmentation and Performance

Understanding the file system methodology

To develop a better understanding of file and disk fragmentation it is vital to have an insight into the Files-11 structure and methodology used by the VMS file system to keep track of file data.

Files-11 ODS-2 is the logical structure which enables the VMS to directly access files stored on disk(s). It is an extension of RXS-11 file system called Files-11 ODS-1, where ODS stands for on_disk_structure. The Files-11 structure is created when a disk is first initialized. The structure is hierarchical in organization and consists of directories, file information and the file data. The VAX/VMS file system implements this structure and allows access to files on disks to be controlled. The internal organization of the files and the different methods of accessing the data within those files is managed through a portion of the operating system called the record management services (RMS). There are several reserved files on any on-disk structure level 2 (ODS-2) that reside in the master file directory [000000] whose purpose and structure are predetermined by the file system architecture. The nine files are 000000.DIR, BITMAP.SYS, BADBLK.SYS, INDEXF.SYS, VOLSET.SYS, CONTIN.SYS, QUOTA.SYS, BACKUP.SYS and CORIMG.SYS.

MFD
The master file directory 000000.DIR is the root of the directory structure. It contains directory records for all files in that directory. It must be read in order to access a directory.

INDEXF.SYS
Contains file header information, and is the final authority on the contents of the volume. Index file structure details are given below:

▸ **BLOCK 1 (BOOT BLOCK)** – indicates bootable or non-bootable disk which tells the operating system whether or not the volume is the system disk. It also shows the location of the boot file

▸ **BLOCK 2 (HOME BLOCK)** – identifies the volume label, owner, protections, maximum number of files allowed, cluster size, etc. Home block is duplicated by the system for data integrity.

▸ **INDEX FILE BITMAP** – home blocks are followed by index file bitmap which has one bit corresponding to each header available in the index file. If a bit is set the corresponding file header is valid; otherwise the file header is available for a new file. File headers are numbered from 1 to n, where n is the number of files allowed on a volume. A file header identifies the location and contents of a file. File headers are divided into six different areas: header area, identification, map area, access control list, reserved area, checksum. To display the header details of the file of your choice, use the command:

DUMP/HEADER/BLOCK=COUNT= 0 < filename >

The area of interest to us from the header details, shown in Table 11.5 on page 91, is the map area and is reproduced here:

Table 20.1 Map area (extract from Table 11.5)

Map area:			
Retrieval pointers			
Count:	12	LBN:	284829
Count:	306	LBN:	465354
Count:	102	LBN:	475725
Count:	1530	LBN:	489588
Count:	714	LBN:	501897
Count:	204	LBN:	502713
Count:	204	LBN:	503127
Count:	102	LBN:	516129
Count:	102	LBN:	520707
Count:	204	LBN:	538344
Count:	1020	LBN:	544572
Count:	34578	LBN:	549957
Checksum: 329187			

This area contains the retrieval pointers for file data, and each retrieval pointer describes an extent, which is a set of logically contiguous blocks on a disk. Each pointer indicates the number of blocks of data associated with each extent and the start of the logical block number. Each file header can store up to approximately 72 mapping pointers. Each mapping pointer represents a file fragment and if the number of file fragments exceeds the 72 limit, the file system allocates additional extension headers to hold the mapping pointers. Extension headers may also be created with the access control list entries. The format of the map area retrieval pointers is shown in Table 20.2.

Table 20.2   Map area retrieval pointers

SIZE	LBN	VBN
The actual size of the extent in blocks. Displayed as count with DUMP/HEADER command.	Logical Block Number. Indicates the starting point of the extent.	Virtual Block Number. Represents the virtual order imposed by the file.

The virtual block number is not displayed with the DUMP/HEADER command shown above, it only represents the relative position of the data in the virtual order applied by the file.

BITMAP.SYS

The file structure is simple. It contains one bit for each cluster on a disk. It denotes information about blocks of the disk currently being used by files, free blocks, and blocks available for allocation on requests. If a bit is set it indicates that the cluster is available for allocation. VMS file system uses BITMAP.SYS information to determine where files can be created and/or extended on the disk volume.

BADBLK.SYS

Contains all known bad blocks on the volume.

VOLSET.SYS

Contains information on the members of a tightly bound volume set (MOUNT/BIND): eg number of members, label identity, etc.

CONTIN.SYS

Identifies the disk as the part of disk saving set using the BACKUP utility.

QUOTA.SYS
Controlled by DISKQUOTA utility stores each account's use of disk space.

BACKUP.SYS and CORIMG.SYS
These are not used by the system.

VOLSET.SYS
Is the volume set descriptor file which contains information for each member of a tightly bound set.

Window turns

By default the file system stores upto seven mapping pointers per file and if the file contains more than seven discontiguous extents additional I/Os are required to make all the data accessible. When a file is opened by the system this part of the extent map is held in memory (ie in nonpaged pool memory, window control block). If the user issues a read to the block of the file not held in memory, the file system refreshes this control block with the new pointers, overriding the old pointers. This is known as a window turn.

A window turn consists of a file header read thus resulting in an additional disk seek, unless the information is stored in the file header cache. Additional I/Os are required to satisfy a file open request, as all header blocks must be read in.

For details on how to reduce the number of window turns on your system, see *Curing the problems of fragmentation - rules of thumb*, on page 148.

Split I/Os

When, on a transfer request, the file system maps the blocks within a file to the logical transfer, it may have to split the I/O. Transfer of data to/from the extents requires additional physical access to the disk for each extent. Each extent is therefore read or written separately and involves additional head movements which is known as a split I/O. In other words, a split I/O is a virtual I/O which cannot be satisfied by a single logical I/O and must be physically serviced through multiple requests to the disk.

File system procedure for accessing data

The steps in the procedure to access data from contiguous and fragmented files are shown in the following sections. If your system is properly configured to suit your applications environment some of the information would be stored in cache memory thus reducing the physical accesses to the disk. For this example we will use our example file TRANSDET.RAN. It is assumed that the user has requested to read the contents of this file in full. The file's directory structure is shown below.

```
DUA0:[MAINDIR]TRANSDET.RAN
```

What is disk fragmentation?

Available free space on a disk is broken into many small areas instead of forming one contiguous space. On a VMS system a degree of disk fragmentation is unavoidable. As the disk is used the free space on the disk is progressively disrupted by the continuous creation, deletion, and extension of disk files. The rate of fragmentation tends to increase with the increase utilization of disk space.

Procedure for contiguous file TRANSDET.RAN

1. Access INDEXF.SYS for the location of information in the MFD, ie 000000.DIR.

2. Access data from the MFD for the file ID of: MAINDIR.DIR.

3. Access INDEXF.SYS for the location of data for MAINDIR.DIR.

4. Access data from the directory MAINDIR.DIR for the file ID of file TRANSDET.RAN.

5. Access INDEXF.SYS to obtain the location of data for the file TRANSDET.RAN.

6. Access data from file TRANSDET.RAN.

Procedure for fragmented file TRANSDET.RAN

To read the fragmented file TRANSDET.RAN the procedure is as follows:

1- 4. As above.

5.   Access INDEXF.SYS for the location of the first seven extents.

6.   Access data from file TRANSDET.RAN.

7.   Access INDEXF.SYS to obtain the location of the next three extents of file TRANSDET.RAN.

8.   Access data from file TRANSDET.RAN.

Disk fragmentation results in file fragmentation which can bring a system down on its knees.

What is file fragmentation?

Data space allocated to a file is broken into multiple smaller extents instead of occupying one large contiguous space. File fragmentation results in excessive disk I/O operations as file I/O requests must be broken into multiple transfers, which in turn result in excessive disk head movements. For each extent there is a corresponding mapping pointer to represent its presence. Each file header is capable of storing approximately 72 mapping pointers providing there are no ACLs.

Why VMS disks tend to become so drastically fragmented

BITMAP.SYS file which resides in the MFD [000000] contains all the information on disk usage – ie which blocks are in use, which are available for allocation on request and which are free. This information on disk usage is held in two caches: Extent cache and the Bitmap cache. The Bitmap cache is part of the general block buffer cache containing information on blocks currently being used, free, and available for allocation.

The Extent cache stores information on the reserved areas (allocated to the files), but not in use. Its contents consist of a simple list of block numbers and lengths that represent free space on the disk. For every create and extend request issued by the user the file system looks at the contents of the Extent cache first to see if the request can be satisfied. If there is enough storage available in the Extent area to satisfy the user request then it is allocated. The Bitmap area is not updated since the information in Extent cache is already marked as allocated.

If sufficient space is not found in the Extent area Bitmap cache is searched to satisfy the request. If necessary it will search the Bitmap area two or three times in order to satisfy the request. At the end of the successful allocation cache information is updated and the information is written to the disk.

For default allocation requests, disk blocks requested do not have to be contiguous and the file system searches these cache areas (beginning with the Extent cache) until it collects sufficient fragments of free blocks or the volume is full. For speedy allocation, the file system returns the first extent it can find. No attempt is made to select an extent of the right size. This is the main reason for the rapid fragmentation of files and free space on VMS systems.

Problems of fragmentation

Fragmentation may result in failure during the creation of some files

Fragmentation can result in the failure (or at least be a hinderance during the creation) of files which require contiguous disk space. For example, the creation and/or extension of the directory files can fail because directory files must be contiguous. When a directory file is extended by the file system, the process involves copying all of the original blocks to a newly allocated large set. Lack of free contiguous disk space may also hinder the creation of some systems files such as, page and swap files.

Fragmentation results in window turns

The file system holds (by default) up to seven retrieval pointers per file in the window control block, where each pointer describes the extent of the file. For files with greater than seven extents the file system has to refresh the old pointers with the new pointers in order to fully retrieve the file. This process of refreshing the old pointer with the new pointers is called a window turn and can greatly affect performance. See *Window turns* on page 144 for a detailed description.

Fragmentation results in split I/Os

A split I/O occurs when a single logical request for file data is serviced through multiple requests to the disk, hence resulting in increasing disk activity. Well-tuned applications can suffer badly from this excessive head movement. In some cases upto 50% performance degradation has been noticed by the author.

Fragmentation can result in extension headers

A file with more than 72 extents and ACLs can result in extension headers which force the file system to perform additional I/Os. All extension headers have a back pointer to the primary (main) header. If your window turn rate is high and the file(s) have extension headers the performance impact can be devastating. This is because the file system has to read repeatedly through the chain of extension headers.

Fragmentation increases with the increased utilization of the disk

As the disk becomes full the rate of disk and file fragmentation increases with creation, allocation, and deletion of files. To fully understand how the VMS file system allocates, de-allocates, creates, and extends files see *Why VMS disks tend to become so drastically fragmented*, on page 146. Despite these disadvantages there are also some advantages associated with fragmentation. It allows the file system to fully utilize the available disk space. Files can be created and extended without the operator having to be concerned about the availability of contiguous disk space.

Curing the problems of fragmentation – rules of thumb

An important factor affecting the performance of DEC VAX running under VMS (with disks), is the degree to which the files are allowed to remain fragmented.

Note: Disk fragmentation left unchecked can have serious detrimental effects on the performance of a DEC VAX system.

To maximize the performance of your disks, the file system, and your applications there are several options available to you. Before taking any of the remedial steps outlined below ensure that disk and file fragmentation is a problem on your system (see section on *Determining if fragmentation is a problem*).

Only after fragmentation has been identified as a problem should you go ahead with the remedial procedure or a combination of the procedures outlined below. Some of the techniques will prevent rapid file and disk fragmentation. Ensure that you follow the preventative procedures precisely as shown.

Option 1: Creating files with contiguous best try (CBT) and allocating appropriate extend size

Do not create files from within a program using the default options. If you know how to create files using RMS system routines, use those routines to create the file with the options of your choice. Ensure that you specify CBT option when creating files from scratch. To make the existing data file contiguous, and to allocate proper extension sizes, follow the steps shown below:

1. Produce the FDL of the file of your choice by issuing the following command:

    ANAL/RMS/FDL filename

    This will produce a FDL file with the extension .FDL.

2. Use the editor you are familiar with to change the 'no' opposite the CBT to 'yes'.

    Contiguous best try no   (before change)
    Contiguous best try yes   (after the change)

    Do not change the 'no' answer to contiguous from 'no' to 'yes'. If your answer to contiguous is 'yes' then the file system fails to create and/or extend the file of your choice if it is unable to find sufficient contiguous space.

    Change the extend size for all the areas (ie data and key areas) to the 25% of the total allocation size for that area. This will ensure that sufficient space is allocated in reasonable chunks rather than in small fragments. Minimum allocation and extend size (default) on a VMS system is 3. It cannot go below this value.

3. Create a new empty file using the FDL just created to ensure proper space is allocated.

    Create this file on a spare disk if possible. The reason being that when the data is loaded from the old file into this new file, the two files will then be on separate spindles which will ensure minimum head movement and hence a faster conversion. Use CREATE/FDL=filename.fdl newfile.

4. Convert the data in the old file to the new format using the modified FDL file:

    CONVERT/FDL=filename.fdl old_file new_file

5. Delete the old file using the /CONFIRM qualifier:

    DELETE/CONFIRM filename.extension;0
    CONFIRM ? YES

6. Copy the new file from the spare to the required disk:

    COPY/CONT filename filename
           (from) (to)

    /CONT ensures that the file is copied back contiguously providing there is enough space on the disk.

Option 2: Making the file contiguous

There are two techniques which can be used to make a file contiguous.

► Method 1 – use the COPY/CONTIGUOUS command:

COPY/CONTIGUOUS old_filespec new_filespec

► Method 2 – use BACKUP/IMAGE to copy one disk to another. BACKUP creates files contiguously on /IMAGE output. The example below copies the entire contents of disk DUB0 to DUB1

Chapter 20

BACKUP/IMAGE DUB0: DUB1:

After the BACKUP is completed successfully, restore the data as follows:

BACKUP/DUB1: DUA0:

Option 3: Changing the size of the window control block

By default, the file system holds upto seven retrieval pointers per file; where each pointer describes an extent. You can increase the size of the window blocks by using any of the commands shown below and hence reduce the amount of window turns

▸ **Method 1** – use the command described below to change the window control block of the mounted volumes.

SET VOLUME/WINDOWS = n

▸ **Method 2** – while mounting the disk, use the qualifier:

MOUNT/WINDOWS = n

▸ **Method 3** – use a cathedral window when opening the file. Specify the number of windows to be –1 (ie 255). This will require you to change the UAF parameter BYTLM to an adequate value and the SYSGEN parameter NPAGEDYN to an adequate value. Changing the UAF parameter BYTLM

```
$SET DEF SYS$SYSTEM
$RUN AUTHORIZE
UAF > MODIFY Username/BYTLM = new_value
UAF > EXIT
```

Option 4: Creating disks with different cluster sizes

If possible, keep static files with very low growth rates on disks with small cluster, and large files (databases) with dynamic growth on disks with a large cluster. The reason being that disks with a large cluster size suffer less from fragmentation. The default cluster size for a VMS disk is 3. You can change this at the time of initialization as follows.

$INITIALIZE/CLUSTER = n

Specify the other necessary qualifiers which you deem to be necessary.

Option 5: Storing files with high extend/create/delete ratios on separate volumes

Wherever possible, keep the files with high creation and deletion rates on separate volumes.

Option 6: Increasing RMS_EXTEND_SIZE parameter

Use a reasonable extend size, do not rely on default values. Setting a reasonable extend size using the command:

$SET RMS_EXTEND_SIZE =n

You can allocate contiguous space for most files, but this will only help if your disk is not already badly fragmented.

Option 7: Introducing volume shadowing

Volume shadowing enables you to combine two or more disks together, so that the two disks remain identical. See *Introduce volume sets (combined spindles)* on page 129 for details.

Option 8: Introducing RMS Buffering

See section on RMS buffering for details.

Option 9: Adjusting ACP cache parameters

A great deal of I/O can be induced through Extent and Bitmap scanning. In these circumstance, it is advantageous if the entire contents of the Extent and the Bitmap file are cached. See *Why VMS disks tend to become so drastically fragmented* on page 146 for details.

Option 10: Avoid transfers on the same disk

Option 11: Avoid extending and deleting files at once

Option 12: Purchase a defragmenter

Part C

RMS Management and
Application Optimization

21   RMS Management

Introduction

A huge number of organizations are lavishing colossal sums of money and time on a bewildering range of caching products to improve the performance of the disk I/O sub-systems. Very little attention is being paid to the optimization of application file design using RMS attributes and the application run-time environment. Once your application is tuned to reap the benefits of RMS features (such as local and global buffering), it can yield much greater benefit at a very low cost and is a more effective alternative. Like many caching products available in the market today, RMS buffering enables you to cache vital data in memory and reduce the direct number of disk IOs required.

This chapter discusses the various techniques which can be used to tune VAX RMS files and applications which use them. It contains a detailed description of local and global buffering, UAF and SYSGEN parameters for global buffering, and the workings of RMS global buffering in a cluster environment. The recommendations are the result of author's experiences with a large number of VAX sites, where he helped make performance gains over the years. There are several RMS parameters which can help you improve the performance of your applications, such as: BUFFER COUNT, INDEX FILL, DATA FILL, ALLOCATION, GLOBAL BUFFERS, BUCKET SIZE.

It is essential that you have a thorough knowledge of the applications if RMS is to be optimized. Also, if you use RMS, ensure that you are not wasting system resources by trying out your embryo structures at the design stage. See Chapter 22: *Rules of Thumb for Designing Files*, for index fill, data fill, allocation, extents, index compressions and bucket sizes.

Types of buffering – local and global

There are two types of buffering available within OpenVMS: local buffering and global buffering.

Local buffers

Buffering enables you to cache index records and hence enhance performance. You can specify buffer values for all three types of file organizations (sequential, relative, and index). Buffer values are specified at run time. The maximum number of buffers one can specify is 127. No set value can be suggested for any file type, it can vary from application to application and you must try out your embryo structure with different buffer values to find the optimal value for a given application. I have come across sites where large buffer values for index files were in force on a system-wide basis for all applications and all users. In fact, it resulted in performance degradation and was a waste of system resources.

Only if applied properly can RMS buffering enhance the performance of your application. Also, do not apply a system-wide universal value for all index files: experiment with buffer values and use the number of buffers that enhances your application performance without exhausting your process quotas. Make RMS buffering part of the command procedure which runs that application. This will ensure that you are not wasting system resources and the CPU is not spending time paging and swapping.

To enhance performance, ensure that your process working set quotas are adjusted accordingly and you have memory to spare. You can set buffer values using the following command:

```
$SET RMS/INDEX/RELATIVE/SEQUENTIAL/BUFFER COUNT = n
```

Note that you need not set buffering for all three types of file organization. To check the default buffer settings, enter:

```
$SHOW RMS_DEFAULT
```

To reset these values use the SET command shown above.

Global buffers

As opposed to local buffers, global buffers are accessible by two or more processes, and it is the most effective way of reducing disk inputs/outputs on files accessed concurrently by a number of users. Global buffers can be used for both relative and index shared files, on a per file basis. If necessary, both the index and the data portion of a file can be cached in memory. The main advantage of global buffers is in caching index buckets. A user may open many files, each with many global buffers. You may set global buffers on a file via the DCL command SET FILE/GLOBAL_BUFFERS=n or during file creation.

Just like local buffers, it is difficult to calculate the correct number of global buffers because of factors such as the amount of memory available on the system, number of user processes using the file, number of reads, number of writes, and keys used. These factors can change suddenly. Global buffers are only allocated after an image has been executed.

Warning: Global buffers can also result in the degradation of performance.

How are global buffers allocated?

Global buffers are mapped as a global section in P0 space, and are pageable and charged against a process working set quota. A process specific list of GBDs (global buffer descriptor) is set up by RMS with one GBD per global buffer. To retrieve a record the entire GBD list is locked and searched sequentially by RMS to check if the desired VBN (virtual block number) is in the global buffer cache. RMS uses two system wide locks to synchronize access to a global buffer section. **Note:** The larger the GBD list, the greater the search time (ie CPU TIME).

How RMS global buffers work in a VAX cluster

Each node maintains its own copy of the global buffers which is kept in a global section along with buffer control blocks and lock value blocks. RMS stores a sequence number in the buffer control block and in the lock value block. The buffer control block is maintained by RMS and the sequence number lock is maintained

157

by the distributed lock manager. Disk I/O is avoided if the sequence number in the lock value block is equal to the sequence number in the buffer control block.

SYSGEN parameters controlling global buffers

The SYSGEN parameters that directly control global buffers are:

- RMS_GBLBUFQUO
- VIRTUALPAGECNT
- GBLSECTIONS
- SYSMWCNT
- GBLPAGES
- LOCKIDTBL
- GBLPAGFIL
- RESHASHTBL

RMS_GBLBUFQUO

This parameter specifies the total number of global buffers over all RMS files that can be active on a system at any one time. The number of global buffers needed by a file is not checked against this quota when a file is first opened. This quota value is not examined until a global buffer is used. Only at that time is this quota value examined. Each global buffer requires a system lock, and these system locks are allocated from the nonpaged pool area (SYSGEN parameter NPAGEDYN).

The RMS_GBLBUFQUO parameter sets an upper limit on how much of the nonpaged pool can be used for system locks on RMS global buffers. RMS uses this mechanism to stop users from flooding the nonpaged pool with system-owned locks. If the total number of requests for RMS global buffers exceed the value of RMS_GBLBUFQUO, no error message is returned to the user and a local buffer is used. Please note that AUTOGEN does not calculate a value for RMS_GBLBUFQUO.

Procedure to determine if a process attempting to create global buffers has exceeded RMS_GBLBUFQUO:

1. Issue the following commands to see if a process has exceeded the RMS GBLBUFQUO:

```
$ SET PROCESS/PRIVILEGE=CMKRNL
$ ANALYZE/SYSTEM
VAX VMS System analyzer
SDA> READ SYS$SYSTEM:RMSDEF.STB
%SDA-I-READSYM, reading symbol table
SDA> SHOW SUMMARY
```

2. Find out the index number of the process using global buffers

```
SDA> SHOW PROCESS/RMS=GBH
```

The value of OUTBUFQUO denotes the number of times the process was unable to create a global buffer because the SYSGEN parameter RMS_GBLBUFQUO was exceeded.

GBLSECTIONS

This parameter indicates the number of global section table entries (GSTE) required; it specifies the upper limit for the number of global sections in a system header. There is one global section for each file with global buffers (ie each data file opened with global buffers needs one GBLSECTION entry), and each global section entry consumes 32 bytes in the nonpageable area of the system header.

GBLPAGES

This SYSGEN parameter specifies the upper limit for the number of pages in memory that can be accessed by more than one user (ie it restricts the number of global page table (GPT) entries on a system). The system page file is used as the backing storage for global pages when they are erased from the modified page list. Calculate the value for this parameter as follows:

(No. of global buffers * bucketsize) + 2 for each file with global buffers.

The lexical function f$getsyi("contig_gblpages") enables you to see if there is sufficient free contiguous space in the GPT to map global buffers. Always check this before assigning global buffers to a file. Lack of this resource – insufficient number of GPT entries – may cause the error shown below:

%RMS-F-CRMP, CRMPSC system service failed to map global buffers

You may also see this error if there is not enough contiguous space (ie the table is fragmented). Entries in the global page table are freed when all processes accessing the global sections have exited and the pages are written to the system page file.

GBLPAGFIL

This SYSGEN parameter specifies the maximum number of system-wide pages allowed for global pagefile sections in the system's PAGEFILE.SYS. It indicates the number of blocks that are allocated for the primary and secondary page files which can be used for pages paged out of global sections. If you are using global buffers in a shared environment then you must ensure that the value of the SYSGEN parameter GBLPAGES is increased using the formula shown below:

(No. of global buffers * bucketsize) for each file with global buffers

VIRTUALPAGECNT

Both local and global buffers are charged against a process's virtual address space which must be big enough to accommodate RMS global buffers. This is controlled by the SYSGEN parameter VIRTUALPAGECNT: it sets an upper limit on the maximum any process's UAF parameter PGFLQUOTA can be increased to. If a process's PGFLQUOTA is insufficient to accommodate all local and global buffers, the following error may be displayed by the system.

RMS-F-DME, Dynamic memory exhausted

If this happens, increase the value of PGFLQUOTA and ask the user to log out and log in again for the new value to take effect.

SYSMWCNT

This SYSGEN parameter sets the quota for the size of the system working set. The global page table is a part of the system working set. Please note that each global page table entry is of 4 bytes in size, and 128 global page table entries use only one page of the system working set. This means that for every 128 global page table entries (GBLPAGES) you should increase the value of SYSMWCNT by 1. The formula is shown below:

```
SYSMWCNT = GBLPAGES/128
```

AUTOGEN calculates the value for SYSMWCNT based on GBLPAGES and PAGEDYN. If this parameter is set too low, it may result in system pagefaults which halt every other activity on the system until they are satisfied.

LOCKIDTBL

As mentioned above, each global buffer has an associated system lock. This parameter specifies the upper limit for the number of entries in the system Lock ID table. LOCKIDTBL entries are built at boot time.

```
LOCKIDTBL per global cache (file) = GBC + 1
```

Allow AUTOGEN to calculate the value of this parameter. Do not specify a hardcoded value in MODPARAMS.DAT. If the number of system lock table entries is too low, it may result in the following error:

```
%SYSTEM-E-NOLOCKID, no lock id available
```

The SYSGEN parameter LOCKIDTBL_MAX specifies the maximum size of the system Lock ID table. As a general rule, it should be twice the size of LOCKIDTBL. When LOCKIDTBL becomes full it expands to LOCKIDTBL_MAX. By default, it is of the same size as LOCKIDTBL.

RESHASHTBL

The value of this parameter can be derived directly from the value of LOCKIDTBL: No. of RESHASHTBL entries = LOCKIDTBL/4.

Note: Do not hardcode the value of this parameter in MODPARAMS.DAT.

Instances when global buffers are not used

The instances which force RMS not to use global buffers associated with a file are described below.

1. The file is opened by DCL.

2. The first process which accesses the files opens it in read only mode and does not allow others to write to the file.

3. File Access Block field is set to zero between an OPEN call and a CONNECT call.

Points to remember about global buffers

1. Most of the time it is adequate to cache the total index structure plus one data bucket to achieve maximum performance.

2. Each buffer should be equal to the maximum bucket size of the file in question.

3. There is no need to specify a large number of global buffers for files being accessed sequentially.

4. Do not specify RMS global buffers on JBCSYSQUE.DAT. The job controller does not use RMS to access this file. This only applies to VMS V5.5-n or below. Quemanager has been rewritten in V6.0.

    Those using V5.5-2 may specify a /BUFFER_COUNT=1500 with the START command.

5. Specify global buffer values for:

    ```
    SYSUAF.DAT
    RIGHTSLIST.DAT
    VMSMAIL_PROFILE.DATA
    ```

    for maximum performance especially if there is heavy MAIL usage and /or batch job submittals.

6. To determine if you should use global buffers on a file, execute the following steps:

    ▸ Enable RMS statistics on the files selected using the DCL command:

    $ SET FILE/STATISTICS

    ▸ Use the MONITOR command to examine the disk I/O rate, first with and then without global buffers using the command:

    $ MONITOR RMS/ITEM=CACHING/FILE=file_name

    If you find that global buffers lower the I/O rate then leave them set.

7. Too many global buffers can make performance worse than if the file had no global buffers. Always perform benchmarks with and without global buffers on selected files before implementing them.

8. For files which are shared, accessed concurrently, and with more than two index levels, cache the topmost levels of the index structure in the global buffers.

    Use the following formula to calculate the maximum number of global buffers (upper bound limit) for an index file:

    Maximum global buffers = total no. of index buckets + 1 (for data) for each index + the average number of users

Optimizing bucket sizes for index files

Bucket size can have a tremendous impact on the performance of your application: it controls the levels of index within an index file. The smaller the index, the greater the performance. A large bucket size does not necessarily help enhance performance, it can adversely affect performance. Always experiment with bucket values at the testing stage. Use multiple areas for data and indices so that you can specify different bucket sizes for each area. While experimenting, record the direct I/Os, buffered I/Os and CPU usage with different settings and then decide on the optimal values.

Remember, large data buckets result in fewer index buckets, which, in turn, reduces the number of direct I/Os but increases the CPU overhead. Small data buckets yield a greater number of index buckets, which, in turn, result in more direct I/Os.

The best strategy is to test the various combinations to determine the optimal bucket size. Time each combination and measure the amount of memory, number of direct I/Os and CPU used.

In a shared environment, a large bucket size can have an adverse affect on the performance because of locking. Consideration should also be given to the potential loss of data in case of a system crash. Also, ensure that your working set quotas are large enough to handle large bucket sizes otherwise it may result in excessive pagefaulting. To optimize your bucket sizes noninteractively for an existing file, use the FDL commands shown below:

```
$ ANALYZE/RMS/FDL data_file.dat
$ COPY data file.fdl new.fdl
S EDIT/FDL/ANAL= data file.fdl/NOINTERACTIVE new.fdl
$ CONVERT/FDL=new.fdl data_file.dat new_data_file.dat
```

22

Rules of Thumb for Designing Files

Introduction

Here are some basic guidelines for you to take into consideration when designing files. Hopefully, these will enable you to achieve optimal performance from your applications.

Keep the number of keys to a minimum

For an index file, a user can specify one main key (primary) and several alternate (secondary) keys. Alternate keys have a major impact on the I/O operations. The number of I/O operations to access a record are directly proportional to the number of alternate keys within your data file.

Use as few alternate keys as possible. The introduction of alternate keys can double the number of I/O operations required to insert or update a record and require additional disk space for alternate indexes.

Consideration should be given to the purpose (use) of the keys at the design stage (ie why a key is necessary, what it is to be used for, how often the file will be accessed using alternate keys, etc). If the index is to be used for some *ad hoc* reports then consider using the VMS sort.

Avoid duplicate keys

Duplicate keys impose additional overheads on the number of inputs/outputs required to add or read records. Where possible avoid introducing duplicate keys.

Keep the size of the keys as small as possible

Use small key sizes if possible as this ensures large packing density.

Greater chunks of indexes can therefore be held in memory which reduces the amount of physical I/Os required to access records.

Avoid changing of alternate key values within a program

Although it's possible to change the value of alternate keys within a program, do not design systems which change key values. The cost of changing key values is higher than adding a new key value.

Avoid using temporary index files

Some programmers create temporary index files to avoid resequencing: this is bad practice. These files are created to avoid resequencing within reports and are later deleted. The process consumes vast amount of I/O and CPU resource and should be avoided at all costs. Use VMS sort.

Use primary key to access records where possible

Less I/Os are required to access a file using its primary key. Use primary keys whenever possible.

Keep record size as small as possible

Create fixed length records of small size. Do not add any spare areas for future implementation.

Design files with primary keys at the beginning of a record

Location and length of the keys also affects the performance and disk space. Primary key should, if possible, be placed at the front of the record. This is because RMS, on deleting records from the file, does not remove any data which is before the primary key value.

Avoid creating files from within high level languages

The most efficient way of creating files is using FDL (file description utility). It enables you to specify several performance options such as the specification of different areas for data and indices on a volume set (bound volumes) and specify the location of a file on a disk volume. Specify the optimization options when the file is first created and/or loaded. Do not create files from within the application programs.

Place closely related files near each other

Before you use this option it is crucial that you have a thorough knowledge of your application file-access mechanism. Only then place the most active and closely related files next to each other using the FDL as shown below.

> Area 0
> POSITION file name "FRED.DAT"

The above clause will place the file near file FRED.DAT on the disk and will reduce the average head seek time. However, data requested from a different group of users may move the head away from the closely related files to a different part of the disk and reduce the gains of careful file placement.

Avoid linking of records using record file address (RFA)

Do not use RFAs as a permanent link between two files. These links are lost when the files are reorganized.

Optimize files using EDIT/FDL/ANAL (reorganize files)

Index files of dynamic growth must be reorganized at least once a week. Your reorganization strategy should cater for the addition of new records until the next reorganization. This will ensure that your file is contiguous. Run-time performance of an existing file may be optimized interactively or noninteractively. The procedure below describes the commands to optimize your existing data file noninteractively.

1. Create an FDL file for the file you wish to reorganize using the command:

   ```
   $ANALYZE/RMS/FDL filename.extension
   ```

2. Copy the newly created FDL:

   ```
   $COPY filename.FDL *.NEW
   ```

3. To optimize the file noninteractively use the following command:

   ```
   $EDIT/FDL/ANALYZE = filename .NEW/NONINTERACTIVE filename.FDL
   ```

4. Edit the '.FDL' file to take into account the growth until the next reorganization. Here, make changes to initial allocation, extension sizes, areas allocation, areas extension sizes and index fill. Calculate the additional allocation using the formulae shown below – but only as a *rough guideline*.

Initial additional allocation =

$$\frac{\text{Ttl. no. of projected records to be added until next reorg.} \times \text{record size}}{512}$$

Total additional disk space allocation = initial additional allocation $\times 2$ (assuming a fill factor of 50%)

Final disk space allocation = space allocated by the system (existing value) + Total additional allocation disk space calculated above

All extension values should be the 25% of the total allocation for that area.

5. Use the convert utility with the new FDL file and the old data file to create a new optimal data file as shown below:

    CONVERT/FDL= modified-fdl-file old-data-file new-data-file

    (as in step 4).

Reduce the CPU overhead on file operations with the use of FDL
Use the techniques described below to reduce the CPU overhead.

1. Specify file access options which are appropriate and necessary for the application. For example, if you wish to read the file then open it for READ ACCESS only.

2. Use nonstring keys where applicable.

3. Specify 'no' to data and/or index compression options when creating and/or converting the file using the FDL utility. This will allow for string keys to be searched via binary searches

Introduce deferred writes
Deferred write processing enables you to keep data in memory until the buffer is needed for other operations or until the file is closed. If deferred write is not enabled, then every write operation to a file results in at least one direct I/O. With deferred write enabled, you may issue several writes to one buffer and incur only one direct I/O. Activate the deferred-write option using the FDL editor by adding the CONNECT DEFERRED-WRITE. Deferred write is more beneficial with sequential access where records are being added/modified one after the other.

Use sequential files for batch updates to indexed files

If your application adds records to the indexed file in batch mode, convert that part of the program to write records to a sequential file and covert that data into an indexed file at a later stage. The CONVERT utility within VMS can accept multiple input files. It can take data from your index, as well as your sequential file, and create the resultant index file in less time.

Allocate appropriate disk space and extension sizes

Pre-expand a file and make it contiguous, if possible. Use the contiguous best try option of the FDL. Ensure that enough blocks are allocated to cater for future records until at least the next reorganization. For each area the extension size should be 25% of its initial allocation. Remember to reduce the frequency of file-extend operations by giving proper allocation and extend quantities at file creation. This will lessen the impact of erase-on-allocate behavior on system performance. Programs can spend more time writing data rather than waiting for the file system to allocate additional disk blocks, and it also reduces disk fragmentation.

Specify WINDOW COUNT when opening files to make retrieval pointers memory resident

A fragmented file can have several extents, each extent requires a retrieval pointer within the file header. Reading a fragmented file with extents requires a greater number of I/Os to the disk than the contiguous file. The file system stores only seven retrieval pointers per file when a file is opened. If access is required to the part of the file not pointed to by the file system, a window turn is performed which requires a file header read. Some high level languages allow you to specify the WINDOW COUNT qualifier with the OPEN statement. Make use of such facility where available, specify a value of –1 (minus 1) to make all retrieval pointers memory resident. This will reduce the number of I/Os to the disk but will consume additional memory, a strategy worth applying.

Reduce locking-related overhead by using client–server techniques

In a cluster, the node which opens a file first locally masters the locks for that file. For other nodes opening the same file, locks are remotely mastered. The overhead of remotely mastered locks is greater than the locally mastered locks. Base your application design on the client–server models to reduce the locking overhead, where you can define the file accessing mechanism as the server and the user interface part as the client. Once these procedures are developed, place the file-accessing mechanism programs on the most powerful node in the cluster to reduce the effect of remotely mastered locks on the other nodes.

Use a fill factor of approximately 70% for index files

Fill factors enable you to allocate free space for each bucket during initial load (ie index initialization). Once a bucket is full, the addition of new records results in a bucket split. Bucket split forces VMS to move 50% of the records from the original bucket to a new bucket and in doing so imposes excessive processing overhead. It also results in file fragmentation.

To avoid bucket split, a fill factor of 70% is suggested, especially for files with extreme growth rates and random record insertions. This will ensure that your application will have 30% of the space free for future write operations without overfilling the affected bucket. In other words, the fill factor helps you reduce the number of bucket splits. Set the fill factor using the FDL for data and indices. Alter the fill factor for existing files by modifying the existing FDL files using the editor you are used to and then use CONVERT to reorganize the file.

Separate indexes from data on a bound volume

For files with frequent write operations, place indexes on a separate drive using the FDL editor which allows you to separate data from indexes on a volume set.

Rewrite programs transported from RSTS/E and other systems if necessary

Re-examine programs from other systems for the following and rewrite them if necessary.

1. Frequent opening and closing of files.

   It is an expensive RMS operation. There were certain restrictions under RSTS/E which forced the users to open and close files. There are no such restrictions under VMS.

2. Creating files for inter-process communications.

   Another expensive file system operation. Avoid it at all costs, use symbols, DECnet, mailboxes, logical name translations, global sections, etc.

3. Packed decimal fields.

    This type of data was mainly used because of limitations on record sizes, and limited disk space. Avoid using it, because it imposes additional CPU overhead. Rewrite the programs to use ASCII and take advantage of the large record size capability of DEC VAXs.

4. Use of virtual arrays.

    Again, virtual arrays were used because of limited memory on PDP-11 systems. Use memory resident arrays rather than the disk arrays.

Part D CPU Management

23 CPU Management

Introduction

The CPU is the heart of all computers. It provides the instruction execution service to user processes and is an expensive resource. When a system is not performing to user expectations, blame is often laid on the CPU. A careful CPU management program can help defer or eliminate the need for expensive hardware and software upgrades.

It can also help to minimize significant expense associated with DEC's software licencing strategy, which is based on the power (capacity) of the various CPUs. The prices of other application programs (both from Digital and other suppliers) are also often directly related to the CPU's capacity.

The CPU is interlinked with the other system resources - such as memory and disk I/O - and the amount of work it can perform is dependent on the speed of other resources and other system variables.

Digital are now producing machines with multiple CPUs that are many times more powerful than the earlier monadic machines. Clustering of machines also enables you to quickly multiply your CPU power. Relative speed of the CPU is often used as a basis for comparison of performance: Table 23.1 provides such a comparison.

Table 23.1   CPU Speed (capacity)

DEC Machines	CPU Capacity in VUPs /SPECmarks	DEC Machines	CPU Capacity in VUPs/SPECmarks
VAX-11/750	0.6	VAX 6210	2.8
VAX-11/780	1.0	VAX 6220	5-5
VAX-11/785	1.5	VAX 6230	8.3
MV II, MV 2000	0.9	VAX 6240	11.0
VAXstation II, VAXstation 2000		VAX 63XX, VAX 6000-3XX,	3.8 - 22
VAXstation 3100 Model 10E	3.5	VAX 6000-4XX	7.0 - 36
VAXstation 3100 Model 30	5.0	VAX 6000-5XX	13 - 72
MVAX 3100 Model 40	5.0	VAX 6000-6XX	32 - 150
MVAX 3100 Model 80	10.0	VAXstation 8000	1.2
MVAX 3100 Model 95	32	VAX 8200	1.0
VAXstation 3200	2.7	VAX 8250	1.2
MV 3300, MV 3400,	2.4	VAX 8300	1.7
VAXserver 3300, VAXserver 3400		VAX 8350	2.3
MV 3500, MV 3600, VAXstation 35XX	2.7	VAX 8500	4.0
VAXserver 3500, VAXserver 3600		VAX 8530	5 5
MV 3800, MV 3900, VAXserver 3800	3.8	VAX 8550	6.0
VAXserver		VAX 8600	4.2
VAX 4000-105	32	VAX 8650	6.0
VAX 4000-200	5 0	VAX 8700, VAX 88XX	6.0 - 22
VAX 4000-300	8.0	VAX 9000, all models	40 - 157
VAX 4000-500	24.0	ALPHA 2000 300S AXP	66 SPEC Int 92
VAX 4000-505	185 TPS	ALPHA 2000 500S AXP	81 SPEC Int 92
VAX 4000-705	45	ALPHA 2100 A500 MP	180–600 TPS
DEC System 5100	18.9 SPECmarks	ALPHA 3000 600S AXP	125 SPEC Int 92
DEC System 5000-240	32.4 SPECmarks	ALPHA 3000 800S AXP	130 SPEC Int 92
DEC System 5500	27.0 SPECmarks	ALPHA 4000 710S AXP	110 SPEC Int 92

Alpha AXP

With the introduction of Alpha AXP (a true 64-bit architecture using RISC technology) DEC moved the CPU technology into the 21st century in the open-system arena. The Alpha uses 64-bit registers to perform all operations. There are 32 integer registers and 32 floating-point registers. Memory is referenced using 64-bit addresses, giving it the potential to address almost an infinite amount of memory – a significant leap forward from the 4Gb that the VAX can address. All instructions are fixed longword (32 bit) length. There is no true stack pointer. Two instructions can be held in one register concurrently. There are no memory-to-memory instructions – all data moves are done through registers – which eliminates slow instructions. Implementation of a pipelining and parallel instruction execution mechanism has boosted the performance of the Alpha AXP as several can be executed concurrently. Alpha AXP also includes a privileged Software Library (PALcode) which enables it to run OSF1, NT and OpenVMS, simply by loading a different PALcode set. There is no microcode.

ALPHA AXP performance

Apart from all the architectural elements designed to make the CPU faster, the physical chip production technology enables it to be run at very high clock speeds (currently 275 MHz, though this is bound to increase).

Measuring performance metrics

Over the years, DEC have used at least three different metrics for declaring system performance. There was the simple VUP: a straight measure of CPU power against a known base. Then came the Specmark which was designed to incorporate an element of the systems I/O processing capability, and now there is a whole range of TPS (transactions per second) measurements. Unfortunately, there is no obvious way of relating one to another and as the Alpha systems are invariably marketed with a different set of ratings from the previous VAX systems, a direct comparison is not easy. Hence the capacity planner at least, finds it difficult to know which Alpha box is appropriate without benchmarking first.

The following table provides some direct comparisons. The performance measure is transactions per second (TPS) and assume the systems are running Open VMS 6.1 and Rdb 6.1. though the figures are only estimates.

Table 23.2   VAX performance statistics

System	TPS	System	TPS
Vax 11/780	8	Vax 7000-620	350
Vax 11/785	12	Vax 7000-630	475
Mvax II	7	Vax 7000-640	590
Mvax 3100-10	19	Vax 7000-660	705
Mvax 3500/3600	21	Vax 7000-710	314
Mvax 3800/3900	30	Vax 7000-740	840
Mvax 3100-30/40	39	Vax 7000-760	1005
Mvax 3100-80	78	Vax 10000-610	210
Mvax 3100-85	110	Vax 10000-620	350
Mvax3100-90	125	Vax 10000-630	475
Mvax 3100-95	165	Vax 10000-640	590
Vax 8250	10	Vax 10000-660	705
Vax 8350	18	Vax 9000-210/410	190
Vax 8500	23	**ALPHA AXP system**	**TPS**
Vax 8530	32	DEC 2000-300	140
Vax 8550	47	DEC 3000-600S	240
Vax 8600	33	DEC 3000-800S	270
Vax 8650	47	DEC 4000-610	200
Vax 8700/8810	47	DEC 4000-710	280
Vax 4000-100A	125	DEC 4000-720	445
Vax 4000-105A	181	DEC 7000-610	340
Vax 4000-200	40	DEC 7000-660	1140
Vax 4000-300	60	DEC 7000-710	400
Vax 4000-400	95	DEC 7000-760	1350
Vax 4000-500A	125	Alpha Server 1000 4/200	285
Vax 4000-505A/600A	185	Alpha Server 2000 4/200-1	265
Vax 4000-700A	225	Alpha Server 2100 4/200-1	265
Vax 4000-705A	280	Alpha Server 2100 4/250-4	662
Vax 6000-210	22	Alpha Server 2100 4/275-1	390
Vax 6000-310	35	Alpha Server 2100 4/275-4	850
Vax 6000-410	55	Note the numbers in the Alpha server system description (Alpha Server xxxx y/zzz-n) have the following significance:	
Vax 6000-510	90		
Vax 6000-610	185		
Vax 6000-620	310	xxxx is the cabinet type	
Vax 6000-630	420	y is the chip evolution (EV4)	
Vax 6000-640	520	zzz is the chip speed in MHz	
Vax 7000-610	210	n is the number of processors (for SMP systems).	

Software performance under Alpha – some considerations

Configure your software to take advantage of the parallel instruction issue and pipelining. Given that there are now 30 usable integer registers and 31 usable float registers, the programmer must attempt to make full use of all of them and avoid, wherever possible, references to the same registers in close proximity.

The programmer must ensure that all blocks of code are longword aligned. Remember that the Alpha chip is able to execute two instructions in one register at the same time. It assumes that the first instruction is in bits 0–31 and the second in bits 32–63. If the instructions are not longword aligned this will not happen and performance is very significantly impaired.

Most compilers are now very intelligent, reordering instructions to maximize the potential for parallel execution and pipelineing. However, the compilers can only work within the confines of the source code provided by the programmer. Wherever possible the compilers will perform all the necessary alignment and re-sequence the lines of code to avoid register conflicts and hence hinder parallel execution and pipelining.

24   Scheduling and Scheduling States

What is scheduling?

Scheduling is the mechanism that identifies/selects a process with the highest priority (providing it is ready for execution, ie COMputable) and places it into execution – makes it the CURrent process. Process priorities range in value from 0–31; whereas 0 is the lowest and 31 is the highest. In general, values 0–15 are used for normal processing and values 16–31 are used for real-time processing. Once executing, a process runs until it:

- enters a wait state
- or a higher priority process becomes executable
- or it reaches its QUANTUM end
- or a hardware interrupt takes priority over the CPU.

The SYSGEN parameter QUANTUM or the execution time interval do not affect a real-time process. A process enters into a wait state when it issues a request that cannot be satisfied straight away, as a result another computable process is selected for execution.

Scheduling states

A process which is not in one of the CUR, COM or COMO states is either waiting for an event to occur or waiting for the availability of a system resource. Use the DCL command SHOW SYSTEM to check the wait states of the processes running on your system. The process becomes computable after the wait condition has been satisfied by the system. These wait states can be categorized into *voluntary wait states* and *involuntary wait states.*

Voluntary wait states

These are listed in the Table 24.1 and discussed below.

°

Table 24.1   Voluntary Wait States

State	Description	State	Description
COM	Computable Resident	HIBO	Hibernate Wait Outswapped
COMO	Computable Outswapped	SUSP	Suspend Wait Resident
CEF	Common Event Flag Wait	SUSPO	Suspend Wait Outswapped

Current state (CUR)

Identifies a process currently being executed. A current process may enter a voluntary or involuntary wait state by making a direct or indirect request for an operation that cannot be completed immediately, or it may enter a COM state when pre-empted by a higher priority process or when it reaches its QUANTUM end.

Computable states (COM, COMO)

A process in COM state is waiting to acquire control of the CPU. A process in COMO state is an outswapped process which is waiting for the SWAPPER to make it resident as a COM process so that it can acquire control of the CPU for execution. Processes in any of the above states are not the cause of any concern, therefore are not discussed in great detail here.

Involuntary wait states

These can be further categorized as follows

▶ **Memory management wait states** – these include processes in PFW, FPG and COLPG states.

▶ **Miscellaneous wait states** – a process in MWAIT state indicates the depletion of a resource; it enters this state when the resource is not available and must be investigated.

Use the DCL command SHOW SYSTEM, or the system utility MONITOR or system dump analyzer (SDA) to check the state of a process in a resource wait state.

Miscellaneous involuntary wait states – in detail

The following sections identify the various involuntary wait states, giving a detailed description of some of the important ones.

Table 24.2   Involuntary resource wait states

State	Description	State	Description
RWAST	AST Wait	RWMPB	Modified Page Writer Busy
RWCAP	CPU Capability Required	RWSCS	System communication Services
RWCSV	Cluster Server	RWNPG	Non-paged Dynamic Memory
RWMBX	Mailbox Full	RWPAG	Paged Dynamic Memory
RWMPE	Modified Page List Empty	MUTEX	Mutual Exclusion Semaphore

RWMPB and RWMPE

RWMPB – *modified page writer busy* – indicates that the modified page writer is writing the modified page list to the pagefile. The process is put in RWMPB state until the modified page writer has flushed pages to the value of SYSGEN parameter:

    MPW_LOWAITLIMIT

Processes should come out of RWMPB state quickly; if they do not, then they must be experiencing problems writing to one of the pagefiles on your system. There could be several reasons for this: it is possible that the pagefile it is trying to write to is full; the disk on which that page file resides is very busy (ie has a very high I/O rate) or there is a problem with the disk on which the pagefile is residing.

RWMPE – *modified page writer emptying the modified page list* – indicates that modified page writer is busy flushing the entire modified list to the available page files. Used by the OPCRASH program on a system crash.

The RWMPB and RWMPE states indicate that the pagefile is full and are usually accompanied by SYSTEM-W-PAGEFRAG and SYSTEM-W-PAGECRIT messages on the system console:

    SYSTEM-W-PAGEFRAG, Pagefile badly fragmented, system continuing
    SYSTEM-W-PAGECRIT, Pagefile space critical, system continuing

The SYSTEM-W-PAGEFRAG error is displayed when the pagefile is nearly 65% full; it does not necessarily mean that the file is fragmented.

The SYSTEM-W-PAGECRIT error is displayed when the file is approximately 90% full as a warning that the file is becoming full and affecting the performance of the system. Check the amount of pagefile space in use by issuing the DCL command:

```
SHOW MEMORY/FILES/FULL
```

Keep at least 40% of the pagefile free. Note that your system can hang if your pagefile becomes full. The follwing points discuss some reasons for a process to enter into RWMPB, and/or RWMPE state.

1. *Heavy disk I/O blocking SWAPPER I/O requests.* In this case you must try to distribute the I/O load evenly across several disks if possible.

2. *Badly fragmented pagefile(s).* A badly fragmented pagefile can also cause this condition.

3. *Little or no free space on page file.* This can also occur when there is very little free space available on the pagefile. Use the DCL command: SHOW MEMORY/FILES/FULL to check the free space availability on the pagefile. To increase the size of the primary pagefile use the DCL command procedure shown below to increase its size, providing there is sufficient free space available on the disk.

    ```
    $@SYS$UPDATE:SWAPFILES
    ```

    You may also create secondary pagefiles to spread the I/O load across several disks. To create a secondary pagefile use the SYSGEN utility as shown below:

    ```
    $RUN SYS$SYSTEM:SYSGEN
    SYSGEN > CREATE disk_name:[000000]PAGEFILE n.SYS/SIZE= n
    SYSGEN > INSTALL disk_name:l000000]PAGEFILE n.SYS/PAGEFILE
    SYSGEN > EXIT
    ```

    Amend your SYS$MANAGER:SYSTARTUP.COM command procedure for the system to automatically install these files after a reboot.

4.   MPW_WAITLIMIT *is lower than* MPW_HILIMIT.

Check the value of the SYSGEN parameters MPW_WAITLIMIT and MPW_HILIMIT. If you find that MPW_WAITLIMIT is lower than MPW_HILIMIT then adjust the value of MPW_WAITLIMIT, make it as large as MPW_HILIMIT. Use MODPARAMS.DAT to make this change.

Alternatively, use the formula shown below to calculate the new size of MPW_WAITLIMIT.

MPW_WAITLIMIT = MPW_HILIMIT + (MPW_WRTCLUSTER*2)

5.   *Processes are faulting heavily.* Heavy page faulting can fill up the modified page list faster than SWAPPER can clear it. If this is the case then you must if possible allocate more memory to those processes which are pagefaulting heavily. For this you need to increase the working set size using AUTHORIZE.

If there is not sufficient memory available then check the value of the SYSGEN parameter MPW_WAITLIMIT. If lower than MPW_HILIMIT, then use MODPARAMS.DAT to make it as large as MPW_HILIMIT. You may also reduce the number of processes that can run concurrently on your system. Use the DCL command $SET LOGINS/INTERACTIVE = n to limit the number of interactive users on the system. You can also achieve this by lowering the value of the SYSGEN parameter MAXROCESSCNT. Use MODPARAMS.DAT for changing the value of SYSGEN parameters.

6.   *A high priority process is blocking* SWAPPER's *activities*. It is possible that a real-time process with a high priority is not giving SWAPPER the chance to carry out its functions.

RWMBX – mailbox full
This condition is signalled when a process attempts to write to a mailbox which is too full to accept any more incoming messages. This sort of condition is caused by an application error when one process is writing to the mailbox faster than the processes reading from the mailbox.

RWAST – AST wait

This condition is signalled when a process is waiting for an outstanding request to complete. Normally, it is due to a process quota not being sufficient in size. A process can be in RWAST state and have no impact on the system. This condition only affects processes requiring the locked resource.

RWCAP – CPU capability required

Used to signal one of the following conditions on your system:

- quorum is lost – used by VMS scheduler
- loss of a device
- loss of processor on a system with more than one processor eg an 8820 or 6320, etc.

RWCLU – cluster transition state

This sort of condition appears when a cluster is in its transition stage, when the system needs to stall a lock request.

RWSCS – system communication services

Can only occur on a cluster system and signals that the lock manager of one node is trying to communicate with the lock manager of another node within the cluster. The process continues to execute after the communication is complete. Occurs on a cluster system where files are being shared and locked. If the condition persists then you must ensure that the most powerful processor on the system is handling most of the locks. See Chapter 25 for details.

RWCSV – cluster server

Can only occur in a cluster configuration. Processes get hung in this state if the cluster server process is missing or not in HIB state. To continue the execution of those jobs start the cluster server process as shown below:

```
$@SYS$SYSTEM:STARTUP CSP
```

RWPAG and RWNPG

RWPAG: *paged dynamic memory* and **RWNPG** – *nonpaged dynamic memory*. These two conditions signal the expansion of the system pool areas. Increase the size of NPAGEDYN and PAGEDYN using MODPARAMS.DAT – providing there is sufficient memory available on the system.

PFW – page fault wait

This condition indicates that a process is waiting for a page to be read in from the disk. If you find a number of processes in PFW state, then you must investigate the following:

1. Check the disk containing the pagefile for I/O contention using the DCL commands shown below:

    ```
    $MONITOR DISK/ITEM=QUEUE
    $MONITOR IO
    $MONITOR DISK
    ```

2. Check disk containing the image files for I/O contention using the commands shown above.

3. Check the status of the above two disks using the following DCL command: SHOW DEVICE/FULL disk_name, to ensure that it is still mounted and functioning properly. Also check these disks for errors.

FPG – free page wait

Signals the depletion of free page list which forces the process to wait for free pages to become available. The following points discuss how to investigate the reasons for the depletion of free page list.

1. Check your system console for any peculiar error messages relating to memory and/or disks.

2. Check your pagefile for free space using the DCL command:

    ```
    $SHOW MEMORY/FILES/FULL
    ```

    Has it become full? If the answer is YES then check if any other processes are in RWMPx state

3. Check for swapfile space using the above command.

4. Check which processes are consuming most of the memory using the DCL command:

    ```
    $SHOW SYSTEM
    ```

Suspend the process(es) temporarily to release memory but with the agreement of the user(s).

COLPG – collided page wait

This condition occurs when a number of processes attempt to access a shared page concurrently. If this is a common occurrence on your system then you must check the disks containing the pagefile(s) and the imagefile(s) for I/O contention as described under PFW.

MUTEX – mutual exclusion semaphore

Processes can enter this state for any of the reasons given below.

1. A process is attempting to obtain exclusive access to Mutual Exclusion Semaphore when another process has that MUTEX.

2. A process is requiring a pool resource which cannot be granted because of insufficient resource.

Use the SYSTEM DUMP ANALYZER to check why a process is in a MUTEX state.

Table 24.3   SYSTEM DUMP ANALYZER and MUTEX states

$ANALYZE/SYSTEM	Invoke SDA
SDA > SHOW SUMMARY	Using this you should be able to find the process in MUTEX state
SDA > SET PROCESS/INDEX = < index >	From the display using the above command use the number in the second 'index' column.
SDA > SHOW PROCESS	Check Job Information Block (JIB) Event Flag Wait Mask, BUFIO Byte Count / Limit, and the Timer Queue entries
SDA > EXIT	Exit SDA

From the SHOW PROCESS display within the SDA, if you find that JIB and event flag wait mask are equal, then the cause for the process in MUTEX wait state is lack of quota, this could be either BYTLM, or TQELM. The quota values for the process can be increased using AUTHORIZE, but the user must log out and then log in again for the new values to become effective.

Rule of thumb
Keep at least 40% of the pagefile free.

25 Locking and CPU Performance Management Within Clusters

Understanding the basics of lock mastering

On a cluster each node should be individually tuned to run its workload prior to any attempts to tune the entire cluster. Remember, one badly performing machine can have a drastic effect on the performance of an entire cluster. On a VMS system, a LOCK is used to co-ordinate the simultaneous access of two or more processes to a shared resource, such as a data record in a file, thus ensuring the integrity of data. Table 25.1 lists the different types of locks which can be granted.

Table 25.1   Lock modes

Mode Type	Description
Exclusive	Prevents the sharing of resource with any other readers and writers.
Protected Write	Provides write access to a resource and inhibits other processes write access to that resource, other processes are allowed to read.
Protected Read	Provides read access to a resource, others are allowed to read but not allowed to write to it.
Concurrent Write	Provide write access to a resource and allows the processes to share this write access.
Concurrent Read	Allow read access to be shared with other readers.

Information on resource locks is held in data structures called resource blocks (RSBs).

Three different types of RSB

Local RSBs

On a node which is not a member of a cluster, all locks are held locally, therefore all RSBs are local to that node and there is very little overhead involved in managing these locks.

Master RSBs

These are created when a resource is first accessed. The node on the cluster that makes the first access becomes the lock master for that resource and controls all access information for that resource until:

1. It leaves the cluster – when this happens lock mastering is distributed among the surviving nodes.

2. All processes on all nodes within the cluster stop accessing that resource.

For example, on a cluster consisting of two nodes *Hamburg* and *Frankfurt*:

If node Frankfurt was first to open a EXCHANGE_RATES file, it will become the lock master of the EXCHANGE_RATES file. Any requests from node Hamburg to access the EXCHANGE_RATES file must request permission from node Frankfurt as it is the lock master for resource EXCHANGE_RATES.

Process copy RSBs

These are created when a master RSB already exists and a member node within the cluster expresses interest in that resource. A node holding process copy RSBs must access all lock information from the node holding the master lock. Overheads in accessing a remotely mastered resource are far greater than accessing local resource.

Distributed lock manager

On VMS, a system distributed lock manager is responsible for managing all locks in a cluster environment. Use the DCL command MONITOR DLOCK to monitor the locking activity on a particular node.

Table 25.3 shows a sample MONITOR DLOCK display.

Table 25.2   LOCK

LOCAL	requests are locks that are locally mastered.
INCOMING	requests for resources from other nodes.
OUTGOING	requests from the local node for access to resources on other nodes
ENQ	is a lock request
DEQ	represents the number of locks that are being removed
Converted ENQ	is the number of ENQs converted from active to null and vice-versa
Directory Function Rate	indicates the number of times the RSB information is being requested
Deadlock Message Rate	gives the rate of deadlock searches

Table 25.3   Sample output from MONITOR DLOCK

VAX/VMS Monitor Utility DISTRIBUTED LOCK MANAGEMENT STATISTICS ON node HAMBURG

	CUR	AVE	MIN	MAX
New ENQ Rate (Local)	8.71	6.71	3.39	9.91
(Incoming)	8.23	8.55	4.58	10.11
(Outgoing)	0.10	3.60	3.52	3.60
Converted ENQ Rate (Local)	9.93	2.11	1.21	9.93
(Incoming)	10.03	9.31	8.21	10.97
(Outgoing)	0.01	3.76	2.00	4.12
DEQ Rate(Local)	8.65	8.23	0.00	8.98
(Incoming)	0.08	0.04	0.01	0.09
(Outgoing)	0.09	0.07	0.03	0.09
Block AST Rate (Local)	0.08	0.08	0.00	0.08
(Incoming)	0.00	0.00	0.00	0.00
(Outgoing)	0.13	0.00	0.00	0.00
Dir Functn Rate (Incoming)	3.57	1.43	1.21	3.58
(Outgoing)	1.19	0.19	0.23	1.21
Deadlock Message Rate	0.00	0.13	0.05	0.51

Lock management and lock directory lookup efficiency is directly proportional to the processor power and is distributed across all nodes in a cluster. Watch out for the lock management activity, especially if you have a wide range of processors in a cluster. Use the DCL command MONITOR DLOCK to examine the incoming and outgoing lock requests to other nodes.

Compared to local locking, remote lock requests consume ten times the amount of CPU resources. On NI and MI based clusters, extra data packets from remote lock mastering can cause significant bottlenecks on Ethernet connections. Impact on performance can be significant resulting in slower response times and reducing the overall capacity of your DEC VAX running under VMS.

Calculating the relative lock cost of a **VAX** cluster system

The table below gives the approximate relative lock costs of CPUs of disparate performance. To obtain the relative lock cost for your cluster, add up the relative costs of individual nodes. **Note:** If the total approximate lock cost is 20 times more than the fastest (most powerful) CPU in the cluster, then there is a possibility that the slower CPU may degrade the performance of the entire cluster.

Table 25.4   Approximate relative lock cost for VAX processors

Processor Type	Relative Lock Cost
VAX-11/750	1700
VAX-11/780	1000
VAX-11/785	670
MV II, MV 2000	1100
VAXstation 3100	300
VAXstation 3200, MV3500, MV3600	370
MV3300, 3400	420
MV3800, 3900, VAX 63XX, VAX 6000-3XX	260
VAX 4000-200	200
VAX 4000-300	130
VAX 4000-505	35
VAX 62XX, VAX 6000-2XX	360
VAX 6000-4XX, 8550, 8650, 8700,88XX	170
VAX 6000-5XX	77
VAXstation 8000	830
VAX 8500	250
VAX 8530	180
VAX 8600	240
VAX 9000	25
ALPHA 2000 300S AXP	20
ALPHA 2000 500S AXP	15
ALPHA 3000 600S AXP	10
ALPHA 3000 800S AXP	9
ALPHA 4000 710S AXP	10

Rules of thumb for handling locks within a cluster

1. While building clusters do not mix CPUs that vary greatly in power rating. The slower CPU can limit the performance of the high performance CPU.

2. Deadlock message rate should be zero on all processors. If not then you must check the application design.

3. It is always a good practice to allow the high-powered system within the cluster to handle lock directory activities. There are several ways of achieving this:

    3.1 LOCKDIRWT value for a fast processor should be larger than all the slow processors in a cluster. Fast processors can handle a greater load of resource directory requests.

    3.2 For systems running VMS V5.0-V5.1-n, boot the faster processor first and allow the powerful node to mount the disks and start the lock intensive applications before the slow processors.

    3.3 Install products which help to reduce the excessive overhead caused by remote lock mastering.

ENQs to VUPs ratio – some notes

- Approximately 200 incoming lock requests (ENQs)/second consume 1 VUP.

- Approximately 300 outgoing lock requests (ENQs)/second consume 1 VUP.

- Ethernet can sustain approximately 150 ENQs/second before showing any degradation in data transfer performance across NI clusters.

- On a VAX-11/780 if the total number of (ENQs + DEQs) are greater than 400 per second, it could be spending over 60% of its time handling lock requests.

26   Diagnosing CPU Limitations

How to determine if the CPU forms a bottleneck

As explained below, the relative health of a CPU can be gauged (checked) by using SHOW SYSTEM, MONITOR STATES, MONITOR MODES, MONITOR SYSTEM and MONITOR SYSTEM/ALL. In addition, you can also check the buffered I/O rate and the amount of locking activity that is taking place on your system.

There are various steps you can take. You are mainly looking for a number of processes waiting to use the CPU (COM and COMO state) and low CPU idle time. Follow the steps below to see if your CPU is forming a bottleneck.

Look for processes in COM or COMO state

To diagnose a CPU bottleneck first determine if there are any processes in COM or COMO state using the SHOW SYSTEM and/or MONITOR STATES commands:

```
$SHOW SYSTEM
$MONITOR STATES
$MONITOR SYSTEM
```

(See Table 26.1 and Figures 26.1 and 26.2). Check the MONITOR SYSTEM display to see if the CPU is at, or very near, 100% busy; if it is, check to see how many processes are in COM state, shown to the right of the CPU BUSY graph (in Figure 26.2). If you consistently find five or more processes in COM state over a period of time, it is possible that the CPU is saturated with the current workload. The solution is either to shift the workload or buy a more powerful CPU.

If you find that there are no processes in COM or COMO state then you can safely conclude that CPU is not a bottleneck and the problem lies elsewhere. But if you find that there are processes in COM and COMO state then you must check to see how the CPU is spending its time by using the MONITOR MODES command.

Table 26.1   Output from SHOW SYSTEM

Pid	Process Name	State	Pri	I/O	CPU	Page flts	Ph. Mem
00000081	SWAPPER	HIB	16	0	0 00:01:19.84	0	0
00002084	BAKER_ST1	LEF	6	924	0 00:00:17.28	3641	3345
00000085	CONFIGURE	HIB	9	21	0 00:00:00.19	102	171
00000087	ERRFMT	HIB	8	5534	0 00:00:34.70	84	129
00000088	OPCOM	HIB	7	2456	0 00:00:14.66	495	160
00000089	AUDIT_SERVER	HIB	10	411	0 00:00:05.99	1365	436
0000008A	JOB_CONTROL	HIB	9	188352	0 00:19:42.51	356	546
0000008B	IPCACP	HIB	10	8	0 00:00:00.16	79	144
0000008C	TP_SERVER	HIB	10	40125	0 00:13:13.53	170	258
0000008D	NETACP	HIB	10	19231	0 00:03:48.23	476	574
0000008E	EVL	HIB	6	49	0 00:00:03.74	151192	46 N
0000008F	REMACP	HIB	9	505	0 00:00:01.26	78	56
00002211	BAKER_865391	LEF	6	633	0 00:00:06.44	1561	287 S
00000092	SYMBIONT_0001	HIB	6	72427	0 00:04:59.38	21895	324
00002213	WALKER_01	LEF	6	13281	0 00:01:21.12	5277	4026
00000095	SYMBIONT_0002	COM	4	37039	0 00:27:36.84	2900	800
00000096	TM_SERVER	HIB	6	18	0 00:00:00.73	306	352
00000097	DA$FCV	SUSP	4	5	0 00:00:00.11	64	94
0000219B	UNWINS	LEF	9	2163	0 00:00:21.38	5079	4001
0000009D	BATCH_629	LEF	4	86661	0 00:34:48.18	467106	275 B
0000009E	VTXCON	LEF	6	5366	0 00:00:12.90	947	682
0000009F	INET CP	HIB	10	14	0 00:00:00.33	133	88
000000A0	UCX$FTPD	LEF	8	15	0 00:00:00.45	210	424
000000A1	NFS$SERVER	LEF	10	48	0 00:00:01.13	1189	1599
000000A2	Autologoff_v5.1	HIB	4	1852	0 00:26:25.69	481	352
000020A7	JONESG_AM	LEF	4	36489	0 00:03:14.62	4838	4041
000020AC	ELSON_JOHN	LEF	7	2906	0 00:00:48.18	4522	3811
0000232E	KITCHENB_3T	LEF	9	4036	0 00:00:26.15	4177	3750
000021B0	MATTHEWS_PI	COM	4	4370	0 00:00:36.38	4545	3865
000022B6	JONES_AM	LEF	8	1817	0 00:00:41.36	4001	3608
00002238	BRACKEN_ST	LEF	7	1809	0 00:00:10.35	3425	2949
0000223A	GM_ENTRY	HIB	4	4315	0 00:00:08.24	669	446
000022BB	DECSUPPORT	CUR	4	5082	0 00:00:24.52	3399	246
000020C2	WHITFIELDAND	LEF	7	1269	0 00:00:20.28	3808	3694
00002343	BROWNMPO1	LEF	6	951	0 00:00:11.38	3418	3071

Table 26.1   (continued) Output from SHOW SYSTEM

Pid	Process Name	State	Pri	I/O	CPU	Page flts	Ph. Mem
000022CS	MANAGERS_DS	LEF	6	2054	0 00:00:30.65	4963	3803
00002049	HALLPJ O1	LEF	9	11510	0 00:00:43.51	4174	3750
000022CC	SERVER_0022	LEF	6	152	0 00:00:02.58	813	317 N
000021CD	BODYCH_OY	LEF	8	475	0 00:00:08.27	3243	2972
0000224E	TARR_11	LEF	6	11481	0 00:01:10.23	5887	4182
00002150	CLARK_ST	LEF	8	40990	0 00:02:33.68	5915	4232
000021DS	WOLLATSJ	LEF	7	17279	0 00:00:57.68	5414	4196
000021D8	BOARDMANGR	LEF	6	6383	0 00:01:29.64	6226	4211
000021DA	CARTERRWST	LEF	6	7980	0 00:00:56.17	5174	3797
00002161	SAUNDERSPI	LEF	7	22676	0 00:01:11.12	4778	3985

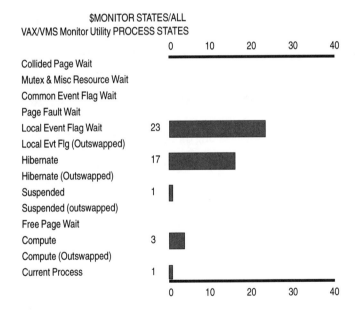

Figure 26.1: Output from MONITOR/STATES

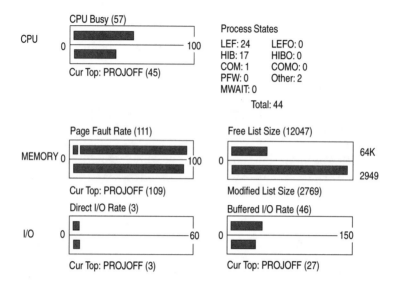

Figure 26.2: Output from MONITOR SYSTEM VAX/VMS Monitor STATISTICS

Check which processes are taking all or most of the CPU time

Use the DCL command MONITOR PROCESS/TOPCPU to display such processes. Use the DCL command SHOW SYSTEM to display the priority of such processes. The processes priorities are listed under the heading 'Priority'. Priority for normal interactive jobs fluctuates between 4 and 9. If you find that the processes consuming the highest amount of CPU are running at a low priority, then you can safely assume that they are not hogging the system: they are merely consuming their share of the CPU because no higher priority job is ready to run. If you find that it is the batch job(s)n and/or the swapper and/or the OPCOM then you must take the appropriate remedial steps as outlined in Chapter 27.

Check the type of work being performed by the CPU

Examine the percentage of time that the CPU is spending in each mode using the MONITOR MODES command.

Table 26.2   Summary output from MONITOR MODES

VAX/VMS monitor utility TIME IN PROCESSOR MODES				
	CUR	**AVE**	**MIN**	**MAX**
Interrupt Stack	1.31	3.31	1.31	5.06
MP Synchronization	0.00	0.00	0.00	0.00
Kernel Mode	12.99	14.04	6.71	26.06
Executive Mode	4.26	5.02	1.63	11.61
Supervisor Mode	3.83	2.24	0.11	10.95
User Mode	6.49	23.25	5.62	50.39
Compatibility Mode	0.00	0.00	0.00	0.00
Idle Time	71.09	52.10	20.63	82.70
PLAYBACK	SUMMARIZING			

To check the percentage amount of time the CPU has been busy performing user work and system work, you can subtract the idle time from 100: ie CPU busy percentage = (100 – idle).

For SMP systems, the CPU busy percentage is calculated as follows:

CPU Busy%= [(100 × No of CPUs) – idle]×100/(100×No of CPUs)

The CPU is not likely to become a saturated resource unless busy percentage exceeds 90% over a sustained period during peak hours. It is important to see the breakdown of CPU activities which you can get from MONITOR MODES display. This will show you where exactly the CPU has been spending most of its time. A high percentage of time in user mode is usually an indicator of good system performance. A brief explanation of the activities under each mode is given below.

Developing a better understanding of CPU modes usage + some rules of thumb

Important! For you to be able to lessen the amount of system overhead (Executive, Kernel and Interrupt) it is important to develop a good understanding of each of the modes.

INTERRUPT stack mode

This is CPU time spent handling interrupts from peripherals such as printers and terminals. It also includes time spent on remote locking activity, SCS cluster traffic, LAVC disk serving and some scheduling activities. A high interrupt stack activity is indicative of a system performing a great deal of I/O activity. This is often the case in NI and MI clusters where high interrupt stack time is most probably directly proportional to the amount of disk serving a node is doing. In this situation the best solution is to keep the I/O intensive applications on the nodes with direct access to the disks.

Rule I
From your MONITOR MODES display, check the percentage amount of time spent in this mode: if greater than 15%, it is possible that your system is experiencing excessive buffered I/O and/or remote locking. If it is consistently over 70% it is most probably a faulty device continually interrupting the processor.

KERNEL mode

Primarily, this is a VMS I/O sub-system with job scheduler, memory management (paging and swapping), and various system services (eg system services that perform logical name translation). If kernel mode activities constitute more than 25% of the CPU usage, it is possible that there is excessive paging and swapping, image activations, local locking and/or excessive file system activities taking place. It is always worth checking for excessiveness of these activities. Some applications are designed to run in KERNEL mode such as ALL-IN-1 and BACKUP; this is because their services execute in that mode. Fragmented files also add to high KERNEL mode time because I/O operations are split into multiple requests to access the fragmented portions of the file, *so always check for file fragmentation.*

Rule 2
On average, KERNEL and INTERRUPT mode time should stay under 40% of the total CPU time.

EXECUTIVE mode

This is mainly associated with RMS file system activities and some VMS system service processing. A high executive and kernel mode activity is indicative of a system making extensive use of RMS files.

202

It is difficult to quote any threshold value for this mode.

Rule 3

If you notice a sudden change in the amount of time your system spends in EXECUTIVE mode (ie over 20%), then you must investigate RMS file system activities.

SUPERVISOR mode

This is mainly associated with the execution of DCL commands. There are no hard figures available for this mode either.

Rule 4

If you see a high percentage of time (ie over 15%) being spent in Supervisor mode, it is possible that DCL use is excessive and you must take steps to reduce it. Consider rewriting the DCL procedures as programs. Some third party products run in SUPERVISOR mode which is normal.

USER mode

Indicates the percentage of time that the CPU is performing work on behalf of users. It is time spent running VAX instructions like application code. The greater the amount of time spent by the CPU in this mode, the better it is. However, if the CPU is spending an abnormally high percentage of time in this mode, it is possible that your system is saturated and can no longer keep up with user demands.

MP SYNCHRONIZATION mode

This is time spent processing spinlocks in multiprocessor configurations.

Rule 5

Investigate locking and/or paging activities if the percentage rate for MP SYNCHRONIZATION mode is greater than approximately 10% of the total CPU utilization.

COMPATIBILITY mode

This is time spent emulating instruction sets for other types of system – eg a BASIC+ program written for a PDP machine under RSTS/E which has been subsequently ported to VAX VMS.

Rule 6

COMPATIBILITY mode should always be zero.

IDLE TIME mode

Shows the percentage of time the CPU has nothing to do. It is a measure of free CPU time, but don't be fooled by this figure. It is possible that the processes were blocked by other resources (eg overloaded disk or insufficient memory) and were not able to consume CPU cycles. You can check if the processes were waiting for any other resources to become available using MONITOR STATES.

Checking the percentage use of the CPU

As mentioned above, the relative health of the CPU can be measured by checking the busy percentage (overall time spent in the modes described above). Assuming that the most of the CPU activity pertains to processing in user mode, a high percentage indicates good system performance unless there are many processes in COM or COMO states and the percentage use exceeds approximately 90% at peak times over a sustained interval.

Rule 7

If you find many processes in COM or COMO states and the percentage use exceeds approximately 90% at peak times over a sustained interval, then the solution is either to shift the workload or buy a more powerful CPU.

27 Rules of Thumb to Reduce CPU Limitations

Rules of thumb

The techniques or processes described in this section may enable you to make efficient use of the CPU resource and hence optimize overall performance. Several common procedures used to reduce the CPU utilization are described below.

Submitting large compute-intensive jobs as batch jobs

If too many jobs are being run interactively which are compute intensive, then some of those jobs should be scheduled to run at off-peak times in a batch environment. This will help to reduce the workload on the CPU at peak times.

Use ACLs (access control lists) to stop an image being run interactively

You may also use ACLs to force users to submit jobs (compute-intensive jobs) through the batch queue, as follows:

```
$SET FILE/ACL= (IDENTIFIER = INTERACTIVE, ACCESS = NONE)
```

Set up batch queues with a low priority

Be careful while setting up the priority for batch queues which also execute jobs at peak times and compete with interactive users at the same time. Interactive users on a VMS system normally work at the base priority of 4, and if you were to set up a batch queue to work at a base priority of 3 then you will be allowing the batch jobs to compete with the interactive jobs whenever they get a priority boost after completing a disk I/O. Batch jobs get a priority boost of 2 after completing a disk I/O operation.

Limit the number of batch jobs running concurrently

Take the precaution of limiting the number of batch jobs running concurrently, especially at peak time. You can control the number of jobs running concurrently at the queue initialization time using the /JOB_LIMIT qualifier.

Dedicate a cluster node to run batch jobs

It may be useful to run compute-intensive jobs from a designated machine within a cluster, dedicated to run batch jobs.

Reduce overall page fault rate

Pagefaulting, whether hard or soft, consumes CPU resources. Check which processes are faulting heavily using MONITOR PROCESS/TOPFAULT and then check the working set quotas of those processes to ensure they are adequate for the jobs being run. You can display the default working set sizes information using the AUTHORIZE utility as shown below.

```
$MCR AUTHORIZE
$SHOW username
$EXIT
```

Use the DCL command SHOW PROCESS/CONTINUOUS to display the amount of memory being consumed by these processes. Lessening the amount of pagefaulting will reduce system overhead, lowering the kernel mode time.

Reduce system pagefault rate

When this occurs, all other activities on the system grind to a halt until the page is recovered from the disk. System fault rate should not be greater than 1. You can use MONITOR PAGE command to check the system fault rate; if it is greater than 1 then you should increase the number of pages allocated to system parameter SYSMWCNT.

Remember: Pages added to the value of SYSMWCNT are considered permanently allocated to the system and are no longer available to user processes. Remember system faults are CPU intensive and you must reduce them.

Allocate adequate nonpage pool caches initially to reduce CPU overhead

The system makes automatic adjustments to the size of the preallocated pool areas (SRP, IRP, and LRP) when necessary. You can examine the initial allocated sizes and the current sizes using:

$SHOW MEMORY/POOL/FULL

See Table 1.1, page 6, for output from this command.

If the Current Total Size value for SRPCOUNT, IRPCOUNT, LRPCOUNT or NPAGEDYN exceeds the Initial Size, pool expansion has taken place. You can reduce the CPU overhead required for expansion by allocating memory adequately.

Reduce locking activity

An excessive lock rate manifests itself as CPU overhead. You can examine the locking activity using MONITOR LOCK. In a file-sharing environment, especially on a cluster, check the rate of lock requests forced to wait by examining ENQs forced to wait. There are no threshold values for this as it largely depends on the type of configuration and applications you are running. If you see an abnormally high value, you must look at the application design to improve the situation.

Ensure optimum bucket sizes for RMS files

Index file design and access methods directly affect the executive mode time. To keep the CPU overhead low, ensure optimum bucket sizes are allocated for all areas, use fill factor values which will minimize bucket splits, use as few keys as possible, avoid the use of duplicate keys and avoid data compression.

Use terminal servers for load balancing on a cluster

Use terminal servers to do the load balancing for you on a cluster. Terminal servers automatically direct the interactive user onto the least loaded system. The service rating which is used to do the load balancing is based on the speed of the CPU and idle time over a recent period.

Avoid excessive use of ACLs

Excessive use of ACLs simply slows down the execution process and imposes additional CPU overhead. Keep to the minimum if their use is really necessary.

Do not raise the priority of compute-bound processes

Do not run a job at a higher priority when there are other interactive users on the system unless it is absolutely necessary. Even then inform the users before the complaints start coming in. This is because it can cause interactive response time to degrade.

High priority compute-intensive jobs pre-empt the execution of interactive processes. This is because the VMS scheduling algorithm always selects the highest priority computable process first and the other processes are denied their fair share of resources.

Set up generic batch queue on a cluster

The job controller ensures that the batch load is proportional to the job limit of each queue pointed to by a generic queue. Increase the number of jobs that can run concurrently on a powerful machine within your cluster using the command:

```
$SET QUEUE/JOB LIMIT = n queue_name
```

Avoid the excessive use of DCL procedures

DCL procedures directly affect the amount of time spent in the supervisor mode. Also, DCL procedures are comparatively slow in performance compared to application programs. If at all possible, rewrite your DCL procedure in a high level language which is compilable. The majority of the tasks performed in DCL can be performed with the calls to the system services routines from the high level languages. These system services routines are part of VMS (ie they are memory resident). Improvements can be five times faster: one can at least gain approximately 50% in performance.

Enable direct memory access (DMA) for direct terminal lines

To reduce the amount of CPU activity in interrupt mode, the SYSGEN parameter TTY_DEFCHAR2 can be adjusted to enable the DMA activity. You can also offload terminal I/O to terminal servers to lessen time spent in interrupt mode; this is because local area transport (LAT) protocol used by terminal servers is more efficiently handled by VMS.

Increase the threshold for deadlock searches

If your application design is such that you are sharing files then it is possible that your system may be performing deadlock searches. This activity consumes a great deal of kernel activity. You can increase the threshold of the SYSGEN parameter DEADLOCK WAIT at which the deadlock searches are made.

The default wait value for this parameter is 10 seconds, which means that your process will wait for the resource to be available for 10 seconds before initiating a deadlock search. To observe this activity use MONITOR DLOCK.

Run BACKUP at a lower priority than the interactive users

The BACKUP utility is fairly compute intensive and should not be run with the interactive users on the system. If you have to, then run it at a fairly low priority so that it is not competing for CPU with interactive users.

Reduce file fragmentation

Fragmentation affects kernel mode CPU time. Keep it low. If the files on your system are fragmented, it will have a direct impact on the kernel mode CPU time to retrieve disjointed sections of the file. Reorganize your index files regularly and/or perform an image backup of the disk and then follow it with 'restore' to make it contiguous.

Adjusting the SYSGEN parameter QUANTUM

QUANTUM defines the maximum time slice a user process is granted when it becomes computable and before control is passed to another computable process by the scheduler.

QUANTUM can be adjusted on the running system without rebooting. The default value for QUANTUM is 20 - ie 200 millisecond time slices.

If you do not see any considerable improvement in performance after changing QUANTUM, then return it to its original value. If you see a significant improvement after the change, then you must note the change in MODPARAMS.DAT.

Increasing the rate of QUANTUM

This is most appropriate where there is a small number of compute-intensive batch processes. This reduces the rate at which the scheduler reassigns the CPU to the next waiting computable process. This has the effect of slightly reducing the VMS overhead on the kernel mode time. In simple terms, increasing quantum means more work will get done by processes when they are allocated their slice of time, but it also means that the overall response will degrade.

Lowering the rate of QUANTUM

By lowering the QUANTUM value you will actually shorten the amount of time a process waits for its share of the CPU. But be careful, it will increase the workload of the scheduler although the system will seem to respond better than before.

Part E

Changing SYSGEN Parameters

28   Changing SYSGEN Parameters

Introduction

Imagine the horror of seeing your DEC VAX/VMS system manager altering the SYSGEN parameters haphazardly in the hope that the changes he/she was introducing would enhance system performance. There are approximately 300 SYSGEN parameters which control various resources that make up the VMS operating system. No one could hope to know the functions of all of these parameters, let alone set them.

System performance tuning is not just about tinkering with SYSGEN parameters. By making changes to SYSGEN parameters one may improve system performance, but imagine the consequences of getting it wrong on a production system; havoc can be created and, at the same time, mask the real cause(s) of poor performance. In altering SYSGEN parameters a disciplined methodology must be observed. Haphazard changes can wreck the system, especially when there is no record of any response time measurements having been taken.

There can be many reasons for the sluggish performance of a DEC VAX; varying from the simple to the complex. There can be situations which may also relate to the settings of the SYSGEN parameters. VMS system and application tuning can also vary from the very simple to the very complex, but before beginning with the tuning exercise targets should be set and weighed against the time and effort needed to achieve them.

Long before you even dream about getting into SYSGEN, you must have a complete understanding of many things which constitute normal behavior on your system. For instance, you must know your hardware, software, user environments and you must have at least a basic understanding of memory management on VMS, disk

I/O mechanism and some understanding of CPU modes of operations and management. You should also know how to use the various utilities, such as MONITOR and ACCOUNTING, for performance monitoring. Table 28.1 lists some of the main items you should be familiar with.

Table 28.1   Understanding your system

Hardware Configuration	Disks (total number, capacity, transfer rate etc.), Total Memory, CPU capacity, Terminals population, etc.
Software Configuration	Layered Products, Installed Images, Location of data files and Application mages, location of Page and Swap files, etc.
User Environment	Average Number of users per day, Distribution of users over nodes, Applications used by various users, etc.
Workload Environment	Average number of users per day, Peak and Off peak period, Average response time, Peak response time, Peak and off peak usage of CPU, Memory, and Disk Utilisation, Page Fault Rate, known problems, and bottlenecks, etc.
VMS Tools	Accounting, Monitor, Autogen, Sysgen, Authorize, etc.

Tip: A word of advice here, before you tinker with SYSGEN parameters and make matters worse, consider the other factors which may be affecting system performance. Only after you have tried everything else, and the system is still not performing as expected, should you even contemplate changing SYSGEN parameters. The chances are that by the time you reach to the stage of altering SYSGEN parameters, you will have a fairly good idea of all the under- and over-allocated resources on your system.

The role of AUTOGEN

Changing SYSGEN parameters is a risky business. A change in the value of a system parameter – perhaps a simple change from the system manager's point of view – *can bring the system down on its knees.* AUTOGEN assists in the modification of system parameters and sometimes helps in adjusting the necessary parameters which are affected by your simple change: acting as your job saviour in avoiding major disasters. SYSGEN parameters are stored in the file:

SYS$SYSTEM:VAXVMSSYS.PAR.

Your system loads these values from this file when it is first booted. There are various categories of SYSGEN parameters, details of these different categories can be found in your *System Generation Utility Manual* supplied by Digital. There are dynamic parameters which can be changed interactively and affect the performance immediately and there are those which require a system reboot to become effective.

AUTOGEN helps you to derive sensible values for all these parameters through its mechanism of feedback. To create a new VAXVMSSYS.PAR it takes input from your current hardware configuration, the system's workload and your loving system manager through MODPARAMS.DAT.

Your system manager has the option of assigning new values in three different ways. He/she can either assign values directly using assignment statements such as ACP_HDRCACHE = 70 or using the ADD statement: ADD_ACP_HDRCACHE= 10 or the MIN statement: MIN_ACP_HDRCACHE= 10

The first technique disables AUTOGEN calculations of the parameter. The second technique allows it to calculate a value and then increment by the amount specified. I always prefer the third option. Always comment your changes in MODPARAMS.DAT showing all the amendments and the reasons for alteration of values. When you add new products, comment the new values and adjustments so that they can be removed easily when necessary. AUTOGEN can also create page, swap and dumpfiles. The utility is written in DCL and is easy to read. If you wish to know how certain SYSGEN parameters values are calculated, print the procedure and study it.

Some useful AUTOGEN commands

A word of caution here: always be consistent in your approach to the change of SYSGEN parameters, do not use different methods to set and/or adjust SYSGEN parameters. Do not change system parameters directly by by-passing MODPARAMS.DAT. You may create havoc by making changes directly.

Make only one or two people responsible for making changes to SYSGEN parameters, and the changes should be agreed *before they are implemented*.

$@SYS$UPDATE: AUTOGEN SAVPARAMS GENPARAMS FEEDBACK

This commands collects feedback data, performs the essential calculations and produces a report for consideration by the system manager, showing the system manager how the feedback data would affect the system.

$@SYS$UPDATE:AUTOGEN SETPARAMS REBOOT

Enables you to create a new VAXVMSSYS.PAR file, setting parameters to the values in SETPARAMS.DAT and reboot the machine with its new parameters.

$@SYS$UPDATE:AUTOGEN SAVPARAMS

Enables a system manager to save the feedback data for later use. The resulting file can be renamed for later use until required for a typical type of load.

$@SYS$UPDATE:AUTOGEN GETDATA REBOOT NOFEEDBACK

Enables the system manager to ignore all feedback information. Useful when a system is being used for the very first time or where the work environment is completely different.

Starting to use **AUTOGEN** for the first time

If you have never run AUTOGEN before and have always made changes using SYSGEN and would like to use AUTOGEN now and also retain the changes made using SYSGEN, follow the steps described below.

1. Save the current parameter settings using the commands:

        $ MC SYSGEN
        SYSGEN > USE CURRENT
        SYSGEN > WRITE SYS$SYSTEM:VAXVMSSYS.OLD

    if you are running VMS V4.5 or earlier.

2. Assuming that you are still in SYSGEN, use the command:

        SYSGEN >SET/OUTPUT=filename.old
        SYSGEN >SHOW/ALL
        SYSGEN >SHOW/SPECIAL
        SYSGEN >EXIT

to create an ASCII file of the current settings and exit. We will later use this file to compare the old settings with the new (see 6 below).

3. Modify MODPARAMS.DAT to include the changes you have made to the system. Use the format MIN_<parameter name> rather than assigning direct values:

```
$ EDIT SYS$SYSTEM:MODPARAMS.DAT
```

to set the parameter to a particular value. Set the flags for pagefile, swapfile, and the dumpfile to 0. It tells AUTOGEN not to adjust these file sizes.

```
SWAPFILE = 0
PAGEFILE = 0
DUMPFILE = 0
```

Include the changes to the system parameters here: eg, if you have made changes to GBLPAGES and/or GBLSECTIONS, make sure you include them in this file.

```
MIN_GBLPAGES = n          Use your current value
MIN_GBLSECTIONS = n       for these parameters.
SCSNODE = """"
SCSSYSTEMID = O
```

4. Use one of the following commands to run AUTOGEN. For systems running VMS V4.n, collect old parameter values.

```
$ @ SYS$UPDATE:AUTOGEN SAVPARAMS SETPARAMS
```

For systems running VMS version 5. Assume, there is no 'feedback' information as you are running AUTOGEN for the first time.

```
S @ SYS$UPDATE:AUTOGEN GETDATA SETPARAMS NOFEEDBACK
```

5. Save the new parameters using:

```
$ MC SYSGEN
SYSGEN > USE CURRENT
```

217

```
SYSGEN > SET/OUTPUT=filename.new
SYSGEN > SHOW/ALL
SYSGEN > SHOW/SPECIAL
SYSGEN > EXIT
```

6. Compare the old parameter file with the new parameter file and write the differences to a new output file:

```
$DIFFERENCES/PARALLEL/OUTPUT = filename.dif filename.old filename.new
```

Print the differences file (filename.dif) and study the differences in the settings. As a general rule, if the new value is lower than the old value then retain the old value because the system may be using the greater amount of resource.

7. Verify that the values specified in the file MODPARAMS.DAT are included

Make necessary adjustments to MODPARAMS.DAT accordingly, repeat steps 5, 6 and 7 and until satisfied.

8. Reboot the system when convenient.

The new parameters will come into effect after the reboot. If you wish to revert to the old parameter settings then use the old file created in step 1 as follows:

```
$ MC SYSGEN
SYSGEN > USE SYS$SYSTEM:VAXVMSSYS.OLD
SYSGEN > WRITE CURRENT
SYSGEN > EXIT
```

Reboot the system when convenient.

A word of warning about AUTOGEN

AUTOGEN attempts to tune your VMS system by providing a value for every parameter. For most SYSGEN parameters it uses the default value as the optimum value. It does not always calculate the optimal value. Use MODPARAMS.DAT to specify the value of parameters critical to the performance of your system.

Making changes to **SYSGEN** – rules of thumb

1. Always set the targets before making any changes.

2. Define and agree ways of measuring performance meaningful to your users; for example, you could measure the response time of a vital application.

3. Make all changes in conjunction with AUTOGEN because it can affect some SYSGEN parameters. It also ensures that the associated parameters are consistent with each other.

4. Use MODPARAMS.DAT to change all SYSGEN parameters, it is used as input by AUTOGEN. Parameter values set via MODPARAMS.DAT override default values calculated by AUTOGEN.

5. Always comment the changes to assist an easy return to the previous values if necessary.

6. Change just one or two parameters at a time and measure the performance after the change: it helps to correct any detrimental changes. Gradual change enables you to assess the impact on other parameters, never rush the changes.

7. Lastly, measure the performance after the change and if it does not result in measurable gain as defined before, do not hesitate to revert to the original settings. Stop tuning when your efforts begin to produce marginal results.

Part F   Tuning Layered Products

29   Tips to Tune ALL-IN-1 Under OpenVMS

Introduction

ALL-IN-1 is a fairly big application that demands a substantial amount of OpenVMS resources and therefore requires special attention to a large number of specific areas to operate smoothly, these being:

- SYSGEN parameters
- Page and swap file(s)
- UAF parameters and user names
- Boosting ALL-IN-1 initialization process
- Disk housekeeping
- Global buffering for shared files
- Reorganization of ALL-IN-1 files.

User authorization file (UAF) parameters

To modify or set user process parameters in SYSUAF.DAT use AUTHORIZE. Set the UAF parameters as shown in Table 29.1; do not use default UAF values as these are insufficient for the load ALL-IN-1 places on user processes.

See Table 29.1 for minimum recommended values.

Table 29.1   Minimum UAF recommended values for ALL-IN-1 user processes

Parameter	Recommended Value	Comments
WSDEFAULT	1,500	Defines the initial working set limit for a process at image activation.
WSQUOTA	1,800	Defines the next limit (general limit). Processes requiring additional memory are authorised to grow to its WSQUOTA value under all circumstances.
WSEXTENT	2,048	Defines the final limit. Memory hungry processes may be allowed to grow to this limit providing there is sufficient memory available on the system. WSEXTENT is limited by WSMAX. A process's extent region cannot be greater than WSMAX. You should set WSMAX to the maximum number of pages required by any application on your system. Normally a working set size of 2048 is sufficient for an ordinary ALL-IN-1 process. Only allocate a bigger working set extent value if the process is page faulting heavily and the I/O activity on your user and page file disks is high, or if you are using DEC WINDOWS, as it requires extra memory. It is suggested that you use system templates to define specific values for different users with the command procedure OA$LIB:MUA_CREATE.COM.
PGFLQUOTA	20,000	Defines the number of pages a user process can use in the system page file.
BYTLM	36,000	See page 139.
FILLM	100	See page 139.
ASTLM	80	Defines the number of asynchronous system trap (AST) requests and scheduled wake-up requests that a process can have outstanding at any one time.
BIOLM	50	Defines the number of buffer I/O operations a process can have outstanding.
TQELM	20	Defines the number of timer entries and the common event flag clusters a process can have outstanding at any one time.
DIOLM	28	See page 139.

SYSGEN parameters

It is recommended that all changes to SYSGEN parameters described in this section should be made in accordance with the rules described in Part E of this book. Please read that section if you have not already done so. Parameters that require some adjustment for ALL-IN-1 fall into two categories as described below:

- Parameters requiring adjustment before the installation of ALL-IN-1.
- Parameters that may require adjustment during normal tuning process.

The values suggested below are adequate for lower end systems only. These suggested values may require adjustment depending upon the needs of OpenVMS and other layered products. Parameters may also need to be adjusted for specific type of terminals or other hardware.

Table 29.2   Suggested SYSGEN values for large VAX clusters

MAXBUF	6,000
WSMAX	Equal to or greater than the largest WSEXTENT value
SWPOUTPGCNT	Equal to WSDEFAULT
SYSMWCNT	See section on system faults in Chapter 4.
VIRTUALPAGECNT	Not less than 20,000
PIXSCAN	Not less than 20 –30 on large DEC VAXs
GBLPAGES	Depends upon the number of active users and shared files
GBLSECTIONS	Depends upon the number of active users and shared files
CHANNELCNT	255
PQL_DENQLM	Not less than 150
PQL_MENQLM	Not less than 150
PIOPAGES	At least 400
RMS_DFMBC	Not less than 16
RMS_DFMBFIDX	2
TTY_ALTYPAHD	Not less than 1,500
TTY_TYPAHDSZ	Not less than 1,500

Page and swap file(s)

As mentioned above, ALL-IN-1 is a large image and therefore needs an abundance of system pagefile space. Under OpenVMS you can have multiple number of page and swap files, so you should try to distribute the I/O load across several available disk spindles, especially on large VAX clusters. There are many guidelines for calculating the size of page and swap file sizes required for the optimum performance of an ALL-IN-1 application, some of these rules of thumb are described below.

Rules of thumb – calculating the pagefile size for a system supporting ALL-IN-1

Allow 3,000 blocks for each concurrent user on the system. Include in this the number of active processes, such as ALL-IN-1 Manager's account, maintenance activities, the sender and fetcher jobs, and any other active processes; or use the formula:

Page File Size = (WSQUOTA * MAXPROCESSCNT * 2)

where MAXPROCESSCNT is the maximum number of processes that can be active on a system at any one time. WSQUOTA is the working set size allocated to each user using AUTHORIZE in their SYSUAF record. Note that the value calculated using this formula is very much higher than the rule number one, but it is always a good practice to over-allocate rather than under-allocate the amount of space required for the pagefile. This is because small pagefiles can become fragmented with use and then may degrade the performance of your application. **If your page file exceeds** the 50% usage, then you must increase the size available pagefile space by increasing the size of the system pagefile, or adding secondary pagefiles. It is always a good practice to have multiple pagefiles rather than one big pagefile.

Rule of thumb – calculating the swap file size for a system supporting ALL-IN-1

Use the formula:

Swap File Size = No. of active ALL-IN-1 processes * WSQUOTA.

Note: Do not underestimate the swap file size. Avoid swapping altogether if possible by ensuring there is sufficient memory available on the system for all active processes.

Rules of thumb – boosting All-IN-1 initialization process

A typical ALL-IN-1 system may take between 10 and 30 seconds to initialize depending upon the power of the CPU, speed of disks, amount of memory available and allocated, and finally the load on the system. Some basic rules of thumb are described below to help you speed up this initialization process.

1. Do not include unnecessary commands and command procedures in user log in and system log in command procedures.

2. Do not allow these log in procedures to grow without reason, this is because every command in these procedures is executed very time someone logs in.

3. Separate the commands required for ALL-IN-1 from other applications command procedures and logical definitions to ensure that they are not executed unnecessarily.

4. Avoid the opening of application form libraries until needed.

5. If possible use precompiled libraries.

6. Allocate large working set sizes to reduce the amount of paging during image initialization.

7. Place ALL-IN-1 executables shareable on a solid state device for rapid image execution.

8. Only display to the user his or her initial menu without any extras to avoid searching any other files.

Disk housekeeping

Efficient use and management of disk space by the users and the system managers is essential for the optimal performance of ALL-IN-1 application.

Guidelines for disk housekeeping

All users should be informed that for the smooth and efficient running of ALL-IN-1 it is essential for them to:

1. *Keep their directories and file cabinets tidy.*

2. *Remove unwanted documents.* All system managers should have some automated procedures to clean-up the directories and file cabinets of unwanted documents. Some clean-up procedures are discussed below.

3. *Purge directories.* Delete temporary files created by the system such as read, delivery and failure notifications.

4. *Only allow users to store documents for a limited period.* Specify an age limit on unfiled mail messages in the READ, OUTBOX and CREATED folders. There are routines available to perform such function and remove messages greater than *n* days old to a wastebasket. It is good practice to notify users before and after removing documents from these folders.

5. *Keep the size of* SDAFs *small.* Especially true on large DEC VAX clusters by unsharing documents referenced in the mail shared areas by a single user. There are tools available to perform such functions.

6. *Archive documents to a magnetic tape media whenever possible.* Note that this action does not reduce the size of DOCDB.DAT and DAF.DAT files in the user directories.

Remember: It is important to keep the users notified of whatever action you may decide to take.

Global buffering for shared files

A global buffer is accessible by two or more processes. Global buffering is the most effective way of minimizing disk I/O operations on files shared by multiple users. You can request global buffers on a per file basis. Global buffers enable you to cache both the index and the data portion of a file in memory if required. The biggest advantage of global buffers is in caching index buckets, not data buckets. It is usually sufficient to cache the total index structure plus one data bucket. As explained in Chapter 21, global buffers can be specified with the SET FILE DCL command when a file is not in use (ie not open).

```
$SET FILE/GLOBAL_BUFFERS=30 0A$DATA_SHARE:PENDING.DAT
```

As most of the ALL-IN-1 files are shared, they constantly remain open, therefore you may need to shutdown the system before global buffers could be applied.

Use the formula: $(n/2 + 1)$ – where n is the number of concurrently active ALL-IN-1 user processes – to adjust and/or set the number of global buffers for ALL-IN-1 files. The exact number of global buffers needed is dependent on the system you are running, the amount of memory available, the amount of mail that is created, read and sent. A cautious approach is recommended. If you discover that the system performance has degraded with additional global buffers introduced, then reduce them and investigate performance.

You may set global buffers for:

- SDAFs
- the User Profile
- the Time Management Meeting and Attendee Files
- the mail Pending File.

Careful consideration should be given when allocating global buffers: you are trading-off system memory to store global buffers and the paging and swapping required for their maintenance against the I/O that would otherwise be performed to access data on disks. For example, the number of global buffers required to cache the index and one data bucket of SDAFs could be very large – especially where SDAFs are approaching a million blocks. See Chapter 21 to estimate the number of buffers required to cache indexes and the parameters involved.

Maintenance of ALL-IN-1 files

Index files are a major contributor to overall system performance and ALL-IN-1 makes extensive use of index files. For optimal performance it is vital that these files are regularly tuned, monitored and carefully maintained. The most important ALL-IN-1 files that require careful maintenance (reorganization) on a regular basis are listed below.

```
OA$DATA_SHARE:PENDING.DAT
OA$DATA_SHARE:PROFILE.DAT
OA$DATA_SHARE:ATTENDEES.DAT
OA$DATA_SHARE:MEETING.DAT
SDAFs (up to five)
```

Keeping PENDING.DAT, PROFILE.DAT and the SDAFs well maintained is essential for the overall performance of an ALL-IN-1 system. See Chapter 22 for efficient file reorganization techniques using the CONVERT utility. Follow the methodology listed below to maintain your ALL-IN-1 files.

1. *Never rely on the default values in the* FDL *files provided with the* ALL-IN-1 *kit.*

2. *Convert the heavily used files as described in Chapter 22 of this guide.* The objective is to ensure that these files remain contiguous (not fragmented all over a disk), bucket splits and window turns are avoided and appropriate extensions including the global buffers are set.

3. *Reorganize the following files once a week*:

    OA$DATA_SHARE:PROFILE.DAT
    OA$DATA_SHARE:ATTENDEES.DAT
    OA$DATA_SHARE:MEETING.DAT

    Reorganize PENDING.DAT at least once a month.

4. *Run File Cabinet Verification and Repair* (FCVR) *once a month to maintain* SDAFs. This will ensure the elimination of 'trash' from SDAFs.

5. *Empty wastebasket folders (user file cabinets* DOCDB *and* PDAF) *once a week.*

    This to be followed by a reorganization.

Important: For good and reliable performance it is essential that the above mentioned files are maintained on a regular basis. Ignoring regular system maintenance will degrade the performance of your system and may result in delay of displaying menus and forms on the screen and of characters not being echoed back rapidly to the screen during an edit session.

30 Tuning OpenVMS for TCP/IP

Introduction

TCP/IP is a suite of common communications services offered by a number of vendors designed to satisfy the need for a multivendor computing environment. Under OpenVMS, TCP/IP application operates through driver software accessing an Ethernet card. Tuning TCP/IP performance should mainly concentrate on reducing the INTERRUPT and KERNEL mode overhead. The guidelines in this section should enable you to:

- configure TCP/IP software optimally
- reduce the impact of overheads generated by TCP/IP software.

Configure TCP/IP software optimally

It is vital that TCP/IP is configured for optimal performance. Speed and buffering ability of Ethernet adapters is important. Considerable performance improvements could be achieved by upgrading Ethernet adapters from DEBNA to DEBNI.

The size of large request packets (LRP) determined by the SYSGEN parameter LRPCOUNT is also critical. This is because the packets requiring system attention are placed in LRP for processing. LRP size should not be reduced from its default value of 1504 as this is the size needed for the Ethernet packet.

TCP/IP software should support setting the buffer count to suit the workload. Sometimes default values are not enough and require adjustment to prevent packet loss, especially if the communication rate is filling the buffers faster than they are processed. Please note that an increase in buffer space might require augmenting UAF parameters for the driver process.

Reduce the impact of overheads generated by TCP/IP software

As mentioned above, TCP/IP packages operate through driver software which generates a great deal of interrupts and kernel mode activity. Under OpenVMS this is partially due to greater cost of process creation, context switching and extensive data protection activity. Excessive interrupt activity can overload the system and should be investigated. SPM and DECPS are good tools to investigate the nature of the interrupt activity. See the SPM SYSTEM_PC report to determine the nature of interrupts. The two interrupts you should lookout for are:

SCH$RESCHED *and* SMP$ACQUIREL

SCH$RESCHED is a reschedule interrupt generated by the OpenVMS scheduler when a process gains or loses control of the processor (ie when it changes the status of the process from or to CURrent). There are a number of SYSGEN parameters which can be adjusted to help reduce this interrupt and kernel mode activity, these are shown below:

QUANTUM, AWSTIME, PFRATH, WSMAX, WSINC, WSDEFAULT, MAXPROCESSCNT, PROCSECTCNT, CTLPAGES, CLISYMTBL, PRIORITY_OFFSET.

SCH$RESCHED is invoked in the following instances:

1. When a current process relinquishes a processor.

2. When another process of higher priority becomes computable and displaces the current process.

QUANTUM end rescheduling should be minimized to reduce the system overhead.

This can be achieved by increasing the size of QUANTUM from its default value of 20 to 40. This should improve response time especially if (interrupt + kernel + MPSYNCH) activity exceeds 40% of the total CPU utilization. Please note that increasing the value of quantum may result in excessive pagefaulting on your system. You may resolve excessive pagefaulting by any of the techniques described below:

- set AWSTIME to 3 times the default value QUANTUM or increase WSINC and WSDEFAULT

and/or

- reduce PFRATH to 20.

Disk I/O and process creation activity associated with SMP$ACQUIREL should also be reduced where possible, especially where process creation rate is high. Lowering the value of the parameters shown below will help reduce the time it takes to create a process and reduce system overhead:

MAXPROCESSCNT, WSMAX, PROCSECTCNT, CTLPAGES, CLISYMBTL

Note: Do not rely on the values set by AUTOGEN for the above parameters. It is worthwhile to monitor the system over a period of time and then define optimal values using MODPARAMS.DAT to reduce the overheads on interrupt, kernel, and MPSynch mode.

Disk and file fragmentation also adds to the activity of SMP$ACQUIREL. To reduce I/O overhead generated by fragmented disks/files follow the guidelines in Chapter 20.

SCH$RESCHED activity also increases if a high priority process is I/O bound or QUANTUM is set to a low value. If the former is true, the process will frequently change its status to and from COMputable, then the SCH$RESCHED activity will increase. For systems with high overheads and/or a non-compute bound system it is worth raising the value of SYSGEN parameter PRIORITY_OFFSET to 4.

This will increase the difference required to displace the current process and thus reduce the interrupt activity but may adversely affect performance of the high priority processes.

233

31 Tuning VMS for X-Windows

Introduction

X-Windows gives you the ability to display information relating to several applications on the same screen. It also allows you to cut and paste information between them. Using X-Windows, users can now create a suite of processes and become more productive. It is for this reason X-Windows applications consume considerably more memory, more CPU time and involve greater process creations and context switches. This behaviour demands a change in tuning methodology from the traditional VMS tuning strategy.

X-Windows tuning methodology

Follow the guidelines below for optimal performance.

Ensure ample memory availability

A key to successfully supporting and running X-Windows under OpenVMS is abundant memory, at least 16 megabytes for reasonably acceptable performance for casual users. However, many X applications are more resource intensive and therefore require much more. See Table 31.1 for approximate details of memory consumption by some of the X-Windows applications.

Table 31.1   Approximate memory consumption by X-Window applications

Application Name	Memory Consumed (approximate VMS pages)
DECW$SESSION	> 3000 (512 bytes a page)
DECW$MW5	> 2000
DECW$MAIL	> 3000
DECW$TERMINAL	> 2000
VUE$MASTER	Between (2000 - 3000)
DECW$CLOCK	> 2000

Table 31.1 (continued) Approximate memory consumption by X-Window applications

DECW$WINMGR	> 1600
DECW$PRINTSC	> 1000
DECW$NOTEPAD	Between (2000 - 3000)
DECW$CALC	Between (1500 - 2000)
DECW$CALEND	Between (2000 - 3000)
DECW$PAINT	> 1000
DECW$LWK_SET	> 1500

Restrict the use of too many colours

Avoid using more colours than necessary as there is a direct link between the number of colours supported, the total network traffic (number of packets and bytes) and the CPU time required to invoke an X-task.

Ensure VMS process quotas are adequately adjusted

System managers supporting X-Windows users should pay special attention to UAF and SYSGEN parameters shown below. Typical OpenVMS process quotas are unsuitable for X-Windows support and impose an additional load on the system.

Table 31.2 SYSGEN and UAF parameters relevant to X-Windows management

SYSGEN PARAMETER	EQUIVALENT UAF PARAMETER
PQL_DWSEXTENT	WSEXTENT
PQL_DPGFLQUOTA	PGFLQUO
PQL_DENQLM	ENQLM
PQL_DBIOLM	BIOLM
PQL_DDIOLM	DIOLM
PQL_DBYTLM	BYTLM
PQL_DASTLM	ASTLM
PQL_DFILLM	FILLM

Workstations have their own command procedure which is invoked when a node is configured, but you should still examine those SYSUAF values. These are set in:

SYS$MANAGER:DECW$CHECK_PARAMS.COM

Keep the cost of process creation and context switches to a minimum

Process creation on X-Windows applications is very resource intensive and therefore it is essential to keep the cost of process creation to a minimum under OpenVMS. For this it is necessary that UAF parameters described above and SYSGEN parameters shown below are adequately adjusted.

CTLPAGES, CLISYMTBL, PROCSECTCNT, MAXPROCESSCNT, WSMAX

All of these parameters are directly related to the cost of process creation and therefore should be reduced as much as possible but should not be reduced to a too low value which may cause the system to hang or prevent users from logging in. There are no threshold values for these SYSGEN parameters as the load on systems differ from site to site. **Warning:** Settings of these parameters should be reviewed carefully.

Minimize the number of process logicals

Creation of a sub-process under OpenVMS comprises the formation and population of a new process logical table, generally by replicating the parent's process table. Therefore, serious consideration should be given to reduce the number of process logicals by using the job logical table, which is shared by the parent process including all its sub-processes. You may achieve this with the /JOB qualifier with your DEFINE or ASSIGN statements in SYLOGIN.COM and LOGIN.COM. Please note that the SYSUAF parameter JTQUOTA would also require some adjustment.

Limit the number of subprocess creation

As a last resort, you may limit the number of subprocess creation by lowering the value of the UAF parameter PRCLM and the SYSGEN parameter PQL_MPRCLM.

Limit the total process creation

To achieve this lower the value of the two SYSGEN parameters MAXJOBS and MAXACCTJOBS. Note that you should only use this option as a last resort as the effects are cluster-wide and apply to the network, batch and interactive environment.

Use PCs or cheap satellite for X displays

Use cheap satellites or PCs for intensive X use. If using a satellite then you can use ACLs to block access to the required images from a certain node.

Upgrade DEBNA network adapters

You can avoid network transmission by improving the VAX's ability to receive packets by upgrading to DEBNIs.

Other SYSGEN-related parameters

For DEC VAX sites using DECNET set the value of the SYSGEN parameters given below as specified.

```
CHANNELCNT 255
MAXBUF 2048
```

Adjust the pipeline quota within NCP to 10,000

Increase the pipeline quota to at least 10,000 and NETACP's default buffer limit to 131,070.

32 Optimizing PATHWORKS Performance

Points to remember before installing **PATHWORKS**

There are a huge number of organizations with PCs running under MS-DOS networked together with Digital's OpenVMS system as a server. Guidelines in this section will enable system managers to optimize PATHWORKS for performance.

- Performance tuning of client–server configurations involves both the client and the server.

- Optimal performance of PATHWORKS requires special attention to memory, server network and disk I/O.

- Client performance is largely dependent on a good network adapter (bus width and local buffer space) and effective memory configuration.

- Conform to Ethernet standards for maximum repeaters, cable length, etc.

- Consider buying a fast Ethernet adapter to optimize OpenVMS network.

- If you are thinking of adding a large PATHWORK load to an already busy system with DEBNA then upgrade it to DEBNI or possibly DEMNA before adding additional load.

- Get a 16 or a 32-bit card which will reduce drop packet rate during periods of high activity.

- Large local buffer space minimizes the likelihood of a packet being lost and reduces the need for a retransmission.

- A poorly configured client or server will ultimately effect the performance of the whole configuration.

- An overloaded network will defeat your finest efforts in both areas.

- Get to the root of the problem before fishing in the dark.

- Alleviate the bottleneck but only after a proper diagnosis and having ensured that it will not reveal a worse problem.

- Reduce the baud rate to hide the slow response if necessary!

- Get the users to store/retrieve/backup large files locally.

Guidelines to optimize PATHWORKS

- Reduce disk I/O load using the techniques described in Chapters 18, 19, 20, 21, and 22. Remember the primary function of the PATHWORK server is to serve files, therefore you must consider ways to reduce the I/O workload.

- Check the CPU MODES utilisation using the VMS MONITOR utility, and if the (interrupt + Kernel + MPsynch) activity exceeds 40% of the total CPU utilization on the server then increase the value of the SYSGEN parameter AWSTIME to twice the size of QUANTUM on the server. This will increase the number of pagefaults per second but you may compensate for this by increasing the value WSINC and/or lowering the value of PFRATH.

- All network activity generates interrupts, therefore, you must consider ways to reduce these interrupts to enhance performance. You may achieve this by increasing the value of the SYSGEN parameter QUANTUM. This technique will enable you to reduce the number of interrupts generated by SCH$RESCHED.

- If possible, reduce the size of MAXPROCESSCNT, WSMAX, PROCSETCNT, CLISYMTBL and CTLPAGES. Reduction in the size of these parameters will reduce the time it takes to create a process and speed-up operations.

- Within NCP, consider increasing the line buffer count and increase the pipeline quota to 10,000. This will require you to increase the quota values for the NETACP process. You may override the original values by redefining the logicals defined in LOADNET.COM.

  Set BIOLM to 131070
  Set WSEXTENT to 3000

- Set CHANNELCNT to greater than 255.

- Set MAXBUF to at least 2048.

Part G   Optimizing RDBMS

33 Understanding Relational Database Management Systems (RDBMS)

Introduction

The relational approach was introduced by Codd and is based on the mathematical theory of relations. Examples of mainstream RDBMS include INGRES, ORACLE, Rdb, SUPRA and SYBASE.

Relational databases are very popular today because of their flexibility, ease-of-use and development productivity which is many times more than the traditional 3GL languages. Development techniques used in a 3GL environment are not relevant with RDBMS. Therefore, it is essential for all those who design, develop, implement and support applications using 4GLs to understand the basics of RDBMS. I hope that this chapter will enable people to develop a better understanding of relational theory and concepts.

A relational database may be defined as a collection of normalized relations and a collection of domains. A normalized relation may be viewed by the user as a two-dimensional table, where each row of the table corresponds to a tuple (record) of the relation, and each column of the table contains entries that belong to the set of values constituting the underlying domain of that column. The relations present in the database are called base relations. A domain is an abstract set of atomic data values (objects), where the domain underlying the column consists of precisely those objects that can appear as entries in that column.

Consider, for example, a database that contains information about some company, and a relation in that database is called EMP, which contains data on the employees of the company. EMP is shown in Table 33.1, described by its table representation. The rows of the table corresponds to tuple (records) of the relation and the columns correspond to instances of particular domains of the database. Loosely speaking, a relation corresponds to a 'flat' file, a tuple to a record and column to a data field.

Table 33.1   The EMP database

Column →	Name	Sex	Salary	Manager	Department
Underlying Domain →	NAME	SEX	MONEY	NAME	DEPT
	Jones Richard	male	£12,000	Jones Richard	Research
	Blackwell Geoff	male	£10,000	Smith Cathy	Sales
	Smith Cathy	female	£11,000	Jones Richard	Sales

Each database relation is created by naming the relation and its constituent columns, and specifying the underlying domain of each column. More than one column in a relation may have the same underlying domain. Column names are unique within a relation. Specifying the underlying domain of each column defines the set of values from which the entries in that column may be selected. There can be any number of rows or columns in tables, with considerable freedom in the format of each column. Records in different tables are related by having the same values in corresponding fields.

All data is explicitly accessible in this tabular form. There are no implicit pointers between records, and no elaborate structure of fields within fields, as in *network* databases. All relationships between records are made explicit in the values of their fields. These relational concepts built into RDBMSs give you a high degree of physical data independence (the ability to alter data structures without changing programs) and logical data independence (the ability to add and delete fields without affecting the application program's view of the data).

These two features – of conceptual simplicity and data independence – greatly reduce the complexity and cost of application programs which use a relational database.

34   Tips to Optimize ORACLE
Applications

Introduction

Tuning RDBMSs is a perplexing task, mainly because database usage, user requirements, conditions and expectations are always changing over time: making it impossible to suggest a clear performance methodology. The generalized approach discussed in this section (configuring ORACLE for optimal performance, tuning INIT.ORA file parameters, the optimization of database structures and the optimization of SQL statements) will benefit all ORACLE users. To tune a database effectively it is *essential* for you to balance the load on memory and I/O equally. This applies to all RDBMSs. You can only achieve this if you have a thorough understanding of your workload environment and ORACLE internals. Below is a list of some of the main items which you should know and the approach you should follow.

1. You should have a good understanding of the internals of ORACLE RDBMS and SQL.

2. You should be able to monitor and evaluate performance using the SQL*DBA command MONITOR and OpenVMS utilities such as MONITOR and ACCOUNTING.

3. You should know hardware configuration details such as, total number of disks, disks transfer rate, disks capacity, total memory and total CPU capacity.

4. You should know your ORACLE configuration details such as location of REDO logfiles, frequency of log allocations, check_point interval, rollback segments, size of the SGA and controlling parameters, location of the tables and indexes,

number of indexes per table, type of tables in use (flat files or normalized), DBWR and LGWR background processes and buffer management details (movement of data from disks to memory and vice versa).

5. You should know your user and workload environment: ie the number of unique ORACLE users connected on average, maximum number of ORACLE users you expect to be connected to the system, average and maximum number of users using SQL*FORMS, average and maximum number of users using SQL*PLUS for *ad hoc* queries, etc.

6. You should also have a good understanding of your applications accessing the data and the underlying data tables. For example, the type of SQL statements that are in high use, indexes used for queries, number of tables used in typical queries, use of temporary segments, number of users allowed to create tables, update tables, delete rows from tables, insert data into tables, and alter grants to tables and the time it takes currently to complete transactions, etc.

A good understanding of your workload environment, SQL, ORACLE configuration (internals), OpenVMS, hardware configuration, application, relational theory (normalization) will enable you to design applications optimally, write efficient SQL code, configure ORACLE in an optimal fashion and hence provide a good service to most of the users on the system.

As mentioned above, the key to successful ORACLE optimization lies in the reduction of I/Os and the effective use of memory. Inadequate allocation of memory can have a colossal impact on performance. It is necessary to allocate memory appropriately to the buffer caches, data dictionary, and the location that holds information vital for the processing of a SQL statement (context areas) to improve the performance of these caches and reduce the amount of paging and swapping on the system. Excessive disk I/O can also have an adverse impact on the performance of software applications. Disk I/Os to ORACLE files can be examined using the SQL*DBA command MONITOR FILE I/O.

Long before you consider tuning your ORACLE RDBMS configuration and start changing the values of the parameters in INIT.ORA it is important for you to have a good understanding of the applications and the problem areas. You should set the targets for tuning; at this stage you should know whether you wish to improve the performance of the whole environment (ie everybody on the system); to improve the performance of a particular database application in question or to improve the performance of some SQL statements accessing the database. Your tuning methodology should somewhat resemble the approach discussed below.

1. Tune your OpenVMS environment to meet the demands placed on it. Observe the performance over a period of time and make adjustments if necessary before embarking upon step 2.

2. Study the SQL code of the programs which are the cause of concern and make necessary changes. Make use of the SQL trace facility and the EXPLAIN PLAN statement to check the execution plan of your SQL statements. Tune your VMS environment to meet the new demands imposed by the changes made.

3. Normalize your table structures to meet the growing demands and the additional load. Tune your VMS environment again to meet the requirements,

4. Make changes to ORACLE RDBMS configuration, and INIT.ORA parameters to make effective use of memory, reduce the I/O load and minimize locking contention. Check your VMS settings again and adjust parameters if necessary.

Some suggestions to improve the performance of your ORACLE applications

As mentioned above, RDBMS tuning is an ongoing process which requires you to review your database design, access methods, ORACLE configuration parameters and the operating system configuration on a regular basis as the database grows in size over time and the user requirements change. The techniques described in this section will enable you to optimize the performance of ORACLE RDBMS in general.

Keep data dictionary cache misses to a minimum

Data dictionary cache is similar to OpenVMS file system caches and holds information about various caches. It contains information such as database table names, view names, names and data types of columns, rights of access, etc. This information is held in a special location in the system global area (SGA) and is shared by all user processes. The size of each cache is controlled by ORACLE INIT.ORA parameters. All cache parameter names begin with 'DC_'. The efficiency of these cache parameters can be examined using SQL*DBA command:

MONITOR STATISTICS USER

If you find that the number of GETMISSES are more than 10% of the total number of GETS, then you must increase the size of the associated cache by at least 10%. Be careful, do not allocate too much memory to these caches, memory allocated to caches is memory taken away from the user processes.

If you find that the USAGE figure is considerably less than the value displayed in the COUNT column then you can actually save memory by reducing the size of the associated cache.

Ensure sufficient number of context areas to accommodate all SQL parsing

As mentioned above, context areas are locations in memory which contain vital information to process SQL statements executed by your applications. For maximum efficiency ensure that there are an adequate number of areas available to parse SQL statements. Once an SQL statement is parsed it can be executed again and again until the cursor information remains in the context area. If a new SQL statement is loaded into the same context area, then the previous statement must be re-parsed again before it is executed. These context areas are controlled by the ORACLE INIT.ORA parameter OPEN_CURSORS which determines the total number of context areas a single process can possess at any one time. The default value of this parameter is 50 and the maximum value that can be specified is 255.

Warning: Do not allocate too much memory to these context areas as it can induce excessive paging and swapping.

There are two more parameters which in conjunction with the OPEN_CURSORS parameter are responsible for the overall speed at which the SQL statements are parsed. These are described below:

CONTEXT_AREA

This parameter defines the initial size of a context area – the default value is 4,096 bytes. The maximum size is operating-system dependent and can be up to 131,072 bytes.

CONTEXT_INCR

This parameter is very similar to the OpenVMS parameter WSINC. ORACLE increments the size of the context area by the value in CONTEXT_INCR (default value is 4096 bytes, maximum is 32,768 bytes) on demand. A value that is too small will require many increments before the SQL statement is executed. On the other hand, a value that is too large will simply waste memory. You may identify unnecessary parsing by examining the statistics produced by the SQL trace facility.

Keep the number of buffer misses to a minimum

The buffer cache is a shared area of memory which holds copies of database blocks containing tables, rollback segments and indexes. The size of the cache is determined by the INIT.ORA parameter DB_BLOCK_BUFFERS. Direct I/O to the disk is not required if the database block is stored in the buffer cache. You may monitor the buffer statistics using the SQL*DBA command MONITOR IO. Compare the logical and the physical reads: if the hit ratio (ie the buffer cache misses) is less than 80% then you must increase the number of buffer caches and monitor performance again. Make sure that the increase in the number of buffers specified by yourself has not induced any paging and/or swapping on the system.

Reduce database file (table) fragmentation

Fragmentation can have a disastrous effect on the performance of ORACLE applications because of the additional overheads required to access the data. Fragmentation occurs when tables run out of disk space and new extents are allocated to store additional rows of data.

Fragmented tables consume a great amount of system resources and can degrade the performance of the whole system. All RDBMS including ORACLE give better performance if your tables are contiguous, especially, if your application is performing full table scans.

To examine the number of extents for your existing tables you can query the data dictionary view USER_SEGMENTS. Follow the guidelines given below to reduce fragmentation on existing tables.

1. Create an empty new table with the appropriate set of storage parameters.

2. Copy the data into the new table from the existing table.

3. Drop/delete the original table.

4. Recreate indexes if necessary.

5. Rename the new table.

You may use disk and file optimizers available from Digital and other vendors to make database tables contiguous.

Warning: Use disk optimizers only after shutting down ORACLE.

To reduce fragmentation on tables always create tables with appropriate INITIAL allocation and storage parameters. For tables where the new transaction rate is very low (almost static), allocate the storage space for the entire table if possible.

You may also decide to store more rows per block. You may achieve this by decreasing the value of storage parameter PCTREE in the CREATE TABLE statement. PCTREE storage parameter specifies the percentage of free space reserved for data expansion. The default value for this parameter is 10. A high value minimizes the likelihood of rows expanding from block to block, this is because there is more free space in each block for rows to expand.

Remember: A low value for PCTREE may give you better performance if your application is performing full table scans. A low value may result in degradation of performance if the table is dynamic. You really need to know your application and data tables before deciding on the optimum value for your application.

One other way of reducing fragmentation is to increase the size of extents allocation by increasing the value of the NEXT or PCINCREASE storage parameters.

Optimize the usage of redo log files

The redo log files contain the modifications made to ORACLE database system and are used to restore the database since the last checkpoint in the event of a crash or a failure. Please note that a database uses one redo file despite the number of instances sharing the database. All instances write to the same database file and if one instance runs out of space in a log file, all instances start writing to the next available redo log file. The background process *log writer process* (LGWR) is responsible for writing the modified data held in the redo buffer pool to the disk on the following conditions:

- when the redo buffer pool is full
- on the initiation of a COMMIT
- whenever the background process DBWR needs to clean the buffer pool.

Redo log file usage can be measured using the SQL*DBA command MONITOR STATISTICS REDO. The time which the user processes wait for space in the redo buffer are shown in the *redo log space* statistics. This should be kept to zero. The following techniques will enable you to optimize redo log files.

Place redo log files on separate disks from database tables
This will enable you to spread the I/O load more evenly and reduce the chances for I/O contention.

Place redo log files on faster disk(s)
If possible use the faster drives for placement of redo log file(s) to attain enhanced performance – especially when a large number of users are accessing the database concurrently.

Reduce the interval at which the data is written to the redo log file(s)
The ORACLE parameter file INIT.ORA contains a parameter called:

```
LOG_CHECKPOINT_INTERVAL
```

This parameter specifies the number of blocks that can be contained in the pool buffer area before they are actually written to the disk since the last checkpoint. The background process DBWR is responsible for this operation. To reduce the contention to the disk, it is desirable to minimize the number of checkpoints in an ORACLE system. This can be achieved in two ways.

- Set the parameter LOG_CHECKPOINT_INTERVAL to a large number. The default value of this parameter is quite low.

- Setup large redo log files to ensure an interval of approximately 10 minutes on a heavily used system.

Increase the buffer size of the log buffers

The ORACLE parameter LOG_BUFFER sets the size in bytes of the log buffers in the SGA. A large value can minimize the I/O to the log file especially if there are a vast number of long transactions.

Determining the size of log files and reducing the frequency of log allocations

ORACLE makes efficient use of the redo log file by allocating a range of the current on-line redo log file. The size of these allocations are determined by the parameter LOG_ALLOCATION in INIT.ORA. Log allocations are expensive and occur whenever an instance needs more space in an on-line redo log file. New allocations are allocated in the current or the next log file.

Log allocations sizes are determined by the INIT.ORA parameter LOG_ALLOCATION for each instance. Follow the rules of thumb below for setting up files:

1. Set LOG_ALLOCATIONS to at least 1000 blocks.

2. Set the size of each redo log file to the sum of all LOG_ALLOCATION parameters.

3. If at all possible, allow five allocations per file per instance.

Understanding and optimizing ROLLBACK segments

Rollback segments, as the name suggests, contain data necessary to restore the database block to its previous pre-transaction state. A rollback entry contains all the information required to reverse all the changes made by one transaction.

Rollback segments are written in a serial and wrap around manner to ensure the availability of rollback data for as long as possible. When a long transaction fills the rollback segment with uncommitted data, the system allocates new extent for rollback segments which are appended to the original rollback segment.

Each user process is assigned a rollback segment for updates and for the duration of the transaction rollback information is only written to that segment. Rollback information is released by the system when a transaction is committed. Rollback segments are updated prior to modification of a database block by a user process.

From the SQL*DBA you can use the MONITOR ROLLBACK to see the rollback statistics. The following techniques will enable you to optimize the performance of rollback segments.

Use multiple rollback segments in a shared environment

By default, only one rollback segment is created (ie the SYSTEM rollback segment) which is used by the kernel and the background processes for housekeeping. Rollback segment entries are written for every transaction processed by ORACLE and at times this can cause contention in the buffers containing the rollback segment blocks.

You can use the SQL*DBA MONITOR STATISTICS CACHE command to check for contention for all buffers in cache. Check the *buffer busy waits* against the sum of *db block gets* and *consistent gets*. If you find that the *buffer busy waits* ratio is >15% then it is possible that buffer contention is affecting performance. The next step is to examine the type of block which is the cause of contention by querying the table V$WAITSTAT. If you find that it is the buffer block containing the rollback segments that is the cause of contention then you must create more rollback segments.

The addition of multiple rollback segments reduces the possibility of locking contention and hence enhances performance. Use the SQL statement CREATE ROLLBACK SEGMENT to create a rollback segment. Spread the rollback segments across several disks if possible to minimize I/O contention. You may use the formula shown below as a rough guideline to decide on the number of rollback segments on a ORACLE system.

Rollback Segment = No. of users/4

Please note that if the number of users are less than 16 then there should be at least four rollback segments for optimal performance.

Ensure that all rollback segments are of the same size
It is vital that all rollback segments are of the same size especially in a shared environment where a large number of users are accessing the database. Oracle writes to the rollback segments evenly despite their size; if one rollback segment is smaller than the others it will wrap round first and overwrite old rollback information – despite the amount of unused space in bigger rollback segments.

Use large rollback segments to support long transaction queries
In a shared environment, the use of large rollback segments is recommended to sustain long running transactions. This enables the system to construct read consistent data from very old rollback information.

Use small rollback segments for better caching performance
For better caching performance use smaller rollback segments to support short transactions. This is because smaller segments are likely to remain in the database buffer pool (cache) for a greater length of time. It is also important that the buffer is large enough to cache these segments.

Understanding and enhancing the performance of the buffer cache (buffer pool)

The buffer cache in ORACLE is used to store the copies of newly modified database blocks. The background process DBWR is responsible for writing the buffers from the buffer pool to the disk. The buffer manager maintains a list of most recently used buffer and the least recently used buffer. The top half stores information on the most recently used buffers and the bottom half the least recently used buffer (LRU).

On the execution of an SQL statement, the top half is searched first to see if the block is already in the buffer cache. Only when it fails to locate it in the buffer pool does it go through the list of LRU buffers. If a free buffer is found, the database block is read into that buffer and the buffer is moved to the top of the buffer list. Over a period of time the least recently used buffers are moved to the bottom of the list and cleared by the background process DBWR. Its contents are then written to the disk and the buffer is declared free.

To view the buffer manager statistics (physical read, physical writes, and the busy buffer waits), you may use the SQL*DBA command, MONITOR STATISTICS CACHE. A high value in the *buffer busy waits* column indicates that there are a number of users trying to access the same block at the same time. You must then reduce the number of rows per block to enhance performance. By doing so you will minimize the chances of different transactions accessing the same buffer block at the same time.

Increasing the number of database buffers
An increase in the size of database buffers will enable you to obtain optimal performance from your ORACLE system providing the paging activity generated as a result of the increase is kept to a minimum. The number of buffers are directly related to the amount of data that can be cached.

The default number of buffer under V6 is 32. As a rough guide allocate 1000 DB_BLOCK_BUFFERS per 100Mb of database storage.

Understanding and optimizing the performance of DBWR process

As mentioned above, the database writer (DBWR) is a background process responsible for the transfer of buffers from the buffer pool to the disk. The buffer manager maintains a list of most recently used buffer and the *least recently used* (LRU) buffer. ORACLE parameters associated with the cleaning and tuning operation of the DBWR process are shown below.

DB_BLOCK_MAX_MOD_PCT
The DBWR process starts cleaning the buffers once the user process has passed the number of ineligible buffers specified by the INIT.ORA parameter DB_BLOCK_MAX_MOD_PCT in its search of a free buffer.

DB_BLOCK_MAX_CLEAN_PCT
The buffer search begins from the bottom of the list and continues until the number of buffers specified by the parameter has been cleaned.

DB_BLOCK_MAX_SCAN_PCT

The search is stopped once it has scanned the number of buffers specified by the parameter DB_BLOCK_MAX_SCAN_PCT. The DBWR process has to wait until a clean buffer becomes available for its use.

DB_BLOCK_TIMEOUT_WRITE_PCT

Specifies the number of buffers to be cleaned at time-outs (ie when the database is idle). **Please note** that since the introduction of version 6.027 of ORACLE RDBMS, The workings of the DBWR process has been greatly enhanced and the process now requires very little attention.

DBWR tuning strategy

Your tuning strategy should be to keep an adequate supply of free buffers available for user processes. Do not allow the system to run out of the free buffer space. Use the SQL*DBA MONITOR STATISTICS CACHE command to check the DBWR statistics.

- **dbwr free needed** - should be kept low, ideally zero.
- **dbwr free buffer waits** - should also be kept low, ideally zero.

If the above two values are not zero, then you *should* consider increasing the value of DB_BLOCK_MAX_CLEAN_PCT, but the number of buffers the DBWR process cleans in each pass should be kept to the minimum required. This will ensure that the DBWR process is not contending with the user processes and locking the LRU list unnecessarily. The following statistics should be kept low and may require the adjustment of the parameters described above:

- buffers scanned
- buffers inspected

You may also increase the value of INIT.ORA parameter DB_BLOCK_WRITE_BATCH to reduce the frequency with which user processes signal DBWR to clean the dirty buffers and also increase the number of blocks it attempts to write. Under OpenVMS it enables the DBWR process to write several blocks in parallel to different disks in a single I/O. A value that is too high may force the users to wait for the block to become available and cause unnecessary delays. The default value of this parameter is 8 and the maximum is 128.

Assign separate tablespace for temporary segments

The assignment of tablespace within ORACLE should be based on knowledge of the application and data. Assign separate tablespace for temporary segments and the creation of database objects.

Spread data across several disks using striping

Striping is the process of separating data stored in large ORACLE tables into small but manageable portions and storing these portions in separate database files across several disks. This enables different processes simultaneous access to different parts of the table without causing disk contention. Striping is especially useful in a shared environment and can enhance the performance of the application using that data.

To create a striped table, first create a tablespace with the SQL statement CREATE TABLESPACE with the DATAFILE clause then create the table with the CREATE TABLE statement using the TABLESPACE and the STORAGE clause. Ensure that each of the datafiles is on a separate disk.

Making efficient use of SQL for optimal performance

SQL is a very flexible and powerful language, it enables you to achieve the same results using a wide variety of constructs. Care is required when writing SQL code, especially if you require better performance, because ORACLE may process one SQL statement considerably faster than the other. ORACLE optimizer examines every SQL statement executed by you or your program and selects the best possible path of execution. The path it chooses depends upon the syntax of your SQL statement, the column names associated with your WHERE clause (conditions), the indexes and your database structures. As mentioned above, use the EXPLAIN PLAN statement in conjunction with the SQL trace facility to determine which statement is more efficient.

Use array processing to reduce SQL statement execution overhead

Array processing enables an application to execute an SQL statement many times with a solitary call to RDBMS and hence reduces the overhead associated with the number of calls to the RDBMS. This is not possible without array processing where all statements are passed to the RDBMS for a connection. The problem is worsened if your application is communicating with the RDBMS engine over the network.

Some ORACLE tools such as SQL*Forms, SQL*Plus, SQL*Loader and the export/import utilities take advantage of array processing automatically. All these tools give you the option of changing the default size of arrays. Notice that the reduction in the overhead described above is directly associated with the size of the array. An array size of 100 is usually sufficient for most applications.

Remove all table lock SQL statements from your V5 programs if you have upgraded

If any of your version 5.1 programs still have LOCK TABLE statements then you should remove those immediately and benefit from the row level locking available in V6 and V7. If you are using V6 or above then ensure the following two INIT.ORA parameters are set to their default values.

Table 34.1   INIT.ORA parameters

Parameter Name	Default Value
SERIALIZABLE	FALSE
ROW_LOCKING	ALWAYS

You may use the SQL*DBA command MONITOR LOCK to view the locking activity.

Use SEQUENCE numbers to reduce serialization

Those who are using ORACLE applications in a shared environment and have upgraded to V6 or above, must remove all reference to serialization and use SEQUENCE numbers for faster access. You can use the CREATE SEQUENCE statement to generate a sequence. Using this statement you can also specify the number of sequence values that can be stored in the cache. The default is 20.

Sequencing reduces locking contention and enhances the performance of INSERT statements. The ORACLE INIT.ORA parameter SEQUENCE_CACHE_ENTRIES controls the number of entries that can be stored in the cache. If a reference is made to an entry which is not in the cache then a disk I/O is performed. For optimal performance ensure your cache is large enough to hold all the entries. The default value of this parameter is 10.

Enhancing performance with the use of indexes

Indexes, if used appropriately, enable you to hike the performance of queries. Indexes are created with the SQL statement CREATE INDEX. Within RDBMS you may create and drop indexes at any time without changing the application programs using those tables. Indexes can be created using single columns and multiple columns where more than one column is used to form an index. Guidelines in this section will enable you to choose the appropriate columns for indexing and also make efficient use of indexes.

Choosing columns to index

When deciding to choose columns for indexing, ensure that you select the columns (fields) that are being used more often with the WHERE clause; columns which are used more often to join tables; columns which are unique (ie no two rows in a table may contain the same value in the indexed column); columns which are often used with the SQL functions such as MIN or MAX. **Please note** that it is not worth creating indexes for very small tables. You can examine the number of blocks that a table is occupying using the ROWID clause. If a table is occupying less than 10 blocks it is not worth creating an index for that table.

Only use indexes for queries that will select less than 25% of a table's rows

It is important that you know your data because such knowledge will enable you to write efficient SQL code. If the resultant query is to retrieve greater than the 25% of data from the table it is not worth using the index, especially if there are other columns in the SELECT clause which are not the part of the index.

Separate indexes from data

For better performance, separate the tables data from the indexes which are accessed often. It enables you to distribute the I/O load across separate disks. This is achieved with the use of the SQL statements CREATE TABLESPACE, CREATE TABLE and CREATE INDEX. The procedure is shown below:

1. Create two tablespaces using the CREATE TABLESPACE and DATAFILE clause on two separate disks.

2. Create the table using the TABLESPACE clause and the first tablespace.

3. Create the index using the CREATE INDEX statement, TABLESPACE clause and the second tablespace.

To change the tablespace for an existing index, drop the existing index and recreate it on the wanted tablespace.

Create concatenated indexes for better performance

Two or more data columns can be combined together to form a concatenated index. A concatenated index provides you a greater degree of selectively. Use the SQL statement CREATE INDEX to create a concatenated index. When deciding on columns which are to form the part of the concatenated index, place the most frequently used column first in the CREATE INDEX statement. A concatenated index can also be used to store additional information; this eliminates the need to retrieve data from the tables if the query refers to all the columns referenced as part of the index.

Note: The 'WHERE' statement must refer to the first column of the concatenated index to force ORACLE to use the index. If the first column is not the first part of the WHERE clause then a full table scan is performed.

Use index column names with your WHERE clause

To avoid a full table scan use index column names with your WHERE clause. Once ORACLE has recognized that you are using an index column it will search for the desired value in the index block and retrieve all records satisfying the criteria. See example below for details:

```
SELECT ...
FROM STUDENT
WHERE SURNAME = 'JONES'
```

In this example as soon as ORACLE has recognized that SURNAME is an index column it will act upon it and search the index column to retrieve all records that match the value 'JONES' from the student database.

Define columns (table items) as NOT NULL

This increases the likelihood of an index being used for queries.

Avoid the use of 'IS NULL' or 'IS NOT NULL' phrase with your WHERE clause

The two examples given below illustrate their use. It is assumed that an index exists on the GRANT column and you wish to extract the records of all students who are receiving a grant.

▸ **Example 1**

```
SELECT ....
FROM STUDENT
WHERE GRANT IS NOT NULL
```

In this example the index column GRANT is not used but a full table scan is performed. Please note that a full table scan is preferred if your statement will extract approximately a third of the records within the database. That is why it is important for you to know your data before executing such statements.

▸ **Example 2**

```
SELECT ...
FROM STUDENT
WHERE GRANT >=0
```

This query will ensure that an index column is searched.

Use unique indexes where possible

With unique indexes, no two rows in a column contain the same value in the index column. When a query refers to more than one index column, ORACLE uses the unique index to drive the query in order to avoid the merge and give faster performance.

Avoid the use of more than five WHERE clauses within a given SELECT clause

Within ORACLE a maximum of five indexes are merged. If your SELECT statement contains more than five WHERE clauses ORACLE will merge as many as five indexes, but will then proceed to check the remaining data manually to retrieve the desired rows as specified.

Suppress the use of least valuable indexes if your query contains more than five indexes

Please note that the use of too many indexes may actually degrade

263

the performance especially if you are using more than five index columns. Sometimes it is useful to suppress the use of least valuable indexes within your query by the use of dummy functions or expressions for the column on which you wish to suppress the index usage. To suppress the index for a numeric column add a zero and to suppress the index for a character column add a null string. See the example below for details.

```
SELECT ...
FROM STUDENT
WHERE DEPTNUM + 0 = 4
AND SURNAME = 'JONES'
```

35

Tips to Optimize Rdb Applications

Guidelines to optimize Rdb RDBMS

To get the most out of your Rdb RDBMS follow the guidelines given below:

1. Familiarize yourself with the Rdb/VMS monitoring tools listed below:

   MONITOR, ACCOUNTING, DCL, RMU/ANALYZE, RMU/ SHOW STATISTICS, Rdb/VMS Logical Names.

2. Develop a good understanding of your logical and physical database design and the applications which access that data.

3. Develop a good understanding of the internals of the RDBMS (logicals and the parameters associated with it). Remember, database tuning is much more beneficial than system tuning. More explicit knowledge of the data and how it is being utilized is required.

Only once you have developed a good understanding of all the topics listed above will you be able to apply the following techniques to improve its efficiency.

Redirect your temporary work files using the logical RDMS$BIND_WORK_FILE

By default, all temporary work files are placed in the SYS$LOGIN or the SYS$SCRATCH directory. SYS$SCRATCH is the same device and directory as SYS$LOGIN. For greater efficiency, distribute these work files on as many spindles as possible.

These files are deleted once the query is completed. You can further improve the performance of these files by using /BUFFER_COUNT and /BLOCK_COUNT qualifiers with the DCL command SET RMS_DEFAULT. You can use the DCL command DEFINE to assign logical names for sort, work, and journal files.

By default only two sort work files are used, the maximum is 10. Using the logical RDMS$BIND_SORT_WORKFILES you can specify the number of work files a sort will use. Each sort work file can individually be controlled by the logical SORTWORK n, where n indicates the number of a work file. If you wish you can place each work file on a separate disk.

Better performance may be achieved with the use of buffering, both local and global

Buffering enables you to make efficient use of available memory and provides faster access to data. With local buffering, user-private buffers are maintained for each process on a system. Even to read the same page, each process has to read that page from the disk in its own buffer area, whereas pages in the global buffer area can be used by more than one process on a system. Local buffering is enabled by default. To enable global buffering use the SQL statement CREATE or ALTER DATABASE with the parameter GLOBAL BUFFERS ARE ENABLED. Global buffers are in effect on a per node basis.

Please note that you can change the value of global buffers on a node using the /GLOBAL_BUFFERs= qualifiers with the RMU/OPEN command. See Chapter 21 for more details on local and global buffering.

To increase the buffer size use the SQL statement CREATE or ALTER DATABASE with the parameter BUFFER SIZE IS. The value specified is applicable to local as well as global buffers. The default is six blocks. For a database with many tables, choose a buffer size which is divisible by all page sizes for all storage areas. This will ensure that effective use of allocated memory is made and none is wasted.

Be careful when assigning buffer values. If the BUFFER POOL is too large, it will induce page faulting. If the value is too small, the database will have to perform more disk I/Os. To monitor buffer cache effectiveness use the command RMU/SHOW STATISTICS PIO.

Calculate the effectiveness using the following formula:

(Ttl No. found in Pool/Ttl No. buffer pool searches)* 100

Any increase in the size of buffer cache requires you to adjust several UAF and system parameters to handle the increased memory requirements. These parameters are shown below along with some suggested values where appropriate.

WSDEFAULT, WSQUOTA, WSEXTENT, BYTLM, PGFLQUOTA, DIOLM, ASTLM, ENQLM and the SYSGEN parameter VIRTUALPAGECNT.

- Set DIOLM to greater than, or equal to the number of database buffers.
- Set ASTLM to the value of DIOLM + 12.

Note: Watch for excessive page faulting. Increase the limit of the working set size to reduce fragmentation.

You may also alter the value associated with the logical RDM$BIND_BUFFERS. The value associated with this logical enables you to specify the amount of memory available to your process for matching operations. The default value is 10,000 bytes and the maximum is 65,000.

Specify a larger value to eliminate the need for Rdb to use temporary disk files. Please note that you cannot specify a value greater than the UAF parameter PGFLQUOTA.

RDM$BIND_BUFFERS is a very powerful and flexible tuning tool. Using this logical name you can define different sets of buffers to suit your batch and interactive session needs. You may define a different value for your batch programs that run in the evening at off-peak hours and a different value to suit your interactive require-ments. You can also define this logical at a system level to affect a large number of user processes.

By default segmented strings are stored in the RDB$SYSTEM storage area

The benefit of greater efficiency may be obtained by specifying a large buffer value for segmented strings using the logical RDMS$BIND_SEGMENTED_STRING_BUFFER.

As a consequence of this increase, if you find that processes are page faulting heavily check their working set size and increase it to reduce excessive page faulting.

You will need to increase the value of UAF parameters WSDEFAULT, WSQUOTA and WSEXTENT.

If you are transferring large data blocks to or from the database

Increase the size of RDB$REMOTE_BUFFER_SIZE logical to 10,000 bytes. The default value is 2048. Local and remote nodes determine the size of this buffer but you only need to define it for the local node.

Overheads of maintaining indexes is quite high

Remove indexes which are unused by standard reports and concatenate indexes where possible to reduce overheads.

Unlike other RDBMSs Rdb provides you with the option of specifying the index usage. If the index is to be used for loading data, specify the usage as update. If the index is to be used for queries, specify the usage as query. Query sets the fullness percentage to 100 and update sets it to 70% reducing the possibility of fragmented tables. Use the RMU/ANALYZE/INDEXES and RMU/ANALYZE/PLACEMENT commands to find out physical information about index levels and the maximum and average number of index records searched to get to the data row.

For optimum performance, define indexes after the rows are loaded into the database. If you define indexes before the loading of the data, the database load program can result in poor performance. If possible, sort the records by the primary key before they are loaded into the database using the RMU/LOAD/PLACE command. It ensures maximum efficiency because the records are physically adjacent to one another. Avoid duplicate keys whenever possible.

Do not commit every single row addition, this keeps the .RUJ file from becoming too big

By default, updated pages are written to the disk as soon as you issue a COMMIT statement. With fast commit transaction processing, updated pages are kept in the buffer pool until a checkpoint is reached. To enable fast commit processing use the SQL statement ALTER DATABASE with the qualifier FAST COMMIT ENABLED. You may also use the RDO CHANGE DATABASE statement with the above qualifier. Use the SQL statement SHOW TRANSACTION to see if fast processing is enabled.

Cluster records together – especially if you are frequently performing join operations over several tables

This will help reduce the number of I/Os required to satisfy your requests and enhance performance. Clustering is done using the PLACEMENT VIA INDEX clause of the SQL CREATE STORAGE MAP statement. When clustering, pay careful attention to storage area parameters such as allocation and page size to avoid degradation in performance due to fragmentation and page overflows.

You can use the RMU/ANALYZE command to determine fragmentation. If you find evidence of fragmentation then you must make these areas contiguous using the SQL statement CREATE STORAGE AREA or RDO DEFINE STORAGE AREA statement. Then you must map all rows to the new storage area using the SQL statement ALTER STORAGE MAP.

Examine your DECLARE/SET TRANSACTION statements to ensure that they allow maximum concurrency

The default is read/write and shared write. Set the transaction to read only and the access mode to shared read for transactions only reading the table. This will lower the locking contention and increase the concurrency, giving you better performance.

Check your deadlocks by reducing the value of the SYSGEN parameter DEADLOCK_WAITS

The default value is 10. Do not lower it to a value less than the number of nodes in a cluster, plus 1. On an SMP machine do not lower it to a value that is less than the number of CPUs plus 1. You can also specify an application-specific wait interval using the SQL SET TRANSACTION or RDO DECLARE TRANSACTION statement. Use the SQL SET TRANSACTION statement to specify exclusive a write option which does not incur the overhead of maintaining locks and writing to the .SNP file. It minimizes these activities and enhances performance.

Turn off the adjustable lock granularity (ALG) if you find many applications stalled in the RMU/SHOW STATISTICS display

This then enables Rdb to use low-level locking. Rdb uses ALG to maintain as few locks as possible. It locks rows of data in the anticipation that additional rows, which may be accessed later, are included in the group. Only enable ALG if transactions need to access clustered data. It then ensures that the maximum number of rows can be accessed with the minimum number of locks. ALG is enabled by default.

Use the SQL ALTER DATABASE statement to disable ALG. You may also specify ADJUSTABLE LOCKING GRANULARITY IS DISABLED to disable ALG before creating the database.

Examine the access strategy of your SQL statements before implementing it in a live environment

To display the access method used and the number of solutions tried and rejected by the optimizer define the logical RDMS$DEBUG_FLAGS as S0.

Use RDM$BIND_RUJ_EXTEND_BLKCNT logical to pre-extend .RUJ files

The default is 100 blocks. Maximum is 10,000. It enables you to reduce the number of extents on a database table. Use the logical RDMS$RUJ to locate this file to a less utilized disk. Default directory is SYS$LOGIN. You can define the logical at the system, group or process level.

Use RDM$BIND_CKPT_TRANS_LIMIT

In Rdb you can use the RDM$BIND_CKPT_TRANS_LIMIT logical to assign the number of transactions as a process specific checkpoint trigger as opposed to AIJ block size limit or the time interval. Note that the growth of the .AIJ file is directly related to the number of checkpoints set using the time interval in seconds and/or the number of transactions.

Re-direct the location of bugcheck dump files to a less utilized disk

The default is the SYS$LOGIN directory. To achieve this redefine the logical RDM$BUGCHECK_DIR. You can also disable the bugcheck by directing the output to a null (NL:) device.

Move your .AIJ file

Move your .AIJ (after image journal) file to a less utilized disk using the RDO CHANGE DATABASE statement. This file should be on a separate disk from the .RDA, .RDB and .SNP files. Allocate an adequate amount of disk space for the .AIJ file using the SQL statement 'JOURNAL ALLOCATION IS' and 'JOURNAL EXTENT IS'. This will ensure that transactions do not need to wait for the allocation of extents.

Disable snapshots

Disable snapshots if the database is not being used in a multi-user environment. Do not incur the overhead of writing to the snapshot file when not necessary. If the snapshots are needed, consider moving the snapshot file to a less utilized disk, but away from .RDA, .RDB, and .AIJ files.

Store historical data

Store historical data into separate tables and make these tables read-only tables to reduce locking contention. Store these tables on a separate disk from the normal data. You may also extract inactive data from your tables and store that separately – this way you can maintain your primary data at its optimum efficiency.

Declare the static data tables as read only tables to minimize locking contention. You can use the SQL ALTER DATABASE statement to achieve this.

36   Tips to Optimize INGRES
                                Applications

Some suggestions to optimize **INGRES** applications

It is assumed that you are familiar with the internals of RDBMS in general and you also possess a very good understanding of INGRES RDBMS and the tools associated with it. Tuning guidelines in this chapter are discussed under the terminology used within INGRES. They are not described in the order of any importance and most of the points mentioned in the two previous chapters are also relevant to INGRES RDBMS as well.

Disk cluster sizes

INGRES works more efficiently with disk cluster sizes of 4, 8, 16 and 32. As a general rule, use a disk cluster size of 4 for small tables and 8 for large tables.

Checkpoints

The II_CHECKPOINT logical specifies the device on which database checkpoints are to reside. Additional locations can also be specified. Under OPENVMS, tape devices can also be used but are not recommended if optimal performance is desired. Checkpoint files have an extension of .CKP. For optimum performance locate these files on a separate device from your data and journal files.

Logfile

II_LOG_FILE is the logical that specifies the location of the logfile for INGRES under OPENVMS. This is one of the most important files within INGRES. The file name is INGRES_LOG.SYSTEM on a single node system and INGRES_LOG.SYSTEM_nodename in a cluster. The logfile records all changes to the database during the database operation, which is followed by a transaction complete stamp after a commit. It is circular in fashion with a logical begin and logical end, and is divided into blocks with special dividers called consistency points which define the size of the blocks and the frequency with which they are written.

As a rule of thumb, a value of 5% is typical for a logfile of 64 Mb. Use a figure of 10% for a smaller file. Consistency points determine the frequency at which log file transactions are journalled and removed. A low value such as 2 will speed up the frequency at which the log file is maintained

Points to remember

- As a general rule the LOGFILE should be kept as big as possible. The actual size for your system will depend on the size of tables and transaction sizes.

- It is vital that this file should have its own standalone device, if not, then you must assign the disk which is least used on your system.

- Allocate more than one device if possible using the logical names.

- Keep a logfile tidy and clean. It is important that the users should close the cursors and commit transactions, as badly handled transactions can block other processes and can even dangle the whole of the INGRES environment.

Journal file

II_JOURNAL specifies the name of the device on which journal log files are stored. Additional devices can also be used. Journal files have an extension of .JNL. They store the transactions journals maintained by the INGRES archiver. The archiver is used to reclaim space from the log file and is activated when a set number of consistency points are reached. Once invoked, it removes all committed transactions from the log file and writes them to the journal file and in the process releases space in the log file. Journal files grow in size until a CKPDB creates a new file. Always backup old files on to a magnetic tape.

Points to remember

- Place journal, checkpoints, data and log files on separate devices.

Dump file

II_DUMP defines the location of the dump file. It is used to record changes to the database in conjunction with the checkpoint. Although the same disk as II_CHECKPOINT can be used it is recommended that you place this file on a separate or a lightly loaded disk. Please note that you can define additional dump locations as well.

4GL code and development directory

ING_ABFDIR defines the name of the directory where all 4GL objects and immediate code is stored when an application is being developed. If possible, specify a separate device from the data device to reduce the I/O contention on the data device.

The executable code

The II_SYSTEM logical defines the location of executable code within INGRES. This device will contain files accessed by INGRES during normal activity. Most of the INGRES main run-time images are installed at start-up time. For good performance you must bear the following points in mind when allocating a device for the INGRES EXECUTABLES.

Points to remember

- Ensure that the executable code is on a separate disk from the data and journal file.

- Select a low I/O throughput disk and regard it as if it were a system disk.

Placement of databases

II_DATABASE defines the default location for database data files. It is also used to store the master database IIDBDB. For good performance it is advised that additional devices are used to store database tables and server sort files, but IIDBDB must reside on

II_DATABASE. For tables it is often better to use smaller faster disks to distribute the I/O load than one large disk. If your disk containing the master database and the tables is being saturated with disk I/O requests then you must consider separating tables from the master database IIDBDB.

Temporary work files

Always include space for temporary files when allocating disk space for end users. Temporary files reside in the users default directory or in the temporary directory defined by II_TEMPORARY, or in the II_WORKDIR_xx_NN logical. These files are deleted once a transaction is completed. Temporary files are required for SQL/QUEL commands (such as create table, copy table, update, and modify), sort files, aggregate temporary files and fronted files.

Performance consideration for a LAVC

For satellite nodes consider using client–server installations to reduce traffic on the Network Interconnect (NI), rather than a full node cluster installation. Install local page/swap files on satellite nodes to reduce the amount of ethernet traffic and give a better response time.

Setting up user accounts

Some of the UAF parameters which are essential for the optimal performance of INGRES are described below along with their recommended values.

Table 36.1   UAF parameters which are essential for the optimal performance of INGRES

UAF Parameter	Comments	Min. Rec'd Value
BYTLM	used for DCL symbol and other process components.	50,000
ENQLM	defines the maximum number of locks a process can hold. INGRES locks are mapped one-to-one to OPENVMS locks.	250
WSQUOTA		Depends upon the table size and transaction sizes.
WSEXTENT		Same as above.
PGFLQUOTA		50,000

SYSGEN parameters

It is recommended that you tune your OPENVMS system twice (before and after you install INGRES). If your system is not performing well before the RDBMS is installed, then the performance of the INGRES system will also be bad. So it is vital that you tune your system before installing INGRES and then apply changes for INGRES to run and work in an optimum fashion. Some of the important SYSGEN parameters which can significantly affect the performance of INGRES are shown in Table 36.2.

Table 36.2   Parameters which can significantly affect the performance of INGRES

SYSGEN Parameter Name	Recommended Values
LRPCOUNT	50
SRPCOUNT	1500
CHANNELCNT	2047
VIRTUALPAGECNT	50000
WSMAX	8000
PQL_DENQLM	250
PQL_DBYTLM	50,000
PQL_DPGFLQUOTA	50,000

INGRES Server Parameters

INGRES servers are detached processes which allow multiple user connections. There are a number of factors which influence the amount of resources needed, such as number of databases to be opened, number of users connected to INGRES and the tasks users perform. These parameters are defined in the INGRES server start-up command file:

[INGRES.UTILITY]IIRUNDBMS.COM

There are several server parameters within INGRES but this section only introduces those which may assist you in obtaining maximum throughput.

Table 36.3   INGRES Server Parameters

/FAST_COMMIT/WRITE_BEHIND/SOL_SERVER	On a single node are set by default. These do not apply to a cluster environment where the database may be accessed from more than one node.
/FAST_COMMIT	Use this parameter for high throughput transaction system where multiple users are accessing a common database. Should be used in conjunction with /WRITE_BEHIND.
/SOLE_SERVER	Reduces the overhead of maintaining multiple database access threads by disabling connection requests from other servers.
/SHARED_CACHE	Enables multiple servers to share a common cache. This cache uses the pagefile as a backing storage.
/EXTENT	Defines the working set size of a server. Should be equal to the SYSGEN parameter WSMAX.
/SESSION_ACCOUNTING	Used for generating accounting statistics. It is recommended that you do not use this parameter as it can seriously degrade the performance of the servers.

Storage structures

There are four storage structures that INGRES uses to store its data. Choosing the appropriate data storage structure can reduce locking contention, save disk space and enhance performance. These storage structures are described below.

Table 36.4   Storage structures

HEAP	This is the default data storage structure. There are no indices, and as a result, queries scan the entire table (every page). There is one main page, and all the others are overflow pages. Do not use this type of data structure for large tables where fast access is required. This type of storage uses a minimum amount of disk space.
HASH	This structure uses an algorithm to control the position of rows in a table, rather than using an index structure. Use this type of storage where a great deal of direct access is required, but not where a scan of the entire table is required. It is fastest on whole key lookups (ie exact matches) but duplicate keys can slow the performance because of overflows. You can also preallocate disk space using this type of structure but can also waste disk space.
ISAM	Tables with this type of storage, structures are sorted by the value of keyed columns. An index is built to point to a page, based on a key value. Use this type of storage structure for small static tables, where direct access is required. Please note that too many appends/inserts may cause overflows and result in poor performance.

Chapter 36

Table 36.4   (continued) Storage structures

BTREE	The BTREE storage structure is similar to the ISAM. However, the index structure is dynamic. Use this type of data storage structure for rapidly changing tables where a direct or sequential access is required. The chances of the overflows is less likely unless there is high key duplicity. It is faster if you are planning to join the entire tables.

INGRES monitoring and control utilities

INGRES also has its own monitoring utility called interactive performance monitor (IPM) which is now available as a supported tool from INGRES release 6.4. It is completely menu driven and enables you to monitor:

- log statistics
- lock statistics
- individual database/user/table activity.

Those using previous releases of INGRES can access these individual utilities from within OPENVMS. See the relevant INGRES manual for details.

Testing applications

When testing programs for efficiency start the INGRES servers with the options /SESSION_ACCOUNTING and /CPU_STATISTICS.

This will force it to send a record to the OPENVMS accounting file when a user session is terminated. You may then extract records from the accounting file pertaining to specific users and obtain CPU and DISK I/O statistics including the front-end and back-end I/Os.

General index

A

ACCOUNTING 214
ACL 208
Adjustable Lock Granularity 270
ALL-IN-1 106, 202, 223, 224, 225, 226,
        227, 228, 229, 230
Alpha 71
AUTOGEN 9, 17, 63, 113, 131, 158,
        161, 214–219, 233
    and SYSGEN 215, 219
    some useful commands 215, 216
    using for first time 216
    warnings 218
Automatic Working Set Adjustment 61
Automatic Working Set Decrementing 37
AWSA 61

B

BACKUP.SYS 141, 144
Backups 138, 209
    and CONTIN.SYS 143
    tuning procedures 138
        and BYTLM 139
        and DIOLM 139
        and FILLM 139
BADBLK.SYS 141
BADBLKSYS 143
Balance set
    slots 52
    swapping 19, 53
BASIC 203
Batch jobs 206
    and batch queues 62, 205
    and indexed files 169
    and swapping 51
    changing characteristics 26
    forcing jobs via batch queues 205

queues 25
queues/quota values 26
to reduce CPU workload 205
Batch processes
    and QUANTUM 210
BITMAP CACHE 110
Bitmap cache 146, 147
    and BITMAP.SYS 106
BITMAP.SYS 141, 143, 146
Bucket sizes 207
Bucket split 170
Buffer wait rate 122
Buffering
    checking buffer settings 156
    index files 156
Buffers
    and process working set quotas 156
    and the three types of file 156
    global buffers 157, 162, 163
        allocating 157
        and GBLPAGES 159
        and GBLPAGFIL 160
        and GBLSECTIONS 159
        and LOCKIDTBL 161
        and RESHASHTBL 161
        and RMS_GBLBUFQUO 158, 159
        and SYSMWCNT 160
        and VIRTUALPAGECNT 160
        parameters controlling 158
    local buffers 156

C

Cache
    adjusting parameters 113
    and SYSGEN parameters 111
    BITMAP CACHE 110
    directory caches 137
    DIRECTORY DATA CACHE 110
    DIRECTORY FCB CACHE 110
    EXTENT CACHE 110

FILE HEADER CACHE 110
FILE ID CACHE 110
hit rate 111
    and AUTOGEN 113
    low hit rate 113
    measuring performance 111
modified page list 15
QUOTA CACHE 110
secondary 13
    and free page list 13
COMO state 50
CONTIN.SYS 141, 143
CORIMG.SYS 141, 144
CPU 175
    Alpha AXP 176, 177, 179
        performance 177
    and COM or COMO states 204
    bottlenecks 197
    calculating busy percentage 201
    checking utilization 197, 204
    idle time 197
    interrupts 202
    management programs 175
    modes 201
        activity in interrupt mode, 208
        and PATHWORKS 240
        COMPATIBILITY mode 203
        EXECUTIVE mode 202
        IDLE TIME mode 204
        INTERRUPT stack mode 202
        INTERRUPT mode and TCP/IP 231
        KERNEL mode 202, 210
            and TCP/IP 231
        MP SYNCHRONIZATION mode 203
        SUPERVISOR mode 203
            and DCL procedures 208
        USER mode 203
    optimization 205
        and pagefaulting 206
        and X-Windows 236
        reducing overhead 207
    processes and time 200

    relative lock cost 194

speed (capacity) comparisons 176
utilization 232
Credit waits 103

D

Data access
    and fragmented files 145
Data bus contention 102
Data transfer
    and busy drives/interface cards 102
    rate of 103
        and striping 123
Database *(see the 'RDBMS' entry)*
Database management 245
Dead page table 36, 37
    reducing scans 37
Deadlock searches 209
Direct memory access 208
Directory and file structures 109
Disk
    achieving high throughput 86
    and caches 109
    average response times 87
    blocks 147
    causes of high response time 87
    checking files open 101
    components of a transfer 67
    disk blocks 109
        logical block numbers 109
    distributing I/O load 101
    dual ported 103
    finding files open 90
    fragmentation 67, 83, 93, 134, 141 *(see also the 'Fragmentation' entry)*
        and backups 138
        and BYTLM parameter 139
        and cache performance 112
        reasons for 146
        what is it 145
    getting read/write statistics 116

heavily used drives 102
hot disks 89
I/O limitations 83
    I/O operation rate 84, 86
    improving I/O performance 95
    investigating I/O problems 83
    problems and global buffers 97
    programs and I/O rate 90
    problem devices 89
I/Os and cache hit rates 111
identifying 'hot files' 101
initialization 133
    and 'Files–11' 141
load balancing 101
monitoring I/O 85
monitoring operation 84
performance 67
queue length 86, 88
    and I/O rate 88
    characteristics 86
quotas 110
RA90 116
RA-series 41, 85, 87
reducing I/O contention 123
relocating key files (I/O problems) 97
response time 87, 93
    and striping 123
    transfer/seek rates, rotational delay 67
selecting (factors in) 67, 69
shadowing 115
    host-based shadowing 78
space is not contiguous 93
virtual unit 123
volume shadowing 73
Disk cluster 105
    and BITMAP.SYS 105, 106
    and RWCLU wait state 186
    size
        and window turns 106
        care when setting 106
        checking size of (for mounted disks) 105
        disadvantage of large 106
        effect on performance 105
        setting size 105

Disk failures
    and volume shadowing 115
Disk files
    BITMAP.SYS (and clusters) 105
Disk I/O
    and global buffers 157
    improving 155
    reducing 13
Disk initialization 105
Disk load balancing 101
Disk space
    checking used and allocated 106
Disk striping 123
    and LBNs 123
    and performance 125
        bus bandwidth 126
        chunk size 126
        contiguous files 126
        disk controller 125
        first LBN 126
        parallel transfers 126
        separate controllers 126
    and VMS version 125
    striping driver 125
    types
        file-based 124, 125
        hardware-based 124
        VMS driver-based 124, 125
    vs file striping 125
Disk queue length 88
Dumpfile 42
    size and adding memory 59

E

ENQs 207
    and VUPs 195
Ethernet card 231
Executable image files 134
Extended addressing 29
Extent area 147

Extent cache 146, 147
Extent map 144
Extra fragment rate 122

F

File header 107
File lookups 110
File system 109
  caches 109, 111
    BITMAP CACHE 110
    performance 111
    the seven different 110
Files
  and deferred writes 168
  controlling number opened 139
  creating 110, 134, 166
  data access 109
  designing 165
    index file 165
  FDL files 167
  fill factors 170
  fragmentation 209, 233
    defined 146
  index files 167, 170, 207, 209
    temporary index files 166
  keys 165, 166
  monitoring access 101
  moving 101
  optimizing with EDIT/FDL/ANAL 167
  primary key 166
  records 109, 166
    linking 167
  with extreme growth rates 170
Files–11 ODS–2 141
Fragmentation 209
  and disk usage 148
  and extension headers 148
  and split I/Os 148
  curing 148
    and 'contiguous best try' 149

  and ACP cache parameters 152
  and RMS Buffering 152
  and RMS_EXTEND_SIZE 152
  and volume shadowing 152
  and window control block 151
  disks with different cluster sizes 151
  making files contiguous 150
  problems caused by 147
Fragmented Request Rate 122
Free list 13
  and BORROWLIM 14
  and FREEGOAL 14, 29
  and FREELIM 14
  and GROWLIM 14
  and soft faults 34
  and SWAPPER 14
  and swapper trimming 47
  and WSDEFAULT 14
  and WSEXTENT 14
  and WSQUOTA 14
  size and memory reclamation 28
Free page list 13
  and swapper trimming 47
  controlling size of 13

G

General block buffer cache 146
Global buffers 97 155 *(see the 'Buffers' entry)*
  for index files 97
  procedure for setting 98
Global section descriptors 6

H

Highwater marking
  disabling 131, 132
HSC controller 115
HSC K.DSI channels 103

HSC performance statistics 103
HSC software 116

I

I/O credit rating 102
I/O credits (defined) 102
I/O performance
    and HSC load balancing 102
Images 131
    frequently used/installing 54
    installed as shared 62, 129, 131
    shared and concurrent processes 130
Index buckets 129
Index file bitmap 142
Index file structure 141, 142
INDEXF.SYS 141, 145, 146
Interactive live users 62
Intermediate request packet (IRP) 5, 6, 7, 9

L

Large request packets (LRP) 5–7, 9, 231
LBN field 93
LBNs
    and disk striping 124
Load balancing 207
    and striping 123, 124
    chunk size for efficient 127
    HSC 102
Lock mastering 191
Lock modes 191
Locks
    and databases 270
    and resource blocks 191
    directory lookup 193
    handling locks within a cluster 195
    lock manager 192
    locking activity and CPU overhead 207

management of 193
output from MONITOR DLOCK 193
relative lock cost 194
remote lock requests 194
resource blocks
    three types 191
        local 191
        master 192
        process copy 192
Logical block numbers 124
Lookaside lists 6
    caches and VMS V5.5-n 5
    configuration and management 8
    SRP, IRP, LRP 5
    structure of 10
    SYSGEN parameters for 5
    uses of 5

M

Mapping pointers 143, 146
    per file 144
Mass Storage Control Protocol *(see 'MSCP')*
Master file directory (000000.DIR) 141
Memory
    adding and tuning (V5) 58
    adding and tuning (V6) 58
    and deferred writes 168
    and free page list 13
    and inducing swapping 53
    and modified page list 14
    and MPW_WAITLIMIT 185
    and processes 24
    and X-Windows 235
    boards 136
    breakdown of consumption 131
    checking amount available 24, 52
    estimating amount needed 57
    four major sections of 4
    installing 58
    management

and V5.5-n 28
and V6.0 29
management mechanism (AWSA) 21
mapping of 3
nonpage pool caches 207
nonpaged dynamic 4
    cache hit rate 113
nonpaged pool
    allocator and deallocator 8
    and data transfers 119
    and global buffers 158
    and OPENVMS 6.0 9
    reclamation (aggressive/gentle) 10
    structure of 5
paged dynamic 4, 6
    cache hit rate 113
pool management and SYSGEN 11
pool management, V6.0 8
proactive reclamation 28
processes residing in concurrently 19
reclamation (idle processes) 28
releasing for other processes 63
requirements and swapping 48
requirements and trimming 47
saving
    and global buffers 97
    and images 129
    and queues 62
steps to take if scarce 53
system pool areas
    and wait states 186
using efficiently 61
virtual memory 3, 31
virtual pages 3, 27

Memory management
    terminology 21
MFD 141, 145, 146
Modified page list 13, 14, 17
    and MPW_HILIMIT 15
    and MPW_IOLIMIT 16
    and MPW_LOLIMIT 15
    and MPW_LOWAITLIMIT 16

and MPW_THRESH 16
and MPW_WAITLIMIT 15
and swapper trimming 47
and VMS executive 14
reducing flushing 17
    and working set size 18
Modified page writer 16, 17
    and MPW_IOLIMIT 15
    parameters controlling 17
Modified page writing
    events that trigger 17
MODPARAMS.DAT 6, 18, 20, 25, 37, 42,
    43, 53, 55, 58, 59, 113, 131,
    161, 185, 186, 210, 215, 217,
    218, 219, 233
MSCP 121, 122
MSCP parameters
    MSCP_BUFFER 119
    MSCP_CREDITS 120
    MSCP_LOAD 119
    MSCP_SERVE_ALL 119
Mutual Exclusion Semaphore 188

O

OPCOM 6
Oracle *(see the 'RDBMS' entry)*
Outswapping 19

P

Page lists
    free and modified 13
Pagefaults 13, 27, 33
    and buffering 136
    and CPU utilization 206
    and pagefiles 43
    and virtual memory pages 31
    and wait states 185

calculating SYSMWCNT 35
checking rate of 32
excessive 28
removing excessive 232, 233
guidelines for acceptable rates 32
handler 3
hard faults 33, 34
  calculating rate of 34
  hard fault and soft fault compared 34
rates and CPU capacity 31
reasons for 31
reducing rate of 206
soft faults 33
  demand zero faults 33
  free list faults 34
  global valid faults 33
system types 35
Pagefiles
allocation 44
and contiguity 41, 95
and disk respone time 89
and dumpfile 42
and I/O problems 96
and swapping 55
and system performance 41
and wait states 183
  badly fragmented and wait states 184
  space in and wait states 184
checking space in 184
creating secondary 41, 42, 95, 96, 184
determining current usage 95
expanding 96
increasing primary 41, 42
reducing size of 43
relocation of 96
PATHWORKS 239
optimizing 240
Performance
reasons for poor 213
tuning 41
  adjusting disk buffers 136
  and bucket sizes 163
  and frequently used images 129

and memory 57
and MSCP_BUFFER 119
and RMS_EXTEND_SIZE 134
and swapfile space 54
and swapping 52
and swapper trimming 48
check free space 130
combining drives 129
contiguous image files 134
data buckets 164
disable ACP_DATACHECK 133
disable highwater marking 131
for X-Windows 235
image level accounting 131
index placement 133
optimize VMS libraries 135
optimizing PATHWORKS 239
reduce fragmentation 134
relink images 135
rewrite DCL procedures 135
RMS index files 134
and TCP/IP 231
the CPU 205
via SYSGEN parameters 213
PQL parameters
changing/privileges 27
Proactive memory reclamation 28
Processes
and low memory (WSQUOTA) 62
and maximum working set list 20
and pagefile allocation 44
and pagefile usage 44
and priorities 181
and section descriptors 20
and states (see also the 'Scheduling' entry)
and swapfile space 55
and swapper trimming 47
and swapping 48
and swapping out of memory 50
and virtual memory 31
and virtual pages 20
and WSQUOTA 23
concurrent in memory 29
detached 26

idle and memory 28
in outswapped state 49, 51
interactive 25
maximum and MAXPROCESSCNT 19
number of (adding pages) 24
pages owned in memory 21

Q

QUANTUM 23–4, 181–2, 209–10, 232, 233, 240
Queue length 87, 88
    and disk response times 89
QUOTA.SYS 141, 144

R

RA81 102
RA9 102
RAID devices 71
    development of 71
    the current position 78
    types of
        other 78
        RAID 0 72
        RAID 0+1 74
        RAID 1 73
        RAID 2 74
        RAID 3 74
        RAID 4 75
        RAID 5 76
        RAID 6 77
RDBMS 245, 246
    and database (table) fragmentation 251
    and global/local buffering 266
    database writer (DBWR) 257
        DB_BLOCK_MAX_CLEAN_PCT 257–8
        DB_BLOCK_MAX_MOD_PCT 257
        DB_BLOCK_MAX_SCAN_PCT 258
        DB_BLOCK_TIMEOUT_WRITE_PCT 258

tuning strategy 258
INGRES 273
    and checkpoints (.CKP files) 273
    and cluster sizes 273
    and dump files 275
    and executable code 275
    and journal files 274
    and location of database files 275
    and logfiles 273
    and monitoring and control 279
    and server parameters 277, 278
    and storage structures 278
    and SYSGEN 277
    and temporary work files 276
    and testing applications 279
    and UAF parameters 276
INGRES, ORACLE, SUPRA, SYBASE 245
Oracle 247, 248
    INIT.ORA 247, 248, 249, 250, 253, 254, 257
        and DB_BLOCK_WRITE_BATCH 258
        and SEQUENCE_CACHE_ENTRIES 260
        parameters for 260
    OPEN_CURSORS 250
        and CONTEXT_AREA 251
        and CONTEXT_INCR 251
    optimization and CREATE index 261, 262, 263, 264
    optimizing 249, 250
Oracle configuration 247
Rdb 265
    and .AIJ files 271
    and .RUJ files 269
    and index usage 268
    and locking 270
    and RDM$BIND_BUFFERS 267
    and RDMS$BIND_SORT_WORKFILES 266
    and RDMS$BIND_WORK_FILE 265
    and temporary work files 265
    optimizing Rdb applications 265
    Rdb/VMS monitoring 265
    record clustering 269
SQL 248
    ALTER DATABASE 269
    CREATE TABLESPACE 259
    efficient SQL parsing 250

EXPLAIN PLAN 249
optimizing the code 259
SET TRANSACTION 270
SQL*DBA 247, 248, 250, 253, 257, 258, 260
and rollback statistics 255
SQL*FORMS 248
SQL*PLUS 248
Record Management Services (RMS) 109, 141
Redistributing files 101
Relational databases *(see the 'RDBMS' entry)*
Requester card (HSC) 103
Retrieval pointers 107, 143
and fragmentation 147
RMS 109, 166
RMS buffering 83, 156
RMS FDL utility 134
RMS files 155, 207
RMS global buffers 157
RMS index files 113, 134
Rollback segments 247, 255
and user processes 255
optimizing 255, 256, 257
understanding/optimizing 254
RSTS/E 170

S

Scheduling
defined 181
states (wait states)
and CPU utilization 197
checking via system dump analyzer 182
computable: COM, COMO 182,197
current state (CUR) 182
involuntary wait states 181, 182
COLPG (collided page wait) 188
FPG (free page wait) 187
MUTEX (mutual exclusion semaphore) 188
PFW (page fault wait) 187
RWAST (AST wait) 186
RWCAP (CPU capability req'd) 186
RWCLU (cluster transition) 186
RWCSV (cluster server) 186
RWMBX (mailbox full) 185
RWMPB and RWMPE 183, 184
RWPAG and RWNPG 186
RWSCS (system communication services) 186
voluntary wait states 181, 182
SCSI connections
and RAID devices 78
SDA 7
Secondary cache 13, 34
determining size of 18
modified page list 15
Security 133
and highwater marking 132
risks and DCL procedures 135
Shadow disk 115
Shadow sets 102, 116-7
Small request packet (SRP) 5, 6, 9
Specmark 177
Split I/Os 107, 144
and fragmentation 148
Split Transfer Rate 88
SPM analysis 116
SPM SYSTEM_PC report 232
SQL *(see the 'RDBMS' entry)*
Storage Works 79, 80
Stripeset 123, 125
and data transfer rate 123
examining existing 127-8
two-disk example 124
Striping *(see the 'Disk striping' entry)*
Swapfile
and contiguity 95
creating secondary 95, 96
determining current usage 95
expanding 96
primary – increasing size 55
relocation of 96
space 55
reducing demand for 55
if full 54

Swapper 4, 185
Swapper trimming 47, 63
    and system performance 48
    defined and explained 47
    first-level trimming 47
    second-level trimming 47
    triggering 47
Swapping 29, 47
    and $GETJPI system services 54
    and balance sets 19
    and batch/interactive jobs 53
    and SWPOUTPGCNT 53
    and system performance 48, 52
    and working set quotas 54
    and WSMAX 18
    and WSQUOTA 53
    how it works 48
    how to induce 53
    inswap rate 53
    reducing 53
SYSGEN 11, 15, 17–18, 21, 159, 160,
       181, 183, 185, 208, 209, 211,
       213–219, 223–5, 232–3, 236–7,
       267, 269, 277
    and AUTOGEN 216, 218
    understanding your system 214
SYSMWCNT
    estimating size of 18
System disk 142
System Dump Analyzer 7, 37, 182
    and wait states 188

T

TCP/IP 231
    and CPU mode activity 231
    CONFIGURING 231
    overheads and 232
TPS (transactions per second) 177
Trimming *(see the 'Swapper trimming' entry)*

U

User Authorization File (UAF) 25, 155,
      160, 223–4, 231, 236–7, 267–8,
      276

V

Virtual addressing 29
Virtual arrays 171
Virtual balance slots 29
Virtual block number 109, 143
Virtual I/O
    and split I/O 144
Virtual page 27, 31
    and hard pagefaults 34
    and soft pagefaults 33
VOLSET.SYS 141, 143, 144
Volume sets 129
Volume shadowing 115, 116
VUP 177, 195

W

Wait states *(see the 'Scheduling' entry)*
Window control block 107
Window turns 107
    and caching 111
    and cluster sizes 106
    and fragmentation 147
    and performance degradation 148
    definition of 144
    Window Turn Rate 88
Working set 21, 28
    adjustments/batch jobs 25
    and buffering 156
    and dead page tables 36

and pagefaults 34
and system performance 24
and WSDEFAULT 22
and WSEXTENT 18, 22, 27
and WSMAX 18
and WSQUOTA 22, 23
automatic adjustment of 23
calculating ideal size 27
controlling system's (parameters for) 35
displaying limits 27
for system executive 35
formula for 18
growth and size 23
limits for development 61
limits/detached processes 26
quotas and V6.0 29
size 62
    and dead page table scans 37
    and low memory 63
    and PFRPATH/WSINC 37
Working set list 21
    defined 21
    size
        parameters controlling 22
        and pagefaulting 24

Working set
    balance set 19
    quotas and minimizing swapping 54
    reducing 54

X

XQP (extended QIO processor) 109,113
XQP I/O buffer cache 6
X-Windows 235
    and network adapters 238
    and process creation 237
    and SYSGEN 236
    and UAF parameters 236
    and X displays 238

Index of parameters

$GETJPI 54
.AIJ file 271
.CKP files 273
.FDL file 167
.JNL files 274
.RDA file 271
.RDB file 271
.RUJ file 269, 270
.SNP file 270–1
/BLOCK_COUNT 266
/BUFFER_COUNT 266
/CLUSTER 105
/CONT 150
/CPU_STATISTICS 279
/ENTRY 26
/EXTENT 278
/FAST_COMMIT 278
/FAST_COMMIT/WRITE_BEHIND/
        SOL_SERVER 278
/GLOBAL_BUFFERs= 266
/HEADER_RESIDENT 131
/IMAGE 150
/JOB 237
/JOB_LIMIT 206
/OPEN 131
/SESSION_ACCOUNTING 278, 279
/SHARED 54, 62
/SHARED image 33
/SHARED_CACHE 278
/SOLE_SERVER 278
000000.DIR 141, 145
0A$DATA_SHARE:ATTENDEES.DAT 229,
        230
    MEETING.DAT 229, 230
    PENDING.DAT 229
    PROFILE.DAT 229, 230

A

ACCOUNTING 247
ACL 146, 148, ,205, 208

ACP 8
ACP_DINDXCACHE 111
ACP_DIRCACHE 111
ACP_EXTCACHE 111
ACP_EXTLIMIT 111
ACP_FIDCACHE 111
ACP_HDRCACHE 111, 215
ACP_MAPCACHE 111
ACP_QUOCACHE 111
ACP_XQP_RES 54
ADD 215
ADD_ACP_HDRCACHE 215
ALLOCATION 155
ASSIGN 237
AST 224
ASTLM 224, 236, 267
AUTHORIZE 22, 25, 37–8, 54–5, 185,
        189, 206, 223, 226
AWSA 21, 23–4, 61
AWSD 25
AWSTIME 23–4, 232–3, 240

B

BACKUP 202, 209
BACKUP.SYS 141, 144
BADBLK.SYS 141
BADBLKSYS 143
BALANCE SET SLOTS 52
BALSETCNT 19, 53, 54
BASIC 39, 203
BIOLM 224, 236, 241
BITMAP CACHE 110
BITMAP.SYS 105, 106, 110, 141, 143,
        146
BLOCK 1 (BOOT BLOCK) 142
BLOCK 2 (HOME BLOCK) 142
BORROWLIM 14, 19, 23
BTREE 279
BUCKET SIZE 155
BUFFER POOL 266

BUFFER SIZE 266
BYTLM 151, 188, 224, 236, 267, 276

C

CEF 182
CHANNELCNT 225, 238, 241, 277
CHUNK_SIZE 127
CKPDB 274
CLISYMTBL 232–3, 237, 241
COLPG 182, 188
COM 181, 182, 197, 198, 204
COMMIT 253, 269
COMO 49, 50, 181, 182, 197, 198, 204
COMPATIBILITY mode 203
CONTEXT_AREA 251
CONTEXT_INCR 251
CONTIN.SYS 141, 143
CONVERT 170
CORIMG.SYS 141, 144
CREATE 261
CREATE TABLE 252
CREATED 228
CRONIC 103, 116
CTLPAGES 232, 233, 237, 241
CUR 181

D

DAF.DAT 228
DATA FILL 155
DB_BLOCK_BUFFERS 251, 257
DB_BLOCK_MAX_CLEAN_PCT 257, 258
DB_BLOCK_MAX_MOD_PCT 257
DB_BLOCK_MAX_SCAN_PCT 258
DB_BLOCK_TIMEOUT_WRITE_PCT 258
DB_BLOCK_WRITE_BATCH 258
DBWR 248, 253, 257, 258
DEADLOCK WAIT 209
DEADLOCK_WAITS 269

DEBNA 239
DEBNI 239
DEC WINDOWS 224
DECNET 5, 238
DECW$CALC 236
DECW$CALEND 236
DECW$CLOCK 235
DECW$LWK_SET 236
DECW$MAIL 235
DECW$MW5 235
DECW$NOTEPAD 236
DECW$PAINT 236
DECW$PRINTSC 236
DECW$SESSION 235
DECW$TERMINAL 235
DECW$WINMGR 236
DEFINE 237
DEMNA 239
DIOLM 224, 236, 267
DIRECTORY DATA CACHE 110
DIRECTORY FCB CACHE 110
DISKQUOTA 144
DOCDB 230
DOCDB.DAT 228
DUMPSTYLE 43

E–H

ENQLM 236, 267, 276
ENQs 195, 207
EXECUTIVE mode 202–3
EXPLAIN PLAN 249, 259
EXTENT CACHE 110
FCVR 230
FDL 150, 164, 169, 230
FEEDBACK 9
FILE HEADER CACHE 110
FILE ID CACHE 110
FILE OPEN RATE 83
FILLM 224, 236
FORTRAN 38–9

FPG 182, 187
FREEGOAL 14, 28–9, 47, 57
FREELIM 14, 17–19, 47
GGBD 157
GBLPAGES 62, 97, 158, 159, 160, 161, 217, 225
GBLPAGFIL 97, 158, 160
GBLSECTIONS 62, 97, 158–9, 217, 225
GETMISSES 250
GLOBAL BUFFERS 155
GPT 159
GROWLIM 19, 24
GSTE 159
HASH 278
HEAP 278
HI 28
HIBO 49, 182
HSC 115–7, 119

I

IDLE TIME mode 204
II_CHECKPOINT 273, 275
II_DATABASE 275–6
II_DUMP 275
II_JOURNAL 274
II_LOG_FILE 273
II_SYSTEM 275
II_TEMPORARY 276
II_WORKDIR_xx_NN 276
IIDBDB 275, 276
IIRUNDBMS.COM 277
INDEX 261
INDEX FILE BITMAP 142
INDEX FILL 155
INDEXF.SYS 110, 141, 145–6
ING_ABFDIR 275
INGRES 245, 273–6, 278
INGRES EXECUTABLES 275, 277
INGRES_LOG.SYSTEM 273
INIT.ORA 247–251, 253–4, 257–8, 260

INSTALL 62
INSUFFICIENT DYNAMIC MEMORY 6
INTERRUPT mode 231
INTERRUPT stack mode 202
IRP 5, 207
IRPCOUNT 5, 9, 207
IRPCOUNTV 5, 9
ISAM 278–9

J–L

JBCSYQUE.DAT 97
JBCSYSQUE.DAT 115, 162
JTQUOTA 237
KERNEL mode 202, 231
LLAVC 276
LBN 109, 123, 124
LEF 28
LEFO 49
LGUTIL 103, 116
LGWR 248
LNM 8
LOADNET.COM 241
LOCK TABLE 260
LOCKDIRWT 195
LOCKIDTBL 158, 161
LOCKIDTBL_MAX 161
LOG_ALLOCATION 254
LOG_BUFFER 254
LOG_CHECKPOINT_INTERVAL 253, 254
LOGFILE 274
LOGIN.COM 237
Lookaside List Name 5
LRP 5, 207
LRPCOUNT 5, 9, 207, 231, 277
LRPCOUNTV 5, 9
LRPMIN 9
LRPSIZE 5, 9
LRU 256, 257

M

MAIL 162
MAINDIR.DIR 145
MAX 261
MAXACCTJOBS 237
MAXBUF 225, 238, 241
MAXJOBS 237
MAXPROCESSCNT 19, 54, 57, 226, 232,
          233, 237, 241
MEMCONFIG.DAT 58
MFD 141, 145
MIN 261
MIN_ACP_HDRCACHE 215
MIN_GBLPAGES = n 217
MIN_GBLSECTIONS = n 217
MMG$GB_VBSS_ENABLE 30
MMG_CTLFLAGS 29
MMT_CTLFLAGS 28
MONITOR 32, 240, 247
MONITOR LOCK 260
MONITOR MSCP_SERVER 120
MONITOR PAGE 33
MP SYNCHRONIZATION mode 203
MPSYNCH 232
MPW_HILIMIT 15, 17, 57, 185
MPW_HILIMIT 185
MPW_IOLIMIT 15, 16
MPW_LOLIMIT 15, 16, 17
MPW_LOWAITLIMIT 15, 16, 17, 183
MPW_THRESH 16, 47
MPW_WAITLIMIT 15, 185
MPW_WRTCLUSTER 17, 185
MPWBUSY 16
MSCP 119, 120, 121, 122
MSCP Parameters 119
MSCP_BUFFER 119–122
MSCP_CREDITS 120
MSCP_LOAD 119
MSCP_SERVE_ALL 119
MUTEX 183, 188

MWAIT 182
MWP_HILIMIT 15
MWP_LOLIMIT 15
MWP_THRESH 15
MWP_WAITLIMI 15

N–P

NCP 241
NETACP 238, 241
NETUAF.DAT 97
NEXT 253
NGRES_LOG.SYSTEM_nodename 273
NL 271
NPAGEDYN 5–6, 8–9, 113, 151, 158,
          186, 207
NPAGEVIR 5, 8
ODS–1 141
ODS–2 141
OPCOM 6
OPEN 169
OPEN_CURSORS 250–1
ORACLE 245, 247–254, 256–9, 262–3
OUTBOX 228
OUTBUFQUO 159
PAGEDYN 6, 8, 113, 161, 186
PAGEFILE 132
PAGEFILE.SYS 58, 115, 160
PAGFILCNT 42, 55
PATHWORKS 239
PCINCREASE 253
PCTREE 252
PDAF 230
PENDING.DAT 230
PFRATH 23–4, 37, 232–3, 240
PFRATL 24, 25
PFW 182, 187
PGFLQUO 236
PGFLQUOTA 160, 224, 267, 276
Ph. Mem 24, 198
PHYSICALPAGES 58

PIOPAGES 225
PIXSCAN 225
POOLCHECK 11
PQL parameters 26–7
PQL_D 26
PQL_DASTLM 236
PQL_DBIOLM 236
PQL_DBYTLM 236, 277
PQL_DDIOLM 236
PQL_DENQLM 225, 236, 277
PQL_DFILLM 236
PQL_DPGFLQUOTA 236, 277
PQL_DWSDEFAULT 26, 27
PQL_DWSEXTENT 26, 54, 236
PQL_DWSQUOTA 26, 54
PQL_MENQLM 225
PQL_MPRCLM 237
PQL_MWSDEFAULT 27
PRCLM 237
PRIORITY_OFFSET 232–3
PROCSECTCNT 232–3, 237
PROCSETCNT 241
PROFILE.DAT 230
PROSECTCNT 20

Q–R

QIO processor 109
QUEMANAGER 97
QUOTA CACHE 110
QUOTA.SYS 111, 141, 144
RDB$REMOTE_BUFFER_SIZE 268
RDB$SYSTEM 268
RDBMS 245, 247, 249, 251, 258, 259,
    265, 268, 273, 277
RDM$BIND_BUFFERS 267
RDM$BIND_CKPT_TRANS_LIMIT 270
RDM$BIND_RUJ_EXTEND_BLKCNT 270
RDM$BUGCHECK_DIR 271
RDMS$BIND_SEGMENTED_STRING_BUF-FER 268
RDMS$BIND_SORT_WORKFILES 266

RDMS$BIND_WORK_FILE 265
RDMS$DEBUG_FLAGS 270
RDMS$RUJ 270
REDO 247
RESHASHTBL 158, 161
RFA 167
RFXX 119
RIGHTSLIST.DAT 97, 162
RIGHTSLIST.SYS 115
RMS 109, 113, 141, 155–8, 160, 162,
    202, 207
RMS GBLBUFQUO 97
RMS_DFMBC 225
RMS_DFMBFIDX 225
RMS_EXTEND_SIZE 152
RMS_GBLBUFQUO 158–9
ROLLBACK 254
ROW_LOCKING 260
ROWID 261
RSB 191–2
RSTS/E 170, 203
RWAST 183, 186
RWCAP 183, 186
RWCLU 186
RWCSV 183, 186
RWMBX 183, 185
RWMPB 41, 183
RWMPE 41, 183
RWMPx 187
RWNPG 183, 186
RWPAG 183, 186
RWSCS 183, 186
RWSWP 54
RXS–11 141

S

SAVEDUMP 43
SCH$RESCHED 232–3, 240
SCSNODE = """" 217
SCSSYSTEMID 217

SDA 7, 188
SDAFs 228–30
SELECT 261, 263
SEQUENCE_CACHE_ENTRIES 260
SERIALIZABLE 260
SETPARAMS.DAT 216
SGA 254
SHOW MEMORY/POOL/FULL 5
SMP$ACQUIREL 232–3
SORTWORK n 266
SPLIT TRANSFER RATE 83–4, 88
SPM analysis 116
SPM SYSTEM_PC 232
SQL 247–9, 250–1, 255–6, 259
SQL$DISABLE_CONTEXT 271
SQL*DBA 247–8, 250–1, 255
SQL*FORMS 248, 260
SQL*Loader 260
SQL*PLUS 248, 260
SRPCOUNT 5–6, 9, 207, 277
SRPCOUNTV 5–6, 9
SRPSIZE 5, 9
STDRIVER.EXE 125
STORAGE 259
SUPERVISOR mode 203
SUPRA 245
SUSP 182
SUSPO 49, 182
SWAPFILE.SYS 115
SWAPPER 14, 62, 182, 184
SWPFILCNT 55
SWPOUTPGCNT 28, 47–8, 53, 62, 225
SYBASE 245
SYLOGIN.COM 237
SYPAGSWP_FILES.COM 42
SYS$LOGIN 265, 270–1
SYS$MANAGER 42
SYS$MANAGERSYSTARTUP.COM 184
SYS$SCRATCH 265
SYS$SYSTEM 131
SYS$SYSTEM:LISTPREPOP.DAT file 10
SYS$SYSTEM:VAXVMSSYS.PAR. 214

SYSDUMP.DMP 58
SYSDUMP.OLD 43
SYSINIT 10
SYSMWCNT 35, 160–1, 206, 225
SYSTEM-W-PAGECRIT 183–4
SYSTEM-W-PAGEFRAG 183
SYSUAF 31, 226, 237
SYSUAF.DAT 97, 162, 223

T–Z

TABLESPACE 259
TQELM 188, 224
TTY_ALTYPAHD 225
TTY_DEFCHAR2 208
TTY_TYPAHDSZ 225
USER_SEGMENTS 252
VV$WAITSTAT 255
VAXVMSSYS.PAR 215–216
VIRTUAL PAGE 27
VIRTUALPAGECNT 20, 158, 160, 225,
    267, 277
VMS INSTALL 33
VMSMAIL.DAT 97
VMSMAIL_PROFILE.DATA 162
VOLSET.SYS 141, 143–4
VUE$MASTER 235
VUP rating 31, 35
WWCB 107
WHERE 261
WINDOW TURN RATE 84, 88
WORKING_SET 27
WSDEC 24
WSDEFAULT 14, 22, 26, 31, 61, 224,
    225, 232–3, 267–8
WSEXTENT 14, 18, 22–3, 26–8, 31, 36–8,
    43, 54–5, 62–3, 224–5, 236,
    241, 267–8, 276
WSINC 23, 37, 232, 233, 240, 251
WSLE 17
WSLIMIT 14

WSMAX 18, 20, 27–8, 37, 43, 224–5,
        232–3, 237, 241, 277
WSQUOTA 14, 22–3, 26, 31, 38, 43, 47,
        53–5, 57, 61–3, 224, 226, 267,
        268, 276
XQP 109, 113
XQP I/O buffer cache 6

VAXWise software offer

a high quality VAX performance analyzer
from Datawise

Dear Reader, as a user and/or manager of a DEC VAX system and responsible for providing services to other departments in your organization, you will be interested to know that a VAX performance analyzer has been developed – especially for non-technical people – to analyze the raw data collected on your system and produce complete reports for management.

VAXWise has been created and developed by the author of this book to meet the needs of *System Managers, Performance and Capacity Management Consultants,* and *Data Processing Managers* to extract, analyze and report on their system's performance. Drawing on standard VMS utilities for its source of information, **VAXWise** not only identifies why your system may not be performing to expectations but also suggests ways of rectifying any shortcomings – *and all this is done in plain English!*

Order form ▶

VAXWise will enable you to:

- ▶ Analyze your system performance *without expert help.*
- ▶ Investigate performance complaints *promptly and efficiently.*
- ▶ *Identify bottlenecks* and highlight the right solutions for your environment.
- ▶ *Reduce the effort* required to analyze raw data.
- ▶ *Shorten the turn around time* for delivering the report.
- ▶ *Minimize the need for specialist skills* required to analyze performance data and produce reports.
- ▶ *Automate* the process of collecting performance data and producing reports.

Using **VAXWise** you can *create a complete report,* including:

- ▶ *Summary of findings* for management presentations.
- ▶ Actions needed to eliminate or reduce bottlenecks *including the reasons.*
- ▶ Node/Cluster configuration details.
- ▶ Processor(s) utilization including analysis *and actions required.*
- ▶ *Memory utilization* analysis including Page Fault statistics (soft, hard, system faults) *and actions required.*
- ▶ *Disk I/O rates* analysis for cluster and single nodes *and actions required.*
- ▶ *Disk fragmentation* analysis and actions required.
- ▶ Data file analysis and optimization.

plus much more!

Datawise Training and Consultancy Services Ltd., Unit V3, Lenton Business Centre, Lenton Boulevard, Nottingham NG7 2BY, England, UK. Tel: (+44) 115 956 188 1 **Fax:** (+44) 115 923 515 5

VAXWise order form: cut out or photocopy this page

Ref BH/OpenVMS

Name: Mr./Mrs./Ms./Dr. _____

Address: _____

_____

Town/City: _____ County/State: _____

Post/ZIP Code: _____ Country: _____

Telephone number: _____ Fax number: _____

E-mail address: _____

Please enclose payment with your order: cheques, international money orders and credit cards are accepted. **Please make cheques/money orders payable to:** Datawise Training and Consultancy Services Ltd.

UK and European Community: **Price:** £500 + £15 shipping and handling.
USA and Rest of World: **Price:** $750 + $30 shipping and handling.

Please supply_____copies of VAXWise at   ❏ £500.00 ❏ $750.00   £/$_____

Add ❏ £15.00 ❏ $30.00 shipping   £/$_____

Total   £/$_____

Signature_____

Please specify your choice of disk: ❏ TK50   ❏ TK70   ❏ PC floppy disk
I wish to pay by: ❏ cheque/money order   ❏ Credit card: ❏ Visa ❏ Access
   ❏ American Express

Card holder's name: _____

Card holder's address: _____

_____

_____

Card Number:

❏❏❏❏   ❏❏❏❏   ❏❏❏❏   ❏❏❏❏

Expiry date: ❏❏/❏❏   Signature: _____

Please send your order to: Datawise Training and Consultancy Services Ltd., Unit V3, Lenton Business Centre, Lenton Boulevard, Nottingham NG7 2BY, England, UK. **Tel**: (+44) 115 956 188 1 **Fax**: (+44) 115 923 515 5.

306

Datawise Training and Consultancy Services Ltd.
Unit V3 Lenton Business Centre, Lenton Boulevard,
Nottingham NG7 2BY, England, UK.
Tel: (+44) 115 956 188 1
Fax: (+44) 115 923 515 5

D

Datawise specialises in the provision of computer-related consultancy services, products and training courses to the commercial and financial business sectors. Datawise is one of the leading suppliers of Information Technology training. At Datawise we recognise the paramount importance of IT to the competitive growth of modern business. Datawise provides a range of courses and seminars to enable the development of an individual's knowledge in the field of *OpenVMS performance and capacity management, Total Quality Management (TQM), software project management and Electronic Data Interchange (EDI)*. The following summary touches briefly on the wide range of services and products we can offer:

Consultancy services provided by Datawise include:

- ❑ Contract and permanent staff recruitment.
- ❑ OpenVMS performance/capacity management.
- ❑ Software project management.
- ❑ Bespoke software development.
- ❑ SWIFT ST400 /SWIFT ALLIANCE support and installation.
- ❑ RDBMS (Oracle and Ingres).
- ❑ Total quality management (TQM).
- ❑ EDI facility development.
- ❑ Data analysis and data modelling.
- ❑ IT strategy development.

Datawise's training is provided in a flexible manner whilst maintaining the highest standards of quality. We at Datawise ensure that our courses and seminars are up to date and incorporate the latest developments in technology. Datawise's courses and seminars can be individually tailored to the needs of your organization and delivered on client's premises to ensure that you receive what you need — when you need it.

Training courses provided by Datawise:

- ❑ OpenVMS performance and capacity management.
- ❑ Data analysis and data modelling.
- ❑ RDBMS (Oracle and Ingres) tuning.
- ❑ Total Quality Management (TQM).
- ❑ Software project management.
- ❑ Electronic Data Interchange (EDI).

For more information on any service or product, please contact **Joginder Sethi** at Datawise.

All Datawise consultants have a minimum of 10 years' experience in Information Technology and have the business and technical skills to work with clients from development of a strategy to full-scale implementation.

Products developed and supplied by Datawise:

SWIFTWise: a report generator capable of analyzing and monitoring international and inter-bank fund transfers effected via the SWIFT global computer network.

continued ►

VAXWise: a performance analyzer program which produces performance enhancement recommendations for Digital's VAX range of computers.

DATAPLAN: a relational database management system.

CRESTWise: a back office system for CREST (the new settlement system for the UK equity industry).